People or Property

Alessandra Jerolleman · Elizabeth Marino ·
Nathan Jessee · Liz Koslov ·
Chantel Comardelle · Melissa Villarreal ·
Daniel de Vries · Simon Manda

People or Property

Legal Contradictions, Climate Resettlement, and the View from Shifting Ground

With writing contributions in chapter seven from Joel Neimeyer and Stacey Fritz

palgrave
macmillan

Author
See next page

ISBN 978-3-031-36871-4 ISBN 978-3-031-36872-1 (eBook)
https://doi.org/10.1007/978-3-031-36872-1

Cover photo by Dennis Davis

This Palgrave Macmillan imprint is published by the registered company Springer Nature Switzerland AG
The registered company address is: Gewerbestrasse 11, 6330 Cham, Switzerland

Paper in this product is recyclable.

Alessandra Jerolleman
Emergency Management
Jacksonville State University
Metarie, LA, USA

Nathan Jessee
High Meadows Environmental Institute
Princeton University
Princeton, NJ, USA

Chantel Comardelle
Houma, LA, USA

Daniel de Vries
Department of Anthropology
University of Amsterdam
Amsterdam, The Netherlands

Elizabeth Marino
Anthropology and Sustainability
Oregon State University Cascades
Bend, OR, USA

Liz Koslov
Urban Planning, Environment
and Sustainability, and Sociology
UCLA
Los Angeles, CA, USA

Melissa Villarreal
Department of Sociology and Natural
Hazards Center
University of Colorado Boulder
Boulder, CO, USA

Simon Manda
University of Leeds
Leeds, UK

The original version of the book has been revised: Missed author names have been included in the chapters. The correction to the book is available at https://doi.org/10.1007/978-3-031-36872-1_11

Acknowledgements

The authors want to thank Dennis Davis, Annie Weyiouanna, Sigvana Topkok, and Julie Raymond-Yakoubian who spoke with us throughout the writing of this book and provided feedback and ideas early on. We thank Elder Chief Shirell Parfait-Dardar for her inspiration and for sharing experiences for this book. We would also like to thank John Lovett who provided language and references with regard to the Scottish Right to Buy and other important concepts. Thank you also to Amitai Heller for constructive feedback on earlier versions of this manuscript. We would like to thank Chris Wolsko for providing sustenance; and Aaron Cook for reading an early version of this book and providing insight. We want to thank Shereen Soliman and Noémie Gonzalez Bautista for help with references and citations. This book was sponsored, in part, by NSF sponsored grant award # 1921045.

Contents

Authorship

This book was a labor of love and collaboration, and is one outcome of years of conversations and relationships. Alessandra Jerolleman, Elizabeth Marino, and Nathan Jessee worked on, wrote on, and edited all parts of this book. Without equivocation, all three are first authors of this manuscript. Liz Koslov and Chantel Comardelle provided essential writing in some chapters, and provided essential insights throughout the manuscript and are second authors. The other authors on this book wrote significant parts of chapters and commented on the manuscript as a whole. It was an experiment to collaborate and write as a collective—to recognize that emergent insights are borne of different perspectives, expertise, and writing styles coming together. Collective writing was challenging; but we are thankful that it was also joyful. This book would have been impossible without the work and wisdom of the whole.

About the Authors

Alessandra Jerolleman has a background in public administration, law, urban studies, and emergency management. She has lived in Louisiana for over twenty years and has spent much of that time working with rural, coastal, and Indigenous communities along the coast, as well as in northern parts of the state. She returned to school in order to pursue a law degree, following decades of working in spaces where law, policy, and bureaucratic discretion consistently led to unjust outcomes.

Elizabeth Marino is an Associate Professor of Anthropology and Sustainability at Oregon State University—Cascades and a chapter lead author of the Fifth National Climate Assessment. She is interested in how people make sense of home, risk, and change and, more recently, how the law enables or disables this sense-making. She is from Louisiana and has long ties to Alaska—but currently has roots down in the desert of Central Oregon.

Nathan Jessee is a Postdoctoral Environmental Fellow at Princeton University's High Meadows Environmental Institute. Nathan's scholarship is focused on community-based participatory research; political ecologies of property, planning, and law; ethnography; ecocide; disaster and development-forced displacement; and climate change adaptation.

Liz Koslov is an Assistant Professor in the Department of Urban Planning and the Institute of the Environment and Sustainability at UCLA. Her research explores the social dimensions of climate change, questions of environmental and climate justice, and how cities are adapting to effects such as extreme weather and sea level rise. Koslov has spoken about this research in outlets that include the New Yorker, WWNO New Orleans Public Radio, and Scientific American. Her writing has appeared in Public Culture, Annals of the American Association of Geographers, and Public Books, among others.

Chantel Comardelle has a deep passion for her community. As Tribal Secretary of the Isle de Jean Charles Choctaw Nation, she serves as the backbone of Tribal operations. Chantel has served in this role since 2000, acting as a Tribal Representative while simultaneously juggling Tribal communications, archival and historical research, and grant writing responsibilities. Her current areas of focus include Federal Recognition, Tribal Resettlement, and the Preserving Our Place Movement. Her educational background includes a Certificate of Museum Studies from the Institute of American Indian Arts and a Bachelor of General Studies from Nicholls State University. She is currently an M.A. student in a Master of Fine Arts in Cultural Administration program at Institute of American Indian Arts. As a lifelong bayou resident, Chantel seeks to positively impact her community for future environmental, economic, and cultural sustainability.

Melissa Villarreal is a Ph.D. Candidate in Sociology at the University of Colorado (CU) Boulder. Her dissertation is an intersectional, multi-level analysis of Mexican immigrant women and their disproportionate vulnerability in post-disaster recovery. Melissa was awarded the National Science Foundation (NSF) Graduate Research Fellowship (GRFP) and the American Sociological Association (ASA) Doctoral Dissertation Research Improvement Grant (DDRIG) for this project. She was also selected for Rice University's Kinder Scholar Program. Melissa works as a graduate research assistant at the Natural Hazards Center at CU, and is a William Averette Anderson Fund (BAF) Fellow, which is dedicated to advancing the success of minority professionals in disaster fields.

Daniel de Vries is an Associate Professor in Anthropology at the University of Amsterdam. Daniel received his Ph.D. in Anthropology at the University of North Carolina at Chapel Hill where he was engaged with several FEMA-funded projects on flood mitigation and buyouts. He subsequently conducted his dissertation fieldwork on the role of history and memory in floodplains across the United States, looking at the collective experience of surprise and vulnerability. Daniel works on the integration of social sciences in preparedness, response, and recovery, including disasters, conflicts, and epidemic threats.

Simon Manda is a Lecturer of International Development at the University of Leeds, UK. He previously was a Postdoctoral Researcher at Oregon State University, Bend Cascades Campus. He worked on a project funded by the National Science Foundation whose centrality pointed to adaptation possibilities for individuals, neighborhoods, and communities who are faced with repetitive flooding. The project specifically focused on the policy options for communities who wish to relocate together. His current research focuses on climate risks and adaptation.

List of Figures

PART I

Conceptualizing Property and Its Contradictions: A Challenge for Climate Justice

CHAPTER 1

Pulling at the Thread

Over the last twenty years, the authors of this book have been enmeshed in conversations about how difficult it is to support communities as they plan relocations and resettlements[1] as an adaptive response to climate change-related flooding. Twenty years ago in Alaska, relocation challenges seemed born of state ignorance and neglect. The flooding that extremely rural, primarily Indigenous communities experienced was mostly invisible to the public. Even as flooding increased, these events often went unnoticed by institutions with the capacity to render aid. Solving for invisibility,

[1] There is a healthy debate over the proper term for community wide relocation. We are choosing to use relocation and resettlement, because they are used among the community leaders with whom we work, and because these terms emphasize the experiences of people instead of infrastructure or investment (Maldonado et al., 2020). Liz Koslov makes a powerful case for embracing the term "retreat," suggesting that retreat should be understood not just in the common sense of a military defeat or withdrawal from an enemy (water), but as an opportunity for spiritual healing, regeneration, and rethinking our collective and urbanized relationships with water and climate risk (Koslov, 2016). Her observation is insightful; but we continue to find the militarized and top-down usage of retreat problematic and so offer "relocation" and "resettlement" as interchangeable notions of more-than-individual movements of people. Moreover, we worry that the currently popular framing of "retreat", in practice, reduces the scope of socio-ecological risks attended to by focusing efforts on exposure to coastal flooding at the expense of confronting other related unevenly distributed risks and vulnerabilities (like threats to cultural survival or inland affordability); displacing local frames, expertise, ways of knowing, and priorities for holistic adaptation; presuming the goal of abandoning land; and foreclosing possibilities for just planning processes (Jessee, 2022).

A. Jerolleman et al., *People or Property*,
https://doi.org/10.1007/978-3-031-36872-1_1

community leaders, academics, and non-profit agencies worked together and attracted media (Callison, 2017) and political attention (Mufson, 2015), wrote books (Marino, 2015), gave interviews (D'Oro, 2014), and provided Congressional testimony (Weyiouanna, 2007) As the climate crisis became more widespread within public consciousness, the places and people actively planning resettlements became emblematic of its impacts.

Likewise, on the Gulf Coast of Louisiana, Tribal and community leaders, environmentalists, religious leaders, and social scientists had long-advocated for addressing risks associated with the destruction of coastal and bayou habitats throughout the Mississippi River Delta. Among the advocates were leaders of the Jean Charles Choctaw Nation,[2] who have been living with and responding to extreme weather and flooding for decades. In 2002, the Tribe began planning their Tribal community resettlement inland responding to recurrent disasters compounded by extreme weather events. As in Alaska, much of this work originally began with no, or minimal, government support. Hurricanes Katrina and Rita in 2005, however, brought new attention to the region. The loss of life, destruction of property, mismanaged evacuation, and the position of the region as a globally important oil and gas exporter and mega-port led to a significant increase in money for recovery throughout the region. Amid the emergence of state coastal restoration and resilience work, scholars also began to consider the legal, cultural, and political dimensions of community relocation (Dalbom et al., 2014; Gramling et al., 2006).

The view in 2023 has therefore changed. The complete invisibility that plagued Alaska's rural west coast and Louisiana's lower bayou communities has, in some important ways, come to an end. Political and public attention to relocation as a possible strategy to reduce risk to environmental hazards, and particularly as an "adaptive response" to climate change, has increased dramatically over the last twenty years (Lustgarten, 2020). This has played out in the news coverage of larger storms and erosion in Alaska (Bronen & Chapin, 2013; Marino, 2015); sea level rise and ecological destruction along the Gulf Coast (Jerolleman, 2019;

[2] Formerly known as the Isle de Jean Charles Biloxi-Chitimacha-Choctaw Tribe. A note of analytic limitation: The research that informed this book was conducted with Jean Charles Choctaw Nation leadership, at tribal and state planning meetings, and focused on the clashing resettlement visions between the state and the tribal community. The experiences of the entire Jean Charles Choctaw Nation, other Indigenous nations in the region, and the totality of experiences and perspectives on the Isle de Jean Charles resettlement are beyond the scope of this manuscript.

Maldonado, 2018), and extreme events, like Hurricane Sandy in the northeast. As a 2020 *New York Times* article claimed, "U.S. Flood Strategy Shifts to 'Unavoidable' Relocation of Entire Neighborhoods" (Flavelle, 2020a, 2020b). Hundreds of journalists have visited Indigenous island communities in Alaska and Louisiana to write stories about the "first climate refugees" (Herrmann, 2017; Marino, 2015). *Politico* wrote a piece entitled the "Case for Managed Retreat" (Panfil, 2020); and from 1987 to 2017, the United States funded more than 43,000 buyouts to remove individuals and families from habitually flooding properties (Panfil, 2020). Yet, despite the increasing visibility, and the decades of community-led advocacy, community-led relocation as a response to habitual flooding is still largely fraught and unrealized in reducing exposure to socio-environmental hazards. Even where community-wide relocations have taken place, what is achieved, whether risks are alleviated, and the role, importance, and centrality of community-held desires remain unclear.

Visibility has also given rise to new challenges. The first is that the growing attention brought with it an oversimplification of climate as a driver of migration (Boas et al., 2019). The people we have worked with who are planning relocations, and the allies that work alongside them, understand that these "environmental" and climate hazards mediate, and are manifested by, structural violence and injustice. For example, over a century of levee and dam building and oil and gas extraction created susceptibility to land subsidence and erosion that, in turn, has led to the deterioration of Isle de Jean Charles. On top of that, the 2002 Army Corps of Engineers decision to exclude Isle de Jean Charles from the Morganza to the Gulf Hurricane Protection Levee System created conditions that made the Island even more susceptible to storms and untenable in the imaginations of regional leaders. Moreover, initial disinvestment by the state and federal government in protecting the road to and from the Island made it difficult for families with school kids or people with off-Island jobs or medical needs to remain due to getting "stuck" when water inundated the road. Under these socio-political circumstances, it is disingenuous and inaccurate to blame risk and exposure simply on the rising temperature and global sea levels.

Second, there is growing concern among those of us that work on, or are living through, these risks, that public attention has turned from ignoring relocation as a critical response to recurrent flooding, to treating it as inevitable. This narrative glorifies relocation or retreat as the only viable option to respond to climate change and sea level rise, regardless of community desires. A new book by science journalist Gaia Vince, *Nomad Century*, makes the case that "large swaths of the Earth will become uninhabitable" or "lethal" leading to mass displacement. The book has been reviewed by the Washington Post, ABC News, and NPR among others, and suggests a, now frequent, and ultimately xenophobic narrative of the "invasion of the climate migrants." The sensationalist story, while not new, of the inevitable displacement of billions of people due to climate change, for social scientists, is, again, oversimplified (Piguet, 2013), irresponsible (Farbotko, 2022; Herrmann, 2017), and largely uncorroborated (Farbotko, 2022; Fussell, 2012). Even human and community migrations that have a climate signal, to date, are rarely driven by the "uninhabitability" of a place. Most environmentally-driven migrants remain internally displaced within a single nation-state; and whether migrations linked to climate will be adaptive or disruptive, and for whom, is a social, political, and economic question (Warnecke et al., 2010).

It is difficult not to see this changing narrative (ignorance to inevitability) as a swing from public and political disinterest to public and political disinvestment—both reactions bearing the mark of colonial responses to locations, homelands, and people who habitually bear the burdens, and lack the benefits, of industrialization (Marino et al., 2022). In the first place, people and communities were "sacrificed" so that industry could access land, labor, and desired materials. Later, these communities were "sacrificed" because they were invisible, ignored, or too costly; and in the third because now destruction is (conveniently) inevitable. None of these narratives foreground the legitimate, empowered, claims of entitlement to land, culture, continuity, and risk protection that we find most prevalent in conversations on the ground and within communities facing repetitive flooding (Farbotko & Lazrus, 2012).[3]

This book confronts another emergent challenge to relocation as an adaptation to repetitive flooding; Whether or not United States and international (Burkett, 2011) legal and regulatory systems are structurally

[3] We use the term "repetitive flooding" to mean repeat flooding, regardless of whether a property is classified as a Repetitive Loss structure under the Federal Emergency Management Agency's definition.

capable, or easily capable, of supporting communities who are considering relocation.[4] Currently relocations, for example, are most often carried out using existing legal mechanisms, such as buyouts, which are often made available following a presidentially declared disaster. Even when funding is available, it is unclear whether these mechanisms are applicable to complex cases of whole-community resettlements (Marino, 2018). There are several examples that have been cited in policy literature as successful community-wide relocations, such as Kinston, NC or Valymeyer, IN, and recently Isle de Jean Charles, LA. But these "successes" are circumspect. As we will see in this book, there is either a lack of information on the outcomes experienced by these individuals, families, neighborhoods, and communities who have relocated; or there is demonstrable evidence that along with benefit, there has been harm. While the federal government has begun to seek governance innovations to better support those who face displacement as a result of the climate crisis (Jerolleman, 2019), including drawing on the experiences of the communities of which authors are part and with whom they have long collaborated (GAO, 2020), the inability, or unwillingness, of governance and regulatory systems to provide just solutions in the context of relocation has, among other things, created divisive and draining experiences among those planning their resettlements.

In the scholarship and attempts at solidarity that inform this book, we have tried to understand the legal and regulatory limitations that frame community-driven relocation processes while also taking seriously the histories and legacies of legal injustice. We think that one profound reason community-wide relocations are challenging is because they embody and evoke some of the central contradictions of U.S. law and the U.S. property regime, even when this broader context is not taken explicitly into consideration. In particular, in this book, we focus on how the legal options for relocating people have tended to conflate complex relationalities within groups (occupants, those with attachments to the land and non-human species and spaces, dwellers and dwellings) into a primary,

[4] This book recognizes that efforts at risk reduction are part of a larger context of disaster policies that have historically often reinforced inequity (Jerolleman, 2019). These disaster policies are bound up in questions such as what constitutes a disaster, and the division of authority and responsibility between federal and state-level actors (Sylves, 2020). As Sylves, and many others have noted, disasters are socially and politically constructed phenomena (2020).

ethnocentric, legally legible, and transactional relationship between a selling property owner and a purchasing government. We have strived to track path dependencies that coalesce around property rights, property ownership, and individual property holders in relocation scenarios and find that prevailing paths extend some of the worst injustices expressed throughout U.S. history.

In our work, we have seen policies and practices that favor property ownership and participation in property markets over-determine relocation planning, giving rise to several challenges for community-driven relocation efforts. Property, most generally, is an abstraction and legal codification of particular forms of land tenure and social organization that creates differentialized power and social relationships among groups of people, both formally and informally (Blomley, 2004). When property ownership is privileged throughout relocation processes, existing disparities may be exacerbated. This is to say, in relocation scenarios, those who have legally illegible relationships to a place, or more precarious rights within the property regime, may be more at risk. Renters, for example, may be further marginalized throughout relocations by their precarious relationships with property, especially if the well-being and compensation of homeowners is prioritized in the allocation of public resources, and if new affordable housing is not created. We know, for example, very little about how renters fared in "community-based" relocations in the Midwest in the 1990s, even though these are often held up as paradigmatic examples of "successful relocations" (Manda et al., 2023).

Market-rate property transactions also sustain historical and ongoing racialized patterns of underdevelopment and geographies of abandonment and exclusion. The environmental justice movement has long documented the inequitable distribution of industrial toxins along racialized lines across the United States (Bullard et al., 2008), leading to lower property values and many other negative impacts to health and wealth. Similarly, protective measures against flooding (like levees and the maintenance of levees) often privilege wealthier and whiter communities (Martinich et al., 2012) and can drive up housing prices or even incentive further development. Thus, property transaction-as-adaptation can externalize historical injustices into lower market values for homes, which may be at risk in the first place because of ongoing race and class dynamics. In practice, this can mean that some "fair market buyouts" may not allow for sufficient purchasing power to buy a home in a less risky area. Given the inequitable production of property values and risk, in the first place, it is even more problematic that disaster aid is governed by policies that actively seek to ensure that no "undue benefits" accrue to those who receive a federal subsidy; and that "market rate" is the standard for "just compensation.[5]" In essence, this restriction means that, after a disaster, federal aid is legally constrained from repairing historical, frequently racialized, inequitable infrastructure investment. These restrictions suggest that adaptive measures may re-entrench historical injustice, and also raises questions around whether restitution or reparative justice can be part of relocation and resettlement without legal action.

Reducing community relocation to a property transaction can also serve to promote individualization and limit the capacity for community organizing and collective action. If market rates for homes in the floodplain limit the options for purchasing a new home for relocating individuals, for example, new homes may be far from friends, family, and social networks. Scattering individuals across a region may not only reduce social capital among people who move, but can render the remaining connections and community less viable due to population reduction, disrupted sense of place and grounded knowledge, and loss of tax base, among other outcomes (Parchomovsky & Siegelman, 2004). The same scattering effect can happen when governments disinvest in "at-risk" locations, or offer only piecemeal support, without clear paths forward for relocation or reconstitution of community relations in a new location (Marino & Lazrus, 2015). Collective action and community organizing can be defined by the creation of "durable institutions ... [that] builds local leadership, giving otherwise fractured communities a unified voice and the collective power necessary to resist oppression" (Schutz & Sandy, 2011). These qualities of organizing can be undermined when governing entities promote individual property owners as the foci of engagement, erasing other community-based entities that might have more power to make demands on a state or federal agency. Community-based entities can also be undermined by the failure to recognize communal rights or communal ownership.

Centering community objectives during relocation has also been challenging because processes which govern relocation and resettlement today

[5] In some buyout programs participants are offered incentive funding on top of fair market price, in part, to create opportunities for buyout participants to afford a house outside of the floodplain. Despite these incentives, fair market value is still the primary determinant of price and purchasing power.

are driven by benefit/cost analysis. As a result, government agencies can be required to foreground and work to diminish risks to *property*, instead of risks to *people*, interpreting success as program participation, and in getting the highest percentage of people off of a piece of land in order to reduce future disaster recovery expenditures by the government (Manda et al., forthcoming, chapter four); not in improving people's lives. Even when people are taken into account, benefit/cost methodologies prioritize areas with higher numbers of persons over those with less population density.

Risks to people are multidimensional and complex. Adaptation and meaningful risk reduction is more than removing people and property from a "hazard-prone" site. In other words, while flooding might constitute the major threat to a property, a person may be balancing the risk of flooding, housing insecurity, childcare needs, gas prices, racism, cultural loss, social dislocation, and other demands and obstacles, as well as the joy and beauty, in their lives. If "relocation" means leaving the risk of hazard, but incurring a risk of houselessness or losing a complex web of social relations that provides support, then what has been accomplished? Reducing "relocation" to market-driven exchange ignores the fact that resistance to relocation almost always entails *reasonable risk calculation* by people who are considering their own complex situations, and that of their broader community. The shared realities of interacting inequities and oppressions (and joys!) cannot be quantified within such an exchange, nor is it easily understood or "solved for" by people outside of communities. Adding insult to injury, resistance to relocation is sometimes cast as irrational or a psychological resistance to change (Esteves, 2018), instead of a nuanced understanding of embedded lives.

It is surprising to many people who are new to the subject of relocation as a response to climate change that carrying out even small-scale relocation of communities in the United States is so expensive and so difficult. Almost 8% of Americans, 26,000,000 people, changed residences in 2021, even during a global pandemic. If this is the case, why is it difficult for small communities of 600, 1000, 10,000, 50,000 people to plan their ways out of floodplains? Is it just a lack of financial investment by the U.S. government? Is it just red tape? The shock and subsequent marveling at the complexity expressed in statements like "If we can't move this tiny community, how will we move Miami?" reflects a paternalism and technocracy that troubles the efforts of small communities. The difficulty of community-based relocations may be better solved for by focusing on the social and political-economic threads through seemingly disparate places in the United States, such as: (1) whether and which communities have access to legal rights and institutions to protect their interests, including property interests; and (2) how the power of property is used as a social institution to demarcate legal rights when faced with risk. The collective set of authors that have written this book want to work toward material changes that promote increased and equitable distribution of funding and possibilities for people experiencing repetitive flooding and harm as a result of the multiple overlapping risk-producers: climate, weather, wind, rain, racism, redlining, colonialism, and theft. As authors, we have long histories of working with and living in local communities and seeing the harms that a lack of just governance solutions has caused to communities directly, including the harms perpetuated by bureaucracies and experts in the name of adaptation.

In the process of writing, one of our authors, Alessandra Jerolleman, made the comment, "I want to be thinking about what will really make a difference, not about how many times Locke (a singular influence on the role of property, just compensation, and governance in the US) has been cited by the Supreme Court." We want to see our family, friends, and collaborators in safe and stable housing and create conditions that foster material support for their livelihoods and honor their cultural integrity. Most of the authors of this book have filled out FEMA forms ourselves after big storms or have done so for our mothers and friends. We want long-term material solutions to repetitive flooding. What we have collectively concluded, however, is that not grappling with Locke, prevailing conceptualizations and legal formations of property, and how those conceptualizations structure planning will result in extending the inequitable distribution of risk during and after relocation and resettlement processes. We have found that assumptions about property, including the primacy of the individual owner, undergird most conversations about relocation and resettlement and that these assumptions are dangerously, and quietly, undermining just climate adaptation.

What this book is not doing is making a universal argument against property, or property rights, as such. We recognize that voluntary buyouts, i.e., a fair market exchange for repetitively flooding properties within the floodplain, are necessary, desired by many homeowners, and should, in many cases, be encouraged. We also recognize differences within our author team concerning our understanding of the role of property in structuring and maintaining limitations on government overreach, as well as the risks and opportunities that accompany government reallocation of property. We all agree, however, that the valorization of property as a singularly sacrosanct right, lack of fairness within the current property regime, and the material legacies of property as a tool for white supremacist European and U.S. conquests, are highly present in the structuring of relocation and resettlement processes. We agree that property law, if taking liberal philosophy at its word, has been contradictorily applied throughout history in ways that produce injustice, particularly in racialized communities and via colonial invasion and dispossession. We agree that without acknowledging, understanding, and trying to unravel these dynamics, we are doomed to repeat them. Finally, we agree that there are just pathways to climate change-driven relocation that exist outside of liberal conceptions of property and should be considered.

Property Law and the Social Creation of Space

Many disparate laws, policies, and regulations come to bear on relocation planning. The Stafford Act, for example, regulates disaster relief and emergency assistance; the Uniform Relocation Act administers relocation costs for people displaced by government planning or development; and, countless local ordinances and regulations impact construction in the places where people move to and from. In addition to these pieces of legislation, the Fifth Amendment to the Constitution codified the protection of property from government seizure without just compensation. It reads:

> No person shall be held to answer for a capital, or otherwise infamous crime, unless on a presentment or indictment of a grand jury, except in cases arising in the land or naval forces, or in the militia, when in actual service in time of war or public danger; nor shall any person be subject for the same offense to be twice put in jeopardy of life or limb; nor shall be compelled in any criminal case to be a witness against himself, nor be deprived of life, liberty, or ***property***, without ***due process of law***; ***nor shall private property be taken for public use, without just compensation.***

The amendment legally gave property a protected status equal even to life and liberty. This statement that no person "be deprived of life, liberty, or *property*, without *due process of law*; *nor shall private property be taken for public use, without just compensation*," encompasses both the *Takings* clause and the concept of *Due Process*, and has created an entire body of jurisprudence in which the relationships and obligations, including processes, among the government and property owners are outlined and debated.

Property rights, as indicated by their presence in the Bill of Rights, are closely connected to the founding of the United States, and the rhetorical and mythological construction of liberalism, a political ideological framework whose proponents argue is a political philosophy committed to the limitation of government, promotion of economic freedom, and protection of the rights of the individual. John Locke is often cited as a central figure in this political philosophy, as he positioned property, labor on the land, and the protection of both from government overreach as central to individual freedom—tied to natural law. Ultimately arguing against the legitimate power of the monarch, Locke located the right to individual, not monarchical, property and inheritance as a natural conclusion of Adam's inheritance of the earth (Locke, 1948). There is some speculation that the modern liberal rhetoric and intellectual heroism of Locke (the "fable" of liberalism) arose, not during the 1700 or 1800s, but in the 1930s and that Locke himself was not so individualistic (Stanton, 2018). This is supported by Alexander's writings that suggest there was more of a dialectic, where property was seen as the foundation of a political, social, and moral order that positioned property ownership as an individual right, but which also incurred civic responsibility (Alexander, 1997). Alexander describes a later-emergent competing sense of property as individual wealth creation, culminating in the protection of the corporate form. According to these lines of thought, the central issue in early American politics was not just how to protect individual freedoms, but also how to protect public rights against the power of government (Alexander, 1997). However, even those who characterize the American legal tradition as not solely committed to the most individualistic form of the Lockean tradition, acknowledge that a market idea of property has had a tremendous impact on American legal thought and jurisprudence. One example of this is the frequency of references to Locke in jurisprudence, even today.

Part of the impact of property on the U.S. legal system lies in the interpretation of the three components within the takings clause of the Fifth Amendment. The components lay out the constituent pieces of legal theory around government involvement in cases pertaining to property, and still have influence and purchase over land regulations and planning.

These include: (1) private property; (2) public use; and (3) just compensation. Some theorists have argued that the Fifth Amendment was written in part to educate land owners about their relationships with property (Fegan, 2006). If land, to white male settlers, was plentiful and cheap, the need for just compensation would have been minimal. If the government needed land for public use, such as a road or port, it would not have been significant at the time to have it put under government control. In this view, the purpose of embedding a Lockean view of property into the Bill of Rights was to render explicit that land and property are protected from government overreach and its best use should be decided by individual owners, unless certain criteria are met. These criteria, particularly what constitutes a public use, have been widely contested.

Even for those who ultimately view the protection of property rights as central to the protection of individual rights and freedom from the tyranny of government and monarchy, it is clear that this narrative diverges from, and "papers over" a complicated and bloody reality that the founding of the United States, and the formation of the U.S. property regime, both relied upon and enabled the colonization of Indigenous lands and livelihoods; genocide; and the enslavement of Black, Indigenous, and other peoples (Banner, 2005; Greer 2018; Park, 2021). These atrocities are intellectually and materially bound to land and property within the United States, despite ongoing legal disagreements about the role of property in early America (Alexander, 2009). Property, as demonstrated so barbarically in the history of the United States, is a set of simultaneously embodied contradictions: protection as theft; freedom as restriction; development as displacement and disinvestment.

On the ground, these competing and irreconcilable counter-forces have found homes within the Takings clause's constituent parts: private property, public use, and just compensation. "Private property" has been taken from some to be protected for others, as is evident throughout histories of colonial invasion, urban renewal, or gentrification. "Public use" creates opportunities for a free market and green spaces for some and restricts use and mobility for others. The history of U.S. treaty breaking to establish national parks, is one example. Another is government involvement in creating conditions that trap people in houses where the value has been depressed by siting of industrial facilities. "Just compensation" is a contradiction in terms when homes in neighborhoods that have been marked for development by city planners get more money in a buyout than homes where disinvestment in infrastructure leads to bad roads, contaminated soils, flooding, or neglected schools. Historical political analysis and contemporary research of community experiences help us to understand where property law (and due process) and its application and interpretation, intentionally and unintentionally, will reproduce injustices during relocation processes. Such notions of how the U.S. property regime has codified and reproduced inequities are increasingly recognized and amplified by critical legal scholars, such as Cheryl Harris, K-Sue Park, and Joseph Singer, for example, but do not seem widely discussed in policy and legislative circles or in the application of the law or treatment of property relations or transactions within resettlement planning processes.

The U.S. property regime, and inherent contradictions therein, affect relocation experiences in four broad ways. First, the property regime plays a large role in shaping landscapes of risk and access to adaptation measures. Land use laws, building codes, and zoning regulations are structured by legal norms and regulations related to property. Such laws, regulations, and norms create, protect, and threaten ecosystems, including people, and influence experiences of emerging hazards associated with climate change. Second, property relations mediate who is pushed toward relocation in the first place. Which built environments and land get protected by hazard mitigation investment or who gets federal subsidies to raise a home, in part, determine also who ends up having to move in the wake of disaster. Third, the property regime structures who is offered a buyout, who is determined to be a beneficiary of public relocation planning, what is considered success by government agencies, what monies are set aside for relocation, and who is able to make future land use decisions. Access to adaptation funding via disaster policies is also directly impacted by the U.S. property regime. We expand upon these aspects in the second part of this book in three geographic regions: the Mississippi River Delta, coastal Alaska, and North Carolina. Finally, the property regime also determines what "new communities" or "receiving areas" look like: Who benefits from migration and relocation events, who is excluded, and what kinds of conflicts or inequalities come to shape experiences for generations to come? These insights into the ways in which the property regime come to bear on processes of relocation are necessary to understand as a mechanism for understanding inequity and pursuing justice.

Four Contradictions of Property and Law

It is no wonder that community-planned relocations and resettlements are challenging to administer from a governance perspective, if the process of relocating communities across landscapes and "property" requires a re-examination of Lockean views of property; and represents an axis on which race, gender, and class politics play out! We can see that debates over how best to create and administer policies that structure relocation and resettlement are inextricably connected to larger questions of why, and how, the protection of certain types of property rights are built into the legal system of the United States. Examining the logics of property law and lived experiences of its application, provides one of the clearest windows into the legal and moral contradictions that undergird the United States, and are implicated in the inequitable distribution of risk as an outcome of climate change.

We consider the following four legal contradictions to expand our earlier observation that property itself exists as a contradiction in the United States. Our observations of the following four contradictions are not simply that the U.S. property regime has been inequitably or unjustly experienced by different communities; but that legally administered property rights and other property-inflected laws and regulations carry within them contradictions about who is able to exercise rights; which rights are prioritized; and who is able to realistically exercise their rights within the material world. These four contradictions are the following:

1. An ethic of the right to land has co-existed with settler state expropriation of land;
2. Despite privileging the rights of the individual, an individual's right to act communally is discouraged and rendered difficult to exercise;
3. At times, the rights of current property owners are privileged above collective protective measures, despite the reality that rights of property owners will, in many cases, be undermined by climate change and that the actions of current property owners may increase the risk to themselves and others; and,
4. U.S. law has consistently been a tool to undermine the rights of individuals and groups through violent displacement, genocide, and dispossession, but it is also seen as a primary mechanism for harm reduction and the restoration and expansion of rights.

As we explain in Chapter 2, these contradictions find expression in some of the worst processes of U.S. history. We will explore these histories more fully in Chapter 2, which, together with this chapter, make up the first part of our book. Understanding these contradictions will also underlay any effort to use the law in service of change.

The second part of the book looks at case studies of communities and different relationships with property to see how these contradictions come into view in case studies and categories of ownership. We call this second section, "Proof of Harm." Before we dive into the legal apparatus that structures these relocations, we feel it is important for our readers to see the lived experience of people and lands as they navigate complex lives, risks, and struggles. For us, these cases should be understood before the law. Chapter 3 relies on experiences from the Jean Charles Choctaw Nation to consider the alternative constructs of resettlement and land tenure imagined and explicated by community leaders, whose plans became subsumed into state-driven development visions that threaten the Tribe's struggle for cultural survival. Chapter 4 discusses an ethnographic account of voluntary buyouts in one community. Here, we confront how relocation processes can splinter communities and create the feeling of coercion among participants. Chapter 5 returns to Isle de Jean Charles and further expands on the ability or inability to articulate needs of a "community" under U.S. law. Chapter 6 engages "precarious possessors" and the complex constellation of people who cannot accept voluntary buyouts as a mechanism for relocation and therefore face higher risk of "forced" displacement. Each of these chapters reveals how property relations define and delimit the kinds of communities that can participate in decision-making around climate relocation. Chapter 7 presents a case study of voluntary buyouts in Alaska and an inquiry into whether "fair market value" is commensurate with "just compensation."

The third part of our book examines laws that shape and constrain possibilities for relocating communities in the United States at the time of our writing in early 2022. Chapter 8 lays out the legal structures that shape relocation. This chapter is a technocratic guide book for community leaders who are looking at novel opportunities to test the law; adaptation specialists who are open to exploring novel legal arrangements, or relocation scholars who might not be versed in the law, legal concepts, and legal tools. Here, we discuss zoning and building codes, takings law, and public trust, among others. Chapter 8 includes an intellectual experiment in what kinds of unique legal and property arrangements might be possible in order to solve constraints on relocating communities and improve outcomes. This is a hopeful chapter—one that points toward possible solutions. Chapter 9 focuses on bureaucratic discretion—the room to maneuver that agencies possess under current legal and policy regimes—and the differences among law, regulation, and policy. Chapter 10 is our conclusion: a caveat about the limits of a legal system when there are differential amounts of power and wealth at play; and a hope for the future.

How to Read This Book

We hope you will read this book as a single manuscript. The book is authored by a collective group of scholars who have entered into the conversation about relocation at different places, with different disciplinary expertise, and in different locations around the United States This manuscript is part of a larger attempt at understanding and articulating the limits and possibilities for mobility that current law and legal norms provide to communities made highly vulnerable to climate change (see also Marino et al., 2022). While a full summation of relevant case law and legal theory, at both the federal and state level, are beyond our expertise and scope here, we examine some contradictions related to legal formations of property rights that come to bear on resettlement planning as we have observed through close partnerships with resettling communities. We recognize that the mitigation of unevenly distributed risk, expressed in climate change, will require broad political, cultural, and legal transformations. We also think that the moment demands transdisciplinary and interdisciplinary investigation and hope that lending our "on the ground" anthropological and public administration insights will be useful in building more robust understanding and more just adaptation. We also recognize the urgency with which many communities are losing ground. Our assumption is that rendering the contradictions inherent in the law and in property regimes visible within the disaster and adaptation world, showing that these contradictions are a foundational aspect to the unequal distribution of risk and adaptation options, and presenting some of the possibilities that communities are already fighting for, will open possibilities for pursuing and supporting, more just planning processes among policymakers, program managers, and their legal teams.

References

Alexander, G. S. (1997). *Commodity & propriety: Competing visions of property in American legal thought 1776–1970*. University of Chicago Press.

Alexander, G. S. (2009). The social-obligation norm in American property law. *Cornell Law Faculty Publications, 94*(4), 745–819. https://scholarship.law.cornell.edu/lsrp_papers/92

Banner, S. (2005). *How the Indians lost their land: Law and power on the frontier*. Harvard University Press.

Blomley, N. (2004). *Unsettling the city: Urban land and the politics of property*. Routledge.

Boas, F. C., Adams, H., Sterly, H., Bush, S., van der Geest, K., Wiegel, H., Ashraf, H., Baldwin, A., Bettini, G., Blondin, S., de Bruijn, M., Durand-Delacre, D., Fröhlich, C., Gioli, G., Guaita, L., Hut, E., Jarawura, F., Lamers, M., Lietaer, S., … Hulme, M. (2019). Climate migration myths. *Nature Climate Change, 9*(12), 901–903. https://doi.org/10.1038/s41558-019-0633-3

Bronen, R., & Chapin, F. S., III. (2013). Adaptive governance and institutional strategies for climate-induced community relocations in Alaska. *Proceedings of the National Academy of Sciences, 110*(23), 9320–9325.

Bullard, R. D., Mohai, P., Saha, R., & Wright, B. (2008). Toxic wastes and race at twenty: Why race still matters after all of these years. *Environmental Law, 38*, 371.

Burkett, M. (2011). The nation ex-situ: On climate change, deterritorialized nationhood and the post-climate era. *Climate Law, 2*(3), 345–374.

Callison, C. (2017). Climate change communication and indigenous publics. In M. Nisbet (Ed.), *The Oxford encyclopedia of climate change communication*. Oxford University Press.

Dalbom, C., Hemmerling, S. A., & Lewis, J. (2014). Community resettlement prospects in Southeast Louisiana: A multidisciplinary exploration of legal, cultural, and demographic aspects of moving individuals and communities. *Tulane Institute on Water Resources Law & Policy, New Orleans, 49*.

D'Oro, R. (2014, January 17). Residents of eroding Alaska village seek federal help. *Fairbanks Daily News Miner*. https://www.newsminer.com/news/alaska_news/residents-of-eroding-alaska-village-seek-federal-help/article_9ce9b1b6-7fc0-11e3-80e6-0019bb30f31a.html

Esteves, L. (2018, September 13). *Climate change: We need to start moving people away from some coastal areas, warns scientist*. The conversation. https://theconversation.com/climate-change-we-need-to-start-moving-people-away-from-some-coastal-areas-warns-scientist-101351

Farbotko, C., & Lazrus, H. (2012). The first climate refugees? Contesting global narratives of climate change in Tuvalu. *Global Environmental Change*, 22 (2), 382-390.

Farbotko, C. (2022). Anti-displacement mobilities and re-emplacements: Alternative climate mobilities in Funafala. *Journal of Ethnic and Migration Studies, 48*, 3380–3396.

Flavelle, C. (2020a, August 26). U.S. flood strategy shifts to 'unavoidable' relocation of entire neighborhoods. *The New York Times* https://www.nytimes.com/2020/08/26/climate/flooding-relocation-managed-retreat.html

Flavelle, C. (2020b, March 11). Trump administration presses cities to evict homeowners from flood zones. *The New York Times.*

Fussell, E. (2012). Help from family, friends, and strangers during Hurricane Katrina: Finding the limits of social networks. In L. Weber & L. Peek (Eds.), *Displaced: Life in the Katrina diaspora* (pp. 150–166). University of Texas Press.

Fegan, M. (2006). Just compensation standards and eminent domain injustices: An underexamined connection and opportunity for reform. *Connecticut Public Interest Law Journal, 6*, 269.

GAO-20-488 (2020). *Climate change: A climate migration pilot program could enhance the nation's resilience and reduce federal fiscal exposure.* Washington, D.C

Gramling, R., Laska, S., Wooddell, G., Forsyth, C., Darlington, J., Green, B., Kappel, B., & Boudreaux, B. (2006). *Anticipating social effects of coastal restoration projects.* Louisiana Department of Natural Resources.

Greer, A. (2018). *Property and dispossession: Natives, empires and land in early modern North America.* Cambridge University Press.

Herrmann, V. (2017). America's first climate change refugees: Victimization, distancing, and disempowerment in journalistic storytelling. *Energy Research & Social Science,* 31, 205–214.

Jerolleman, A. (2019). *Disaster recovery through the lens of justice.* Springer.

Jessee, N. (2022). Reshaping Louisiana's coastal frontier: Managed retreat as colonial decontextualization. *Journal of Political Ecology, 29*(1). https://doi.org/10.2458/jpe.2835

Koslov, L. (2016). The case for retreat. *Public Culture, 28*(2), 359–387.

Locke, J. (1948). *The second treatise of civil government and a letter concerning toleration.* B. Blackwell.

Lustgarten, A. (2020, September 15). *Climate change will force a new American migration.* ProPublica. https://www.propublica.org/article/climate-change-will-force-a-new-american-migration

Marino, E. (2015). *Fierce climate, sacred ground: An ethnography of climate change in Shishmaref*. University of Alaska Press.

Manda, S., Alessandra, J., & Elizabeth, M. (2023). Assumptions and understanding of success in home buyout programs. *International Journal of Disaster Risk Reduction*, https://doi.org/10.1016/j.ijdrr.2023.103863

Marino, E. (2018). Adaptation privilege and voluntary buyouts: Perspectives on ethnocentrism in sea level rise relocation and retreat policies in the US. *Global Environmental Change, 49*, 10–13.
Marino, E., & Lazrus, H. (2015). Migration or forced displacement?: The complex choices of climate change and disaster migrants in Shishmaref, Alaska and Nanumea, Tuvalu. *Human Organization, 74*(4), 341–350.
Marino, E., Jerolleman, A., Jessee, N., Weyiouanna, A., Topkok, M. S., Keene, E., & Manda, S. (2022). Is the Longue Durée a Legal Argument?: Understanding Takings Doctrine in Climate Change and Settler Colonial Contexts in the United States. *Human Organization, 81*(4), 348–357.
Martinich, J., Neumann, J., Ludwig, L., & Jantarasami, L. (2012). Risks of sea level rise to disadvantaged communities in the United States. *Mitigation and Adaptation Strategies for Global Change, 18*(2), 169–185. https://doi.org/10.1007/s11027-011-9356-0
Maldonado, J. K. (2018). *Seeking justice in an energy sacrifice zone: Standing on vanishing land in coastal Louisiana*. Routledge.
Maldonado, J., Marino, E., & Iaukea, L. (2020). *Reframing the language of retreat,* Eos, 101, https://doi.org/10.1029/2020EO150527. Published on 10 November 2020.
Mufson, S. (2015, September 1). Obama visits receding glacier in Alaska to highlight climate change. *The Washington Post*. https://www.washingtonpost.com/politics/obama-visits-receding-glacier-in-alaska-to-highlight-climate-change/2015/09/01/dfacfe1e-50f6-11e5-9812-92d5948a40f8_story.html
Panfil, Y. (2020, July 14). *The case for 'managed retreat'*. Politico. Retrieved July 15, 2022, from https://www.politico.com/news/agenda/2020/07/14/climate-change-managed-retreat-341753
Parchomovsky, G., & Siegelman, P. (2004). Selling Mayberry: Communities and individuals in law and economics. *California Law Review, 92*(1), 75–146.
Park, K. S. (2021). The history wars and property law: Conquest and slavery as foundational to the field. *Yale Law Journal, 131*, 1062.
Piguet, E. (2013). From "primitive migration" to "climate refugees": The curious fate of the natural environment in migration studies. *Annals of the Association of American Geographers, 103*(1), 148–162.
Schutz, A., & Sandy, M. (2011). *Collective action for social change: An introduction to community organizing*. Springer.
Stanton, T. (2018). John Locke and the fable of liberalism. *The Historical Journal, 61*(3), 597–622.
Sylves, R. (2020). *Disaster policy and politics* (3rd ed.). Sage.
Warnecke, A., Tänzler, D., & Vollmer, R. (2010). *Climate change, migration and conflict: Receiving communities under pressure?* Washington, DC: The German Marshall Fund of the United States.

Weyiouanna, T., Sr. (2007). *Shishmaref erosion and relocation coalition concerns.* Immediate Action Workgroup Hearing.

CHAPTER 2

Property Law and Its Contradictions

Contradictions in the Property Regime of the United States

Despite its ubiquity, "property" is a difficult legal concept to pin down. The property regime and case law regarding property encompass many different forms of tangible and intangible property such as land and structures, intellectual property, hunting rights, personal possessions, and much more. Even when only thinking about land and structures, which pertain to resettlement planning most immediately, defining property can be challenging. For example, sometimes property is described as a set of entitlements, protected by laws, for the rights of exclusion from a physical space at the discretion of the person or people who hold title. Under this explanation, each title holder is comparable to a sovereign, and finds metaphorical support in the naming of legislation like "Castle Doctrines," which are state-designated laws that permit a property owner, in some circumstances, to use force to remove an intruder from their property. Alternatively, property is described as reflecting the social norms of the time, with protections in place to prevent property owners from causing harm to non-owners through activities described as nuisances. This can include the rights of all citizens affected by ownership to have some reasonable say on what the title holder(s) may or may not do. Zoning as a method of urban planning, EPA regulations on dumping, and prohibitions on who you may or may not exclude are indications that property entitlements are malleable to current conceptualizations of the rights of

A. Jerolleman et al., *People or Property*,
https://doi.org/10.1007/978-3-031-36872-1_2

non-property owners in relation to property owners. These conceptualizations are not static, but change over time through social (including legal and regulatory) encounters, that are themselves mediated by access to justice and by focusing events such as disasters (Sylves, 2020).

Broadly, we can understand property law as a negotiation, contestation, and compromise between rights of exclusion and rights of inclusion across title and non-title holders, or the rights of the individual property owner weighed against the rights of the common good (Fitzpatrick, 2006). For example, the doctrine of private necessity in tort law allows for some trespass such as in the event of a life threatening emergency, but what constitutes an emergency is mediated by a history of jurisprudence. In some states, laws of adverse possession, commonly known as squatter laws, are "the transfer of a legal interest in property from the original owner to one who has acted as if she owned the land for a certain period of time," particularly when the legal owner is absent (Clarke, 2005). These laws focus on the value of *use* of property, and on retaining property within a marketplace instead of, for example, allowing it to sit derelict. Laws also protect the established rights of owners from being impinged upon by other owners, such as liabilities incurred by an owner who builds a dam and floods a neighbors property. Additionally, nuisance laws broadly protect non-title holders from even being unreasonably "annoyed" by a title-holder's actions on their own property. For example, noise ordinances limit a property owner's ability from conducting any activity that makes too much of a racket. The most prominent example of the malleability of property ownership to the common good is that the federal government can take any property, with "just compensation," to be put to public use via eminent domain, following due process. Property law and the property regime, therefore, have always been bound by the responsibility the law assigns to a title holder to uphold the rights of others, and the power the law grants to a non-title holder on their right to access, put limits on, or make demands on the rights of a title holder.

Property rights are sometimes described as being like a bundle of sticks, or firewood, a metaphor often credited to Justice Benjamin Cardozo (Ellickson, 2011). This metaphor is useful in describing rights that accompany title, as being possible to aggregate or disaggregate among different owners (Wyman, 2018). Under this metaphor, there are three primary types of rights: the use of the property (such as occupancy), the right to its fruits (such as agricultural products or rental income), and the right to sell (market exchange) or encumber the property (such as burdening a property with a mortgage). These rights can be legally disaggregated in specific ways. For example, an owner may grant usage rights to their property through a mechanism such as leasing the "fruits of the property" to a farmer to develop agricultural products, while the original owner retains the ability to occupy and sell the property. An owner may also sell future development rights or grant a conservation easement. In this case, the owner sells future "fruits" of the property, while maintaining the right to sell the underlying land. The law typically provides some protections for the legally recorded owner of such rights, such as timber rights, when the land rights are connected to changes hands. Another common right is a usufruct granted to a widow or widower, where a property title may pass to children, but the right to occupy the house remains with the living spouse. Perhaps the most common example of disaggregated property rights is that an owner may give the rights of occupancy to a renter, earning the "fruits" of the property and retaining a right to sell. These disaggregated rights create complex webs of property rights and relationships, which include and implicate non-owners.

As prefaced in the introductory chapter, we outline four contradictions in the application of U.S. property law that we have seen come to bear on efforts to resettle from flood hazards associated with climate change:

1. An ethic of the right to land has co-existed with settler state expropriation of land;
2. Despite privileging the rights of the individual, an individual's right to act communally is discouraged and rendered difficult to exercise;
3. At times, the rights of current property owners are privileged above community protective measures, despite the reality that those rights will in many cases be undermined by climate change and that the actions of current property owners may increase the risk to themselves and others; and,
4. U.S. law has consistently been a tool to undermine the rights of individuals and groups through violent displacement, genocide, and dispossession, but it is also seen as a primary mechanism for harm reduction and the restoration and expansion of rights.

Contradictions within the property regime, within disaggregated rights holders, and within the legal system broadly which then serve to interpret whose rights hold precedent, all mediated by access and power, have had important implications for the histories of displacement and relocation throughout the history of the United States, including relocations occurring now under conditions of, and hazards stemming from, climate change.

An ethic of the right to land has co-existed with settler state expropriation of land

A recent analysis geospatially referenced and quantified the amount Indigenous dispossession of lands and changes in resource base that accompanied colonization of the United States (Farrell et al., 2021). Farrell and colleagues found a 98.9% reduction in cumulative coextensive lands and a 93.9% reduction in non-coextensive lands (Farrell et al., 2021) from the early colonial period compared to today. This was despite the fact that protection of private property ownership was integrated into both the U.S. Constitution and the Bill of Rights. Both documents were inspired by the Magna Carta, which codified the responsibility of governments to compensate their citizens for any land taken (Ely, 2008; Epstein, 1985). In one of many legal decisions that justified dispossession from Indigenous peoples, the founding fathers and U.S. courts embraced the Doctrine of Discovery, a set of principles that European colonial nations (including then the United States) had the right to dispossess millions of Indigenous peoples of the land and ecosystems that sustained them, in part because according to the racist and ethnocentric lens of European and U.S. settlers, the land was not put to so-called productive use (Barker, 2008).

While we often take this theft as inevitable, it is interesting to point out that international law at the time typically required a conqueror to integrate members of the conquered population while maintaining their property rights. In the case of the colonies that would become the United States, European powers chose to ignore this precedent on the grounds that Indigenous peoples could not be readily integrated into the social life of the nation and did not make the *fullest use* of the property (Kades, 2000). This contradiction (right to land/dispossession of land) has often been justified by a Lockean view that land holds little to no value prior to the expenditure of labor on its development and improvement (Epstein, 1985). Settlers who codified liberal property relations into law largely misrecognized, ignored, and displaced Indigenous ways of relating to land and existing forms of land tenure despite widespread sophisticated forms of land cultivation and productive ecological relationships maintained by Indigenous peoples throughout the continent during both pre-

and post-Columbian times (Denevan, 1992; Newcomb, 2008). While this misrecognition included misunderstanding Indigenous agricultural communities, the law is particularly blind to land relations that included seasonal migration or informal ownership without clearly demarcated property lines. As Carol Rose (1994) has noted: "It is doubtful whether the claims of any nomadic population could ever meet the common law requirements for establishing property in land. Thus, the audience presupposed by the common law of first possession is an agrarian or a commercial people – a people whose activities with respect to the objects around them require an unequivocal delineation of lasting control so that those objects can be either managed or traded" (Rose, 1994, 19).

Modes of seasonal settlement, shifting settlement, and mobile infrastructure, conflict with fixed, enclosed forms of private property (Bhandar, 2018; Marino, 2015). These biases against multi-locality or seasonal settlement are present in our case studies. In Chapter 7, Indigenous Alaskan modes of mobility are current and traditional solutions to coastal changes, but are difficult to fund through existing policy mechanisms. Nicholas Blomley has also noted that the colonial "conjunction of permanence and possession" continues to delegitimize mobile populations, such as renters, in urban environments (2004, 92), and in Chapter 6 we see that renters and other populations with precarious relationships to property are marginalized in relocation scenarios. Throughout the case studies, we also see a legal preference for a narrow, ethnocentric conceptualization of highest and best use re-emerge in the way land management and hazard mitigation is prioritized. For example, state and local governments in Louisiana continue to issue land use permits for industrial actors and for the engineering of mega-projects along a sinking coastline, while the inland migration and largely uncompensated abandonment of traditional lands by Indigenous, Black, and other marginalized communities is treated as a foregone conclusion (Esealuka, 2022). In coastal Alaska, sea wall revetments and other infrastructure projects that protect coastlines are used specifically to protect homes and businesses and not subsistence equipment or land and seascapes that are critical to Alaska Native ways of life (Marino, 2015). These prioritizations create the ecological and socio-political conditions which lead to relocation.

Historically, dispossession and expropriation of Indigenous land by the United States was also persistently insisted upon as legal, voluntary, and protective of communities, even when those protections were demonstrably false. The Indian Removal Act of 1830 practically enabled the forced displacement of hundreds of thousands of people, dispossession of millions of acres of land, and the mass killing of many thousand citizens from the Cherokee, Choctaw, Creek, Seminole, Chickasaw, and other nations who traditionally inhabited land east of the Mississippi River (Thornton, 1984), but was passed by Congress under the auspices that it would be entered into voluntarily by tribes and that they would be adequately compensated (Cave, 2003). The legislation reads:

> Be it enacted by the Senate and House of Representatives of the United States of America, in Congress assembled, That it shall and may be lawful for the Presidents of the United States to cause so much of any territory belonging to the United States, west of the river Mississippi to be divided into a suitable number of districts, for the reception of such tribes or nations of Indians ***as may choose*** to exchange lands where they now reside, and remove there [our emphasis].

In accordance with the Lockean understanding of best use and value, the Act furthermore states,

> Sec. 4. And be it further enacted, That if, upon any of the lands now occupied by the Indians, and to be exchanged for, there should be such improvements as add value to the land claimed by any individual or individuals of such tribes or nations, it shall and may be lawful for the President to cause such value to be ascertained by appraisement or otherwise and to cause such ascertained value to be paid to the person or persons rightfully claiming such improvements.

The Act codified a long-standing policy of forced removal that had begun centuries prior and continued well after the 1830s by local militias and national forces (Bowes, 2014), but contains language that frames the exchanges as "voluntary," and following the payment of an appraised value. The law, in that case, created cover for violent displacement. That such a globally condemned historical act has a similar legal structure to contemporary buyouts, including a similarly fraught understanding of voluntariness, should give us pause. As legal historian Stuart Banner (2005) writes, conquest and contract should be seen as a spectrum upon which at various places lies the transfer of land from Indigenous peoples to settlers.

Histories of forced displacement are partially why buyouts and acquisitions must be "voluntary" today, and that there are protections in place to make them such. However, as we'll see in the case studies in this book, contemporary relocation is still framed as a success when there is full "participation," i.e., the removal of everyone, or almost everyone, and that participation can be subjectively experienced by communities and individuals as coercive even when individuals formally choose to go. As legal scholar Stuart Banner wrote, "There is no sharp distinction between voluntariness and involuntariness. The difference between them is one of degree, not kind (2005, 5)." Though these historical examples are used here to be instructive, and not conflated, we want to point out that some of our collaborators in Louisiana who identify as Choctaw see direct parallels between the Trail of Tears and contemporary development-forced relocations, and talk about contemporary relocations as such. Some scholars and local tribal leaders along the Gulf Coast, have in fact explicitly referred to the current patterns of government supported displacement as a "modern day trail of tears" orchestrated via land use regulations and property laws, coupled with the violence of a tribal acknowledgment process that renders tribes invisible in the eyes of the law (Sand-Fleischmann, 2019).

Despite privileging the individual, the individual's right to act communally is discouraged

Another contradiction lies in the law's inability to reconcile the well-being of locally meaningful communal social structures, and communal ownership, with the legal primacy of the individual or household as social and property-holding units. U.S. legal forms and planning conventions have historically discouraged collective, social approaches to land tenure. In some cases, the friction is imposed intentionally. For example, assimilationist movements within the U.S. government advanced the 1887 General Allotment Act, also known as the Dawes Act, to convert Tribal lands into individually owned parcels under the assumption that individuation of land would promote industriousness and that unused land should be made available for agricultural use. In practice, the policy undercut Tribal sovereignty and created real estate markets out of Tribal territories, expropriating approximately 100 million acres from Indigenous nations and created checkerboard patterns of ownership. Melissa Watkinson-Shutten has written that the Bureau of Indian Affairs (BIA) is still trying to make up for the error of Allotment by working with tribes to buy back allotments that have since become fractionated, or owned by multiple (in some cases, up to 90) heirs. In some cases, this buyback program is a method of asserting sovereignty so that tribes can plan for climate change adaptation, including relocation, to contiguous, tribally-held land (Watkinson-Shutten, 2022).

Throughout the history of Indigenous/U.S. relations, it has been difficult to integrate legal protections of property with notions of land held collectively. During the Alaska Native Claims Settlement Process, enacted in 1971, these complexities were attempted to be reconciled by making tribal members shareholders in a corporate structure, as the easiest way to hold property and assets as a group. In Alaska, there is often significant respect given to the elder Indigenous statesmen and women who implemented ANCSA, given the difficulty of their position, and how quickly they had to organize. The ANCSCA example is instructive to see how difficult it was under U.S. law to protect collective holdings, and that the corporate structure seemed like the only legal option under which to organize Tribes without the land ultimately being held in trust by the federal government, as is the case on reservations.

The propensity toward individuation can also be seen through the exporting of collectively-held risk onto individuals, as evidenced in the suggested solutions for rising national losses from flooding and flood-prone development. Construction of homes in the floodplains was facilitated by the construction of levees by the U.S. Army Corps of Engineers (USACE), and by local permitting decisions. These same homes were then marketed to families as being free from risk by developers and local officials. The availability of insurance through the National Flood Insurance Program (NFIP) also directly contributed to that development. Families that purchased these homes have since experienced repeat flooding, are expected to pay rising flood insurance premiums and to bear a portion of the financial costs of relocation from the floodplain. The NFIP continues to be subsidized by the government and rates are not actuarially priced, but there are repeated calls for reform across the political spectrum (Teirstein, 2022), including from the Biden administration. Reorganization or changes to the NFIP are likely inevitable, however, it is useful to point out that this is an individual market solution to risks incurred by collective development and land management decisions. It is also important to point out that without accounting for the historical patterns of risk creation, any effort to charge actuarial rates will disproportionately harm lower-income homeowners. We already see lower-income homeowners opting out of flood insurance because of rising rates, and recognize that this has implications for recovery following future flooding, including the loss of a great deal of federal assistance.

In Chapters 3 and 5, we'll describe the difficulty Isle de Jean Charles had in claiming collective ownership of relocation processes. Both there and in Kinston, North Carolina, which we encounter in Chapter 4, we see that "community" itself is challenging to identify and involves negotiation and contestation within and among groups. It is also the case that it is often seen as "easier" or "more equitable" from a governance perspective to buy-out multiple individual properties as an adaptive response to climate change, rather than resettling or relocating a community. We want to suggest that this is not "natural" or the result of logic, but that it is due to the particular way property and use is conceptualized within laws and norms in the United States. And yet, as discussed in Chapters 3 and 7, there are real reasons that communities need and want to stay together. In Chapter 8, we propose some legal formations that could encourage this possibility but that have been overlooked or sidelined in the resettlements we have observed.

The rights of current (or future) property owners to develop their property for economic gain are privileged above community protective measures, despite the reality that those rights will, in many cases, be undermined by climate change and that the actions of current property owners may increase the risks to themselves and others

Another contradiction appears when we consider the clear need for land use constraints that would limit development to avoid risk, but may impinge upon the immediate economic enjoyment of some current property owners. In other words, at the same time, some communities are being pushed toward relocation, there is development occurring continuously along the coast which is largely protected by laws that have prioritized development without undue interference from the government. As summarized in the writings of Platt, Joseph L. Sax has pointed to a fundamental tension between requiring land to be left in its natural, undeveloped condition, and the goals of private property law (Platt, 1999). As a result, property interests related to development are almost always privileged above allowing property to remain in a natural state. These property dynamics happen via decisions by government agencies when they choose to protect tourist areas using beach nourishment, for example (Marino, 2018). The relatively few cases, where property is left in an undeveloped state, or returned to a more natural state, tend to occur through mechanisms that exclude human habitation and interaction, such as nature preserves.

In Chapter 8, we tell the story of an elder who flooded multiplied times on the coast of Louisiana. Her insurance rates increased and the flood damage became overwhelming. She sold her mostly undeveloped land to the highest bidder who put up a bigger house and subdivided the remaining property. Is this climate relocation? We would argue, but with the overlay of our 3rd contradiction, that the right to develop property is so prioritized that even under conditions of risk that would drive *some* people out of a landscape, development retains a foothold and then expands. In some cases, development then becomes "too big to fail" or enjoys the benefits of insured protection or armorment. There are currently plans to try and limit development in the floodplain by withholding flood insurance through NFIP (Teirstein, 2022), and changes to building regulations have been suggested by FEMA as a way for local governments to offset risk (FEMA, 2021), but it is difficult to put restrictions on development.[1] It is particularly difficult for the federal government to restrict coastal development as land use decisions occur at the state and local level, and municipal finance is deeply impacted by limitations on development.

This difficulty was rendered most visible in the case of Lucas vs. South Carolina Coast Council. Here, a local land owner purchased two residential lots on a barrier island in 1986. In 1988, the state passed a law which prohibited development and Lucas sued the government for a per se Takings case, arguing that the state law was essentially a government taking of the "fruits" of his property without compensation. The case went to the Supreme Court, where the court sided with Lucas that this did constitute a Taking and Lucas received compensation. This case and other cases related to takings are further described in Chapter 8. The case suggests however, as Platt (1999) observes, that states have an incentive to avoid the political burdens of regulating land use, especially when such regulations might render the land less valuable. Municipal governments are particularly vulnerable to resisting limiting development via zoning because they are more likely to need the tax funding that comes from development and are less likely to have the funds to pay for a Takings violation. In this contradiction, we recognize that land use regulations are a tool that can transfer the financial costs of avoiding disaster

[1] Homeowner's insurance, including catastrophic wind coverage, is beyond the scope of this book but also presents some challenges to habitation along coasts. Coastal states have created various programs and policies to attempt to ensure continued availability of coverage for residents and to limit price increases.

impacts to the property owner or developer, by limiting development, however, this also protects future owners, renters, and neighboring residents. Finally, developers may be in a better financial position to bear the costs of limiting development compared to the homeowners who, following development, are left to bear the costs of continually rising insurance payments.

An exception to privileging development may be the increasing use of conservation easements in large undeveloped portions of the northern United States. Conservation easements originated as a way for national parks to purchase development rights from adjacent land holdings as a means of preserving the viewscape (Teicher, 2021). However, most recently conservation easements have been used more by the wealthiest Americans as a pledge to limit development on their vast landholdings. The top 1% of wealthiest Americans currently hold 40% of the "non-home real estate" (Teicher, 2021). These conservation easements protect wealthy homesites and offer tax credits for large parcels of land that are being used for recreational purposes by their owners. We revisit conservation easements in Chapter 9, as we think through who is being paid "not to develop." It is instructive to consider here the elder we write about in the beginning of this section that wants to remain on less developed land in the floodplain, or the Indigenous communities in Alaska that are fighting mining developments, such as pebble mine (Greenfield, 2021), and compare them to the tax break for wealthy landowners to not develop recreational property.

Overall, privileging development is one means of prioritizing government decisions that can be justified using cost-benefit analysis models that are blind to the impacts to people and persons. These decisions habitually prioritize economic uses and economic gain, particularly in relation to property, and often without consideration of historical culpability for previous decisions, or long-term culpability for future harm. The longitudinal aspects of this contradiction are present in arguments with regard to what constitutes just compensation and the emphasis on market value. Chapters 7 and 9 explore this further.

U.S. law has consistently been a tool to undermine the rights of individuals and groups through violent displacement, genocide, and dispossession, but is also seen as a primary mechanism for harm reduction and the restoration of rights

There are, and have always been, examples where government interference with property rights are seen as permissible when in support of "societal" goals, or the goals of the powerful (Ely, 2008). This is true when the U.S. government found it permissible to confiscate land from Indigenous land holders, or for example, or in the Civil Rights Act of 1866, which granted equal rights to own property regardless of race, or legislation in the 1960s which allowed women to possess equal rights to marital property. All three of these examples illustrate legislative interference in property rights. The former as a means of undermining Indigenous rights, and the latter as a means of limiting the ability to discriminate in the sale, use, and ownership of properties. None of these legislative acts entirely accomplished their purported ends. Indigenous peoples have worked tirelessly to hold lands and property remains highly segregated across race and gender. However, these attempts to both eradicate and protect the rights of certain citizens did have an impact and made substantive changes to the property regime.

This history of interference with property rights suggests that property law in the United States is at least in part based, and reflects, norms and values that can change (Singer, 2014). As Singer points out, "property is about the social order; it reflects and enables our conception of what it means to live in a free and democratic society" (Singer, 2014, 1299). If property is always a permeable boundary of exclusion and inclusion, rendered differently at different moments in social history, then the law may change in order to bring about, and respond to, shifting understandings of the public good. This is the hope that many people, including ourselves, bring to climate-driven relocations: that the law can change sufficiently enough, and fast enough, to bring about greater climate justice in relocation scenarios so that individuals, families, and communities that need to relocate will be able to do so in a dignified way with minimal disruption. We build on this hope in Chapters 8 and 9 when we discuss novel ways of using existing legal structures and areas where change might lead to improved outcomes.

What all of these legal formations of property have in common, however, is ultimately that legislation reflects an assumption that citizenship within the democratic system should generate the ability to own property, seen as fundamental to democracy (Singer, 2014). As we've shown before, the Constitution protects property from government overreach just as it ensures protections of life and liberty, and the tax system in the United States is set up to encourage owning a home. Legislation like the ones mentioned above prohibits discrimination within the property regime, but does not question its overall good. We trace this protection back to the philosophical and metaphysical orientations of the founders of the country, and stemming back to the legal, philosophical, and metaphysical orientations of much of Western Europe. Locke organized his view on property through natural law, which he locates as stemming from the relationship between inheritance, Adam, and God as described in the Bible (Locke, 1948).

Cash Ahenakew and colleagues have noted that the institutions that organize modern life make it difficult to "provincialize the West" (Chakrabarty, 2009). They write that "modernity's epistemological trap" (Ahenakwe et al., 2014, 217) is that even struggles against oppressive forces must be legible in the "grammar of modernity that is bound by specific metaphysical choices" (217). Land as property is among these metaphysical choices. A real question for us is, Does the law have the capacity to protect social norms that exist outside of Euro-centric and ethnocentric assumptions? While philosophical and epistemological in origin, these "traps" are not abstract. In Chapters 3 and 6, we discuss the potential dangers of market orientation and what Keeanga-Yamahtta Taylor (2019) calls "predatory inclusion." In these chapters, we encounter the impacts of state-enforced reimagining of traditional territory into real estate and generational wealth into home value. These struggles raise the question of whether or not U.S. law is ever capable of protecting values that exist among other epistemological traditions (though these boundaries are fuzzy), and, if not, whether conditions of extreme climate change and relocation will make these misalignments in value and worldview lead to ongoing harms and climate injustice, during solution-making processes.

Finally, we wonder whether any legal formation is ultimately determined, not by the structure of the law itself, but by the power dynamics of access to the law. The same body of law, for example, that held up the rights of freedom of the individual has been used as a tool for genocide and dispossession. Is it possible, then, to expect the law to protect a different set of actors now? Climate change, erosion, disasters, and development all push relocation. These are sometimes direct, but often indirect. For example, land grabs are a socio-political formation that can be a significant driver of displacement during both development investments and following a disaster. Land grabs can also lack visibility in legal and policy mechanisms (Manda et al., 2019), and be treated as an inevitable part of development (Deininger et al., 2011). If the law protects displacement as an outcome of development, can it be rendered useful to protect the human rights of displaced communities in Alaska linked to erosion?

Many people, including the authors, look to the law and legal structures to uphold societal goals of mitigating climate change, adapting to climate change, and seeking climate justice. We consider both how the law and legal structures might be used, and also might be changed. This is done despite the fact that we, along with many other academics, affected communities, journalists, and the American public at large, also recognize that the government is largely ineffectual and/or inequitable at preventing, managing, or distributing risk and benefit through law and policy. This lack of effectiveness is due in part to the many levels of government that interact with each other, as well as their interactions with broader societal pressures and histories of inequity.

There is reason to be circumspect of the law's capacity to render justice. The history of internal displacements within the United States includes both climate-induced migrations, such as during the Dust Bowl era of the 1930s, and those driven by socio-economic factors and racializing policies, such as the Great Migration, which spanned a period of over fifty years and resulted in the movement of millions of Black workers and their families (Wikerson, 2010). It also includes Japanese Internment, managed by the War Relocation Authority, which moved over 100,000 people without any compensation for the loss of land and properties (Tulane, 2014; although reparations were later paid to some families). It includes the displacement of African American communities for urban renewal and highway projects (Fullilove, 2005; Ronald & Lindell, 1997), and the repeated displacement of Native American Communities including, more recently, the Bureau of Indian Affairs Urban Relocation Program of the 1950s (Keene, 2017). Indigenous communities in Alaska and Louisiana, described in Chapters 3, 5, and 7, who are facing the choice of relocation now because of repetitive flooding, have homes in precarious places, in part as a result of histories of forced relocations linked to colonial decision-making that moved Tribes to geographically vulnerable landscapes and imposed forms of development in those locations that limited their ability to adapt to changing ecological conditions (Maldonado et al., 2013; Marino, 2015). In these cases, the law largely did not protect people from the risks that pushed relocations as a result of colonial intrusion, or the risks communities incurred because of the outcomes of those intrusions.

There are also, however, important reasons for hope, and inspiration to push for change. While civil rights laws and protections have not eradicated racial injustice within the court system itself (Clair, 2020), they have been used to successfully render justice for plaintiffs bringing suit against discriminatory practices. The following chapters will show that real harms are being done in communities that are facing displacement as a result of relocations that stem from socio-political circumstances and climate change impacts. However, we believe that ongoing legal work to point out the inconsistencies in application of the law, and promoting legal formations that support climate justice for people going through relocation, are critical and may have material impacts, even if these relocations have ongoing disparities and challenges.

Gregory Alexander argues that there is a demonstrable legal obligation to foster the capabilities essential to human flourishing (Alexander, 2009). In other words, the law could be put in service of remedying harms. While historical efforts to do so have often failed, it isn't wasted time to point toward legal possibilities that address systemic injustices which take these historical lessons into account as part of broader strategies geared toward addressing current challenges. This includes legal and property possibilities that repair historical harm. As Singer points out: "... property rights are justified if they are part of a political and economic system that enables every person to become an owner, and if it is not possible for every person to use self-help to enter the property-owning class, then it follows that refusing to share one's property with the poor deprives them of resources needed for human life" (2006, 327).

References

Ahenakew, C., Andreotti, V. D. O., Cooper, G., & Hireme, H. (2014). Beyond epistemic provincialism: De-provincializing Indigenous resistance. *AlterNative: An International Journal of Indigenous Peoples, 10*(3), 216–231.

Alexander, G. S. (2009). The social-obligation norm in American property law. *Cornell Law Faculty Publications, 94*(4), 745–819. https://scholarship.law.cornell.edu/lsrp_papers/92

Banner, S. (2005). *How the Indians lost their land: Law and power on the frontier*. Harvard University Press.

Barker, J. (2008). Gender, sovereignty, rights: Native women's activism against social inequality and violence in Canada. *American Quarterly, 60*(2), 259–266.

Bhandar, B. (2018). *Colonial lives of property: Law, land, and racial regimes of ownership*. Duke University Press.

Blomley, N. (2004). *Unsettling the city: Urban land and the politics of property*. Routledge.

Bowes, J. P. (2014). American Indian removal beyond the removal act. *Native American and Indigenous Studies, 1*(1), 65–87.

Cave, A. A. (2003). Abuse of power: Andrew Jackson and the Indian removal act of 1830. *The Historian, 65*(6), 1330–1353.

Chakrabarty, D. (2009). The climate of history: Four theses. *Critical Inquiry, 35*(2), 197–222.

Clarke, J. A. (2005). Adverse Possession of Identity: Radical Theory, Conventional Practice. *Oregon Law Review, 84*(2), pp. 563–655.

Clair, M. (2020). *Privilege and punishment: How race and class matter in criminal court*. Princeton University Press.

Denevan, W. (1992). The pristine myth: The landscape of the Americas in 1492. *Annals of the Association of American Geographers, 82*(3), 369–385.

Deininger, K., Byerlee, D., Lindsay, J., Norton, A., Selod, H., & Stickler, M. (2011). Rising global interest in Farmland: Can it yield sustainable and equitable benefits? World Bank. https://openknowledge.worldbank.org/handle/10986/2263

Ellickson, R. C. (2011). Two cheers for the bundle-of-sticks metaphor, three cheers for Merrill and Smith. *Econ Journal Watch, 8*(3), 215–222.

Ely, J. W., Jr. (2008). *The guardian of every other right: A constitutional history of property rights*. Oxford University Press.

Epstein, R. A. (1985). *Takings: Private property and the power of eminent domain*. Harvard University Press.

Esealuka, M. (August 29, 2022). 'They want us gone': Black Louisianans fight to rebuild a year after Ida. Southerly. https://southerlymag.org/2022/08/29/they-want-us-gone-black-louisianans-fight-to-rebuild-a-year-after-ida/

Farrell, J., Burow, P. B., McConnell, K., Bayham, J., Whyte, K., & Koss, G. (2021). Effects of land dispossession and forced migration on Indigenous peoples in North America. *Science, 374*(6567).

FEMA BRIC. (2021). https://www.fema.gov/sites/default/files/documents/fema_fy21-bric-technical-criteria-psm_111521.pdf

Fitzpatrick, D. (2006). Evolution and chaos in property rights systems: The third world tragedy of contested access. *Yale Law Journal, 115*, 996–1048.

Fullilove, M. T. (2005). *Root shock: How tearing up city neighborhoods hurts Americans and what we can do about it*. One World Press.

Greenfield, N. (2021). *Alaska natives lead a unified resistance to the pebble mine*. NRDC. https://www.nrdc.org/stories/alaska-natives-lead-unified-resistance-pebble-mine

Kades, E. (2000). The dark side of efficiency: Johnson v. M'Intosh and the expropriation of American Indian lands. *University of Pennsylvania Law Review, 148*(4), 1065–1190. https://doi.org/10.2307/3312840

Keene, E. (2017). Lessons from relocations past: Climate change, tribes, and the need for pragmatism in community relocation planning. *American Indian Law Review, 42*(1), 259–289.

Locke, J. (1948). *The second treatise of civil government and a letter concerning toleration*. Blackwell.

Maldonado, J. K., Shearer, C., Bronen, R., Peterson, K., & Lazarus, H. (2013). The impact of climate change on tribal communities in the US: Displacement, relocation, and human rights. *Climate Change, 120*(3), 601–614.

Manda, S., Dougill, A., & Tallontire, A. (2019). Large-scale land acquisitions and institutions: Patterns, influence and barriers in Zambia. *Geographical Journal, 185*(2), 194–208.

Marino, E. (2015). *Fierce climate, sacred ground: An ethnography of climate change in Shishmaref*. University of Alaska Press.

Marino, E. (2018). Adaptation privilege and voluntary buyouts: Perspectives on ethnocentrism in sea level rise relocation and retreat policies in the US. *Global Environmental Change, 49*, 10–13.

Newcomb, S. T. (2008). *Pagans in the promised land: Decoding the doctrine of Christian discovery*. Fulcrum Publishing.

Norton, A., Selod, H., & Stickler, M. (2011). *Rising Global Interest in Farmland : Can it Yield Sustainable and Equitable Benefits?* World Bank. https://openknowledge.worldbank.org/handle/10986/2263

Platt, R. H. (1999). *Disasters and democracy: The politics of extreme natural events*. Island Press.

Ronald, W. P., & Lindell, M. K. (1997). Principles for managing community relocation as a hazard mitigation measure. *Journal of Contingencies and Crisis Management, 5*(1), 49–59. https://doi.org/10.1111/1468-5973.00036

Rose, C. M. (1994). *Property and persuasion: Essays on the history, theory and rhetoric of ownership*. Routledge.

Sand-Fleischmann, M. G. (2019). *Circumventing the next trail of tears: Re-approaching planning and policy for the climatologically displaced indigenous communities of coastal Louisiana* (Doctoral dissertation). Cornell University.

Singer, J. W. (2006). After the flood: Equality & humanity in property regimes. *Loyola Law Review, 52*(2), 243.

Singer, J. W. (2014). Property as the law of democracy. *Duke Law Journal, 63*(6), 1287–1335. https://doi.org/10.2139/ssrn.2407966

Sylves, R. (2020). *Disaster policy and politics* (3rd ed.). Sage.

Taylor, K.-Y. (2019). *Race for profit: How banks and the real estate industry undermined black homeownership*. UNC Press Books.

Teicher, J. G. (2021). This land is their land. *The Baffler*. https://thebaffler.com/latest/this-land-is-their-land-teicher

Teirstein, Z. (2022). Biden's new vision for the National flood Insurance Program. *Grist*. https://grist.org/housing/bidens-new-vision-for-the-national-flood-insurance-program/

Thornton, R. (1984). Cherokee population losses during the Trail of Tears: A new perspective and a new estimate. *Ethnohistory, 31*, 289–300.

Tulane Institute of Water Resources Law & Policy. (2014, September). *Community resettlement: Prospects in Southeast Louisiana. A multidisciplinary exploration of legal, cultural, and demographic aspects of moving individuals and communities*. Tulane University Law School.

Watkinson-Schutten, M. (2022). Decolonizing climate adaptation by reacquiring fractionated tribal lands. In M. Walter, T. Kukutai, A. A. Gonzales, & R. Henry (Eds.), *The Oxford handbook of indigenous sociology*. Oxford University Press. https://doi.org/10.1093/oxfordhb/9780197528778.013.42

Wikerson, I. (2010). *The warmth of other suns: The epic story of America's great migration*. Vintage Book.

Wyman, K. M. (2018). The new essentialism in property. *Journal of Legal Analysis, 9*(2), 183–246. https://doi.org/10.1093/jla/lay002

PART II

Proof of Harm

CHAPTER 3

Market Orientation as an Environmental Hazard for Resettling Communities

Introduction

For better and worse, community resettlement as climate adaptation can disrupt regional land and property relations. Government officials in U.S. jurisdictions have raised concerns that resettlement threatens municipal budget stability by potentially decreasing the property tax base and stifling future development (Koslov, 2016; Shi & Varuzzo, 2020). Threats of ecological disaster can drive up housing and land costs in nearby, supposedly safer locations (Keenan & Bradt, 2020; Taylor & Aalbers, 2022). Finally, new displacements happen simultaneously, and wholly outside of climate risks, due to development, gentrification, the corporate consolidation of land and residential housing, and mass incarceration, among other forces. There is a lack of anti-displacement policies throughout the country (Anguelovski et al., 2019). These various dynamics can interact within the contexts of ecological disaster, amplifying demands for public investments in affordable and social housing (Fleming et al., 2019; Li & Spidalieri, 2021; Morris, 2021) as well as creating debate on the inequities and structural violence already baked into the housing market (De Vries & Fraser, 2012; Siders, 2018).

Efforts to link mobility and adaptation policy in the United States therefore evoke long-standing and urgent questions about the relationships between land as property, U.S. housing policies, and environmental and climate justice. In what ways do histories of uneven development, forced displacement, and racialized or gendered housing precarity come

A. Jerolleman et al., *People or Property*,
https://doi.org/10.1007/978-3-031-36872-1_3

to bear on community and Tribal-driven resettlement processes and outcomes? How do property relations endure in the wake of climate disasters that seem to lay bare the unjust conditions produced, in part, by the U.S. property regime in the first place? In coastal Louisiana, policies intended to restore coastal environments and create resilience among coastal communities have habitually accommodated socio-environmental risk producers, like land speculators and the fossil fuel industries, who have both shaped and leveraged the U.S. property regime for profits. In this chapter, we consider the reconfiguration of property relations in the wake of the environmental catastrophe of coastal habitat loss as colonial, insofar as Black and Indigenous ecological and social relations are further fractured and industrial actors standing as stakeholders are sustained, despite the damage they have caused (Barra, 2021; Jessee, 2022).

Building on observations throughout one resettlement planning process in Louisiana, and taking seriously insights provided by climate migration and urban studies scholarship, this chapter considers the peril created by narrowly framed climate adaptation policy and planning. Given the historical scope of socio-environmental risks and the known effects of existing real estate practices and inadequate government protections, we explore how narratives of market value limited adaptation options produced by the state. Additionally, the chapter takes up several themes raised throughout the book, including, how the unjust existing property regime shapes human mobility in relation to environmental and climate change; divergent conceptualizations of community and how people are encouraged or discouraged to act communally; and interactions among the market, market actors, and law throughout displacement and resettlement.

Community Resettlement as a Real Estate Transaction

Privileging land as real estate and resettlement as a real estate transaction may undermine local climate adaptation. This was especially vivid as the state of Louisiana administered federal funds in a way that exploited Jean Charles Choctaw Nation leaders whose resettlement planning began in 2002, garnered state support in 2014, and was awarded federal funding in 2016. Prior to the funding, resettlement was envisioned by Tribal leaders as a struggle for cultural survival in the wake of multigenerational experiences of land grabs, ecological destruction caused by oil and gas extraction and river development, and forced displacement (Comardelle, 2020; Maldonado et al., 2021). As discussed further in Chapter 5, Tribal leaders prioritized the reunification of displaced Tribal citizens and rekindling traditional ways of life on higher ground. Among other initiatives, their plans included enhancing collective Tribal land stewardship both on the Island via continued ownership, occasional temporary habitation on the Island, new investments in ceremony, and tribal economic development activities at a new inland location via the establishment of a community land trust. Tribal leaders articulated these goals of collective land stewardship as an overall risk mitigation strategy with the understanding that individual households who moved would be safer from hurricanes and could be better supported by the Tribe if tax burdens increased, or insurance costs rose. The Tribe's plans were used by Louisiana's Office of Community Development to acquire $48.3 million through the federally sponsored National Disaster Resilience Competition, however, upon receiving the money, state officials imposed a different framework of resettlement that prioritized ongoing land commodification, and individualized household property ownership. During planning meetings and conversations, Louisiana's lead resilience administrator working on the resettlement repeatedly emphasized, "At its core, the resettlement is essentially a very complicated real estate transaction."

State planners articulated the real estate framework alongside their exploitation of Indigenous planning and as they reduced commitments to their partnership with Tribal leadership (Jessee, 2022). In 2018, Louisiana's Office of Community Development began what local leaders experienced as a divisive planning process that undermined years of work by the Tribe. Simultaneously, the agency released eligibility requirements for those moving to the resettlement site. These requirements surprised Tribal leaders and departed from the initial resettlement goals. The guidelines provided multiple "options" for individual households depending on their relationship to the Island and financial capacity. Option A consisted of a parcel of land and new house in the resettlement site. Eligibility was limited to only those who lived on Isle de Jean Charles at the time of the grant allocation (2016) or those who had left since 2012—the regulatory "tie back date," which is the year of the congressional appropriation of funds. That same demographic also could choose Option D, a house outside of the new location and outside the flood zone. Initially, the state tried to establish 40-year mortgages for Island properties, so that eventually property would be transferred to the state, but the Tribe resisted.

After a mobilization against the state's attempt to take Island property, the state used a contract to guarantee that families who resettled would not lose their Island property, at least as part of the resettlement. However, these homeowner contracts also created the risk of future loss of those properties if restrictions were not met. The agreements however are also pretty restrictive, prohibiting those who resettle from making substantial repairs to Island property if damaged in storms and prohibiting the use of Island property as fishing camps or rental properties, a limitation on use by which the white campers and few Indigenous households who did not apply for a new home in the resettlement do not have to abide.

Many Island residents, including some Tribal leaders who have led the resettlement effort, had been displaced or left the Island in the wake of storms or because of road flooding prior to 2012 and were therefore ineligible for either Option A or Option D. Some of this group was eligible instead for Option B, an empty lot in the new location, but no house. Eligibility for this option, however, was limited to those who could demonstrate the ability to finance the construction of a new house themselves and who would let go of any existing housing that they own due to the regulatory prohibition on public funding for second homes. The qualification to demonstrate financial capacity meant that low-income former Island residents could not meet this requirement and would thus be prevented from moving closer to friends, family, and other social networks that were relocating to the new site. Leaving out low-income households from the resettlement may also have meant that the Tribal members who could have most benefited from the resilience plans Tribal leaders had envisioned were left out of the new resettlement. The qualification to let go of existing homes deterred many other Tribal citizens and at least some Tribal leaders who argue they could have added organizing capacity to the new community. Option C allowed for the public auctioning of properties that do not get claimed through the planning stages with current and former Island residents. According to state documents, "Any unused lots in the new community will be made available to the public through other housing programs or public auction for residential housing development" (LOCD, 2019, 8). This was rarely, if ever, discussed publicly by state planners or policymakers and never disclosed in the state's promotional or informational materials related to the resettlement.

State officials saw the resettlement as a way to manufacture a real estate market and establish the conditions for subsequent development of commercial real estate and businesses as part of their view of sustainability while excluding Tribal input. In an important reflective analysis, Rachel Isacoff, who worked as part of the subcontracted market analysis team, emphasizes that she never met the Tribe, never got to consider their needs and desires, but just had to run numbers on highest and best use, a concept, as applied by planners and the real estate industry, links a Lockean notion of individual property relations to economic value above all:

> I was on the team that conducted a market analysis of the new resettlement site and made recommendations for housing, commercial, and retail schemes that reflected the "highest and best use" of the site. This technocratic approach to planning did not mirror the economic characteristics of the existing community and did not directly consider how well the proposed uses responded to the needs of or supported the workforce training and livelihoods of the IDJC tribe. In fact, because of the way our team (and all consultants) valued and capped time through billable hours and leaned heavily on experience from conducting past economic development analyses, no one from my firm met with the tribe during the process. (Isacoff, 2021, 198–199)

The approach to land and economic development aims were thus subsumed by state planners within what Samuel Stein refers to as the "real estate state," decontextualized from Indigenous-led struggle to enhance or honor tribal cultural survival, land justice, livelihoods, social relations, and practical needs. According to the state's lead resilience administrator who was leading the administration of the federal funds for the resettlement, "Like founding any new town over the course of Western history [...] it's all wrapped around the idea of, how do we generate revenue? [...] In Louisiana, that could mean fitness companies, pharmacies, and supermarkets chip in with funding in exchange for footholds in the new community, much like a city would on a new real estate development." "Unlocking that financial [support] (sic) is something that will determine the success of [relocation] (sic) projects," adds Mr. Sanders. "Ultimately we want to show that there would be the same amount of incentives the private sector has every time in any real estate development" (Gass, 2017).

Planners also decided that common areas of the new site, such as the cultural center and outdoor spaces, would serve broader publics instead of the Tribe's distinct needs and would be maintained by Terrebonne

Parish, rather than the Tribe, as was articulated in the state's resettlement prospectus and the funded National Disaster Resilience Competition application. When Tribal leaders requested ownership of community property throughout the site to fulfill their plans for traditional herb gardens, walking paths, Tribal government offices, and several other ideas generated as part of the Tribal community-driven plans, the Office of Community Development informed them that the Tribe would have "use rights" to common areas of the resettlement but not ownership of any land. Therefore, as it currently stands at the time of this writing, the Tribe—a landowner on the Island and historical Island social institution—will have no formalized sustained collective presence at the resettlement site, and only limited individual use rights along with any other citizen or organization.

Approaching resettlement as a real estate transaction among individuals distorted the Tribe's goals. First, it denied the Tribe itself a full set of property rights, aka the three sticks in the bundle (see Chapter 2), limiting their rights, authority, and role as the designated beneficiaries of the relocation, broadly. Second, it focused on individuals without simultaneous investment in the Tribal community as a whole as described in the state and HUD's descriptions of beneficiaries for the grant. Third, it established a frame that prioritized the act of moving over long-term investments and ongoing Tribal consultation and resilience. Fourth, it undermined the rearticulation of Indigenous collective land tenure as a functioning land ethic and practice. Finally, framing resettlement as a real estate transaction among individuals prioritized economic development, creating new terrain for the real estate market, and enticing non-Indigenous residents. The outcome of which expropriated land and potential land rights to highest bidders instead of keeping land and land rights to support the collective well-being of the Tribe. It is difficult not to see the resemblance between these events and historical colonial land grabs and assimilation policies. The General Allotment Act of 1887, for example, enabled the President of the United States to forcibly divide land previously held in trust for Indigenous nations into parcels of property that were then allotted to individuals along with U.S. citizenship. Unallotted land was taken by the U.S. government for agriculture or sold to settlers. Allotment policy disrupted traditional forms of land tenure, place-based ecological relations, and Indigenous adaptation. The policy also came following a period of rapid U.S. imperialism westward intensified by the California Gold Rush and 1848 Treaty of Guadalupe Hidalgo, which annexed lands occupied by Mexico to the United States. Much like the reservation system and removal policies, allotment was driven by settlers' desire for land within a cloak of paternalistic reforms aimed at assimilating Indigenous peoples. The federal government ended allotment in 1934, but by then, Indigenous lands were reduced by over 100 million acres and split up into dispersed parcels and subsumed within the colonial state's property regime (Echo-Hawk, 2010). Option C, the public auctioning of land purchased with federal funds initially allocated for the Tribe's community resilience mirrors the sale of "surplus" Tribal lands under allotment.

Individuation and Limitations on Receiving Community Engagement

Louisiana's Office of Community Development emphasized residential engagement and bifurcated their approach to administering resettlement funds so that activities focused on the Island and leaving the Island were driven by a distinct set of policy objectives that differed from activities focused on redevelopment at the new site. On the Island, the primary goals articulated by the state were to move people away from coastal flood risk and to prevent those who resettle from living and rebuilding on the Island (i.e., reducing economic costs of flooded properties). It is, however, worth noting that the state's legal inability, or unwillingness, to restrict Island redevelopment for recreational camps, created skepticism among those resettling about the state's intentions to un-develop the Island. The state's focus at the inland site was to nurture conditions for population and market growth as a receiving community.

The distinct modes of "community engagement" on the Island and in Schriever (the location of the inland resettlement site) reflected narrow constructions of risk and possible adaptations. State planners and contractors imposed a haphazard and individualistic outreach process on the Island that seemed aimed at decontextualizing the resettlement from existing Tribal community action for cultural survival and justice after generations of colonization, exploitation, and marginalization. As discussed further in Chapter 5, the state and contractors organized individual household interviews with some residents, and published misrepresentations and assumptions about the Island's social organization. Practically, this de-emphasized the Tribe as a community that consisted of on/off Island Tribal relations, and instead portrayed the Island as a discrete community of individuals. While the state organized three community meetings on the Island, when these convenings became difficult for the state to manage due to ongoing debate among participants, planners and subcontractors switched to utilizing a format for meetings whereby some "stakeholders" were invited to meeting locations during a specified window of time to engage with state planners and contractors one on one. This approach enabled the agency to better control information flow and shared narratives by displacing messy group conversation and collective processing of information, and putting the responsibility of engaging on the individual, and the weighing of individual testimony, on the state agencies. The switch limited the ability to organize in larger numbers, making participation as communal action more challenging.

Meanwhile the state's outreach to the predominantly white property owners who lived in the Schriever area adjacent to the new site was more open to the assertion of a right to act communally in so far as state planners adjusted their initial meeting format from an open house tour of plans to a group discussion where people listened to the concerns of others in a shared space face to face with state planners when the residents demanded such a conversation. The state's administration of the resettlement funding stirred conflict within the receiving community as well. Resistance and "NIMBYism," or "Not in My Backyard," attitudes were expressed by the mostly white Schriever residents who lived adjacent to the inland location purchased by the state for the resettlement in ways that surprised state administrators. In addition to expressing concern about water drainage issues at the site, which continue to worry both those resettling and onlookers (Dermanksy, 2022), residents raised objections to the discrepancies between the Tribe's initially proposed and funded plans and the state's vision during a planning meeting hosted by the state once site designs were developed in 2019. "We were told this was going to be an Indian community," yelled one man. "We were ok with that, but this is different. We don't want HUD housing or Section 8. Or who moves in if these people move out?!" Fears of the resettlement site becoming "section-8" and a "normal HUD subdivision" may have been an expression of the widespread stigmatization of public housing and coded anti-black racism in the United States. It also reflects the extent to which real estate values, racial formations, and the white management of exclusion and inclusion of urban space remain mutually interdependent, including during climate resettlements.

While community outreach with individual residents is essential, research has demonstrated that the conflicts that tend to emerge in receiving areas are typically mediated by existing political economic forces and conditions. Scholars focused on environmental migration have located some sources of conflict within, for example, an existing lack of governing capacity, inadequate resource provision, and political instability in destination locations (Reuveny, 2007; Warnecke et al., 2010). Reuveny (2007) refers to these as "auxiliary influences" on resettlement outcomes. As the next section describes, such influences in the United States are shaped in large part by predation and extraction within finance, land, and real estate industries which exploit and reproduce racialized disparities in housing, wealth, and climate change-related risk, among other institutions. This means that perhaps more meaningful than funding community engagement among new neighbors, there must be more fundamental, transformative, and enduring investments into life sustaining institutions, like for example, affordable housing, in receiving areas for better resettlement processes and outcomes.

Out of the Kettle of Coastal Flooding and into the Fire of Predatory Inclusion

As the section above emphasized, while there is a lot of attention to the conflicts that can emerge throughout resettlement among resettlers and people who live in the places they are moving to, such conflicts are not typically driven by interpersonal interactions between new neighbors but rather aggravated by institutionalized inequities and power. Taking seriously the effects of auxiliary influences in producing resettlement risks in "receiving areas" requires a recognition within climate adaptation planning that the climate crisis is at once a racial capitalist crisis, an affordable housing crisis, a land crisis, a financial crisis, and a governance crisis that is produced at multiple sites and levels of government. For example, local governments determine land use and housing availability with federal funding and federal policy and rules are locally interpreted within program implementation and project development.

During the Isle de Jean Charles resettlement, Louisiana's Office of Community Development frequently evoked legal and regulatory constraints when explaining the deviation from the Tribe's plans and development decisions at the inland site. Among them was the Fair Housing Act—the federal policy that prevents housing discrimination based on race, color, religion, sex, disability, familial status, or national origin. According to Louisiana's Office of Community Development, "The program is open to all residents of the island, and in later phases to past residents of the island, regardless of tribal affiliation, race, color, religion, sex, national origin, familial status or disability" (LDOA, 2019). The evocation of fair housing laws while reducing possibilities for Tribal inclusion in the resettlement was striking and seemed contradictory. According to Jean Charles Choctaw Nation Chief Albert Naquin during an interview, "This doesn't seem very fair. We know the Fair Housing was meant to prevent discrimination, but I think what they are doing is discriminating against the Tribe."

This evocation of Fair Housing to undercut tribal planning is but one example of a long history of inconsistency in enforcing fair housing policy that goes back to the Federal Civil Rights Act of 1866, which prohibited racial discrimination in housing (Taylor, 2019; Zonta, 2019). More recently, compare HUD's approach when the Obama Administration administered an anti-segregation rule "further affirming fair housing" by incentivizing more aggressive desegregation policies at the municipal level to the position of subsequent HUD Secretary Ben Carson's dismissal of such efforts as "failed socialism" (Carson, 2015). Once Carson took over as HUD Secretary in 2017, HUD aggressively regulated some jurisdictions—like Los Angeles, for insufficient accessible housing availability—while turning their back on racial discrimination elsewhere and fighting to roll back the regulations against a disproportionate adverse effect on protected groups under the Fair Housing Act (Kasakove, 2019).

Two basic questions regarding the Fair Housing Act and the resettlement confounded Tribal leaders and their allies. First, why would HUD have funded something that was intended to support a Tribe's resettlement if that was impossible under existing Fair Housing law? And second, if administering the Tribal community resettlement as was proposed and funded was illegal, then why was there not a sustained collaborative conversation and formalized agreement as to how to use discretion in order to accomplish the Tribe's central goals of reuniting their Tribe and embracing their heritage in a way that did align with the Fair Housing Act before moving on with a more top-down planning process? According to Maldonado and Peterson (2018), one problem lies in the inability of U.S. laws to recognize communal social structures that have been prioritized in the resettlement planning. They point out that the Fair Housing Act protects the rights of individual citizens and not community rights, which are seen as essential for many "Indigenous and culturally connected communities" (ibid.). This aligns with insights of Lisa Kahaleole Hall, who has described the individualism internalized within civil rights discourse, and how this produces a tension with Indigenous nationalism:

> In the United States the contemporary conception of race is firmly anchored in civil rights ideologies, the idea of equality of individuals within one nation, and does not address very different concepts of Indigenous nationhood. The logics of some forms of antiracist struggles paradoxically can undermine group identities by advocating for a form of social justice based on the equal treatment of individuals. (2008, 277)

Well-intentioned policies to protect individuals from discrimination may therefore have the unintended consequence of harming collective realities. However, there are also reasons to think that state officials may have been overstating the extent to which the Fair Housing Act was a policy barrier to using federal funds to support the Tribal community resettlement and that the matter was one of state political will and discretion.

There is also noteworthy historical precedence of exceptions to the Fair Housing Act approved by HUD when it seemed egregiously inappropriate, but these examples depended upon the exercise of bureaucratic discretion and the willingness of officials to work toward solutions. One example comes out of the fight against gentrification in San Francisco. The city wanted to use an anti-displacement "neighborhood preference" for low-income residents from certain areas in their applications to the new publicly funded Willie B. Kennedy Apartments. Essentially, the plan was to offer those who came from certain neighborhoods a priority spot in new public development "to stem the exodus of African Americans and members of other minority groups from neighborhoods that are rapidly gentrifying" (Dineen, 2016). HUD originally rejected the city's proposed "neighborhood preference" policy because it violated the Fair Housing Act. However, after the city appealed the ruling, HUD permitted, "40 percent of the 98 units in Willie B Kennedy to be prioritized for residents who live in low-income neighborhoods undergoing displacement and experiencing advanced gentrification, as defined by a research analysis conducted by UC Berkeley" (Dineen, 2016).

Furthermore many of the legal victories that have protected at least some rights for Indigenous peoples in the United States stem from treating Tribes as political entities and not as a racial group. This has sheltered tribes from discrimination suits and from unintended consequences of the Fair Housing Act, but is a practice that is currently under attack in the Supreme Court (Nagle, 2022) and does not apply to non-federally recognized tribes. With the Indian Housing Block Grant program, HUD has also adjusted individualistic logics of the Fair Housing Act when needed. The program has waived the restrictive aspects of Fair Housing for both federally and state recognized Tribes, and if the federally funded housing is not located on land in which the Tribe has jurisdictional authority and if the federal funds are used in conjunction with other funding sources, Tribes have been able to devote housing to Tribal families. Section 201(b)(5) of Native American Housing Assistance and Self Determination Act of 1996 allows a preference for Tribal members for a subset of housing.

More generally, federal efforts to confront unfair housing, segregation, and racialized inequality have largely failed due to government accommodation of the real estate industry. In *Race for Profit: How Banks and the Real Estate Industry Undermined Black Homeownership*, Keeanga-Yamahtta Taylor describes how the end of redlining at the Federal Housing Administration and the passage of fair housing law in the late 1960s established new institutional footing for racialized structural violence, discrimination, and exploitation. Taylor tracks how programs created by the Housing and Urban Development (HUD) Act of 1968 intended to promote black homeownership, instead led to what she termed "predatory inclusion" because of the actions of appraisers and banks provided capital and new terms for the real estate industry to continue to garner profits at the expense of potential Black homeowners. The new subsidies enabled exploitation and theft at multiple levels: "Real estate agents and speculators familiar with the landscape of the Black housing market were newly partnered with appraisers, mortgage bankers, and, of course, the [Federal Housing Administration] itself, which was quite inexperienced when it came to Black buyers and the urban housing market" (2019, 147). As a congressional investigation eventually documented, speculators bought property to sell to those who would qualify for the new program and went so far as to bribe appraisers to inflate values as much as three to four times the actual worth. Many families were unable to continue paying new mortgages, resulting in HUD possessing

78,000 single-family homes from the program by 1974. Furthermore, HUD openly demonized Black families for a failure to practice responsible homeownership. Ultimately, the programs exacerbated racialized inequalities, segregation, substandard and uninhabitable housing, and ultimately stifled the ability, once again, of Black Americans to accrue wealth and benefits linked to homeownership. The failure of the program was also used by the Nixon administration as evidence that government intervention was inappropriate in housing markets and that HUD should not be housing poor and low-income families.

Keeanga-Yamahtta Taylor's critique of predatory inclusion extends beyond uneven enforcement of Fair Housing law to provide a detailed indictment of the extractive principles and racial structures that drive capitalism. Taylor points to layers of extraction, describing, for example, widespread exploitative practices including the use of land installment contracts, which impose higher costs on poor people and profits for those who own the mortgage as homebuyers make their payments and other rent-to-own schemes that continue in the present moment, and predatory lending, which despite the Fair Housing Act and Community Reinvestment Act continue to segregate and extract from communities of color throughout the United States (see also Bond et al., 2009; Mehkeri, 2014). Such practices have undermined wealth equality and prevented Black, Latinx, and other communities of color from wealth afforded to white families. According to Anderson (2020), the result of legal discrimination in housing through redlining accounts for a reduction of $212,000 in home equity for Black families and racialized national disparities in current homeownership, with 44% for Black families and 73.7% for white families. Additionally mortgages have become a financial asset disconnected from the land and house whose value they supposedly reflect, and investment firms and real estate giants continue to buy up property in predominantly neighborhoods inhabited by communities of color at an unprecedented rate (National Low Income Housing Coalition, 2022; Raymond et al., 2022). They acquire property cheaply perpetuating segregation and a long history of devaluing Black homes (NLIHC, 2022). Recent important scholarship on risk and uneven development reveals how interaction among real estate, insurance, visions of sustainability or resilience, and gentrification are now shaping racialized inequities in different locations across the United States (Aidoo, 2021; Checker, 2020; Keenan et al. 2018; Knuth, 2016; Taylor & Aalbers, 2022).

Resettlements are thus subsumed within wider political and economic processes—not simply the exposure to hazards and rational planning responses. Take, for example, the ways in which the resettlement funding rationale cited by the state in their application for federal funds—the deterioration of the Island Road and the unwillingness of federal agencies to enhance the road after storms—was undermined following the resettlement allocation. In 2008, the Federal Emergency Management Agency refused to fund "enhancements" to protect the two-lane, flood-prone road despite concerns from Tribal leaders. Then, the state's resettlement funding application to HUD explicitly cited the expectation that the road will soon be impassable as a rationale for the millions in federal resettlement funding. However, since the resettlement funding allocation, multiple investments in protecting and enhancing the Road to cater to recreational fishing have materialized (Jessee, 2021). In December 2019, for example, the state provided $300,000 to the hunting and conservation non-profit Ducks Unlimited for marsh restoration south of the Road. The following year the state completed five fishing piers and small parking lots and a rock levee on Island Road using $2.4 million in BP Disaster Settlement funds. Louisiana's Department of Wildlife and Fisheries said the piers will allow "anglers" to "take advantage of the bounty in our Sportsman's Paradise." When these investments were initially mentioned to state planners involved in the resettlement, they were unaware of the plans and even dismissed them as rumors.

This begs the question of actual management and hubris among the planners involved who had narrow views of risk and successful adaptation shaped by status quo development and liberalism. At key points throughout the broader planning process, state officials asserted a belief that they had control of beneficial outcomes and risks when deflecting criticism. One Louisiana planner working on the resettlement shared their view that securing property ownership for individuals who move reflected the ideal of property as wealth creation. "I just think about the kind of generational wealth we are creating for Celie [an Island resident] and her family, who would probably never be able to own a home otherwise," they reflected. "She can sell it in five years. I mean, Celie's son will be able to go to college because of this." This view, however, relies on multiple assumptions regarding property, value, and community not shared by Tribal leaders. First, there is the assumption that the value of the house will appreciate, and that property owners would sell or refinance, which runs counter to the notion of remaining in a new community for future generations. Second, Tribal leaders and their partners were concerned about emergent whole housing costs, like increased tax burden and utility costs, that those resettling would incur alongside new ownership of higher appraised property. Third, for at least six years following the resettlement funding, state officials maintained an all or nothing approach whereby individual property ownership came at the expense of Tribal land ownership.

Conclusion

The reality is that resettlements, and other socio-ecological adaptation strategies for that matter, do not start or end with a real estate transaction. We worry that there is not enough critical attention to the enduring structural inequities produced by the predatory practices of market actors within resettlement processes and adaptation planning more broadly. This leads to local, state, and federal accommodation of risk production, whereby institutional processes designed to reduce inequities can further entrench them. The conclusions that can be drawn about how such dynamics will shape resettlement outcomes within the Isle de Jean Charles resettlement are limited. We still do not know how development will occur at and around the new site over time, as the initial move-in of individual houses is still unfolding and disbursement of unclaimed lots and corporate development has not yet happened. We do know that the state chose an individual real estate transaction approach instead of exploring legal possibilities for nurturing collective land relations, despite the Tribal leadership's interest in it. We also know that even the state's vision of the resettlement was at times undermined by other agencies and private actors.

Our observations have convinced us that this is not only a matter of flawed policies at the highest level, but also that the work of defining and realizing policy and programmatic goals is never done. This points to the importance of and limits to critical exploration of legal possibilities throughout adaptation planning processes. Power influences the ways that safety and value are interpreted within policy development and, perhaps more importantly, program implementation, as well as how they change over time. More recently, safety has been aligned with value preservation as part of arguments for protection. But the ways in which public safety has been used to justify racialized violence both within the property regime and beyond (like for example to promote mass incarceration). As discussed more in the next two chapters, community structures (and communal rights) are advanced differently from individual rights as opposed to being integrated in a progressive, gradual, cautious, and prudent coordination arrangement vis a vis institutionalization of structural inequities through the markets and the state.

Existing federal policies, like Fair Housing law and the Uniform Relocation Act of 1970 (URA, 1970) discussed more in Chapter 6, as they are currently implemented, do not do enough to protect people from inequitable outcomes. In some cases, they fail to prevent the structural dynamics, racist and reactionary frames of understanding, and greed that produces inequity. For example, drawing on her work administering buyouts in New York City after Hurricane Sandy, Deborah Helaine Morris wrote, "The URA does create an assistance floor capable of providing minimum costs of a physical move from one location to another, but it does not push managed retreat programs, like mine, to imagine assistance in any other form than a remittance. Rather than address the disinvestment and exclusion that have placed certain populations in communities of risk, our program placed the burden on these vulnerable households" (Morris, 2022). Housing justice advocates and scholars have long argued for an array of approaches and more forceful regulations of the real estate industry at local, state, and federal levels, reiterating these demands in the wake of recent disasters to prevent displacement (Climate and Community Project, 2022; National Low Income Housing Coalition, 2022; Zonta, 2019).

Yet, despite the increasingly evident failures of existing policy, development, and planning norms and the seemingly novel complexities posed by the climate crisis, the fundamental challenges of risk production are not new, and perhaps neither are some of the possible solutions. Li and Spidalieri (2021) argue that receiving jurisdictions have a special role and responsibility to create more affordable housing and combat generations of racialized inequality. Carolyn Kousky, Billy Fleming, and Alan Berger's 2021 volume, *A Blueprint for Coastal Adaptation* offers a multitude of existing possibilities to confront inequality and institutionalized racism within climate adaptation planning, including the expansion of public funding for affordable housing and community-driven resilient redevelopment. The NDN Collective's 2021 *Required Reading: Climate Justice, Adaptation and Investing in Indigenous Power* also provides important analysis, and recommendations from their memo on "Mobilizing Climate and Environmental Justice Investments to Indigenous Frontline

Communities" (NDN Collective, 2021). While the memo is focused on increasing federal investments in infrastructure like roads, utilities, and water on Indigenous territories; Native financial institutions and businesses; funding for Tribal capacity building; creating better processes for Tribes to access resilience dollars; investing in clean energy and resilience planning employment among Tribes to build and implement their adaptation plans, these goals as well as the aims of restoring Indigenous land rights and ecologies at the forefront of their landback campaign are salient to policymakers and planners at multiple levels of government and practitioners in multiple sectors. See also Climate and Community Project 2022 which warns against the influence of privatization in the midst of climate disasters and recommends investing in community planning and community institutions, public housing, local workers and unionization, decarbonization, and supporting and utilizing Traditional Ecological Knowledge. We offer additional suggestions at the end of this book, but at its core, regulating the financial extraction perpetuated by real estate markets, considering anti-displacement laws and planning constructs, and valuing communal relations in addition to property must be front and center.

References

Aidoo, F. S. (2021). Architectures of mis/managed retreat: Black land loss to green housing gains. *Journal of Environmental Studies and Sciences, 11*(3), 451–464.

Anguelovski, I., Connolly, J. J., Pearsall, H., Shokry, G., Checker, M., Maantay, J., Gould, K., Lewis, T., Maroko, A., & Roberts, J. T. (2019). Why green "climate gentrification" threatens poor and vulnerable populations. *Proceedings of the National Academy of Sciences, 116*(52), 26139–26143.

Anderson, D. (June 11, 2020). Redlining's legacy of inequality: $212,000 less home equity, low homeownership rates for black families. *Redfin News*. https://www.redfin.com/news/redlining-real-estate-racial-wealth-gap/

Barra, M. P. (2021). Good sediment: Race and restoration in coastal Louisiana. *Annals of the American Association of Geographers, 111*(1), 266–282.

Bond, P., Musto, D. K., & Yilmaz, B. (2009). Predatory mortgage lending. *Journal of Financial Economics, 94*(3), 412–427.

Carson, B. S. (2015, July 23). Experimenting with failed socialism again. *The Washington Times*. https://www.washingtontimes.com/news/2015/jul/23/ben-carson-obamas-housing-rules-try-to-accomplish-/

Checker, M. (2020). *The sustainability myth: Environmental gentrification and the politics of justice*. New York University Press.

Climate and Community Project. (2022). Toward just disaster response in the United States and US Territories. https://www.climateandcommunity.org/_files/ugd/d6378b_594920722a1b4e3393ea57629e29fbb0.pdf

Comardelle, C. (2020, October 19). Preserving our place: Isle de Jean Charles. *Nonprofit Quarterly*. https://nonprofitquarterly.org/preserving-our-place-isle-de-jean-charles

De Vries, D. H., & Fraser, J. C. (2012). Citizenship rights and voluntary decision making in post disaster U.S. floodplain buyout mitigation programs. *International Journal of Mass Emergencies and Disasters, 30*(1), 1–33.

Dermanksy, J. (2022, September 8). *Isle de Jean Charles community members moved into the first federally funded resettlement project in Louisiana despite visible engineering issues*. Desmog. https://www.desmog.com/2022/09/08/isle-de-jean-charles-relocation-new-isle-climate-change/

Dineen, J. K. (2016, August 17). Feds reject housing plan meant to help minorities stay in SF. *San Francisco Chronicle*.

Echo-Hawk, R. C. (2010). *The magic children racial identity at the end of the age of race*. Routledge.

Fleming, B., Cohen, D. A., Graetz, N., Lample, K., Lillehei, X., McDonald, K., Brave Noisecat, J., Paul, M. (2019). Public housing at risk: Adaptation through a green new deal. https://www.filesforprogress.org/memos/public_housing_at_risk.pdf

Gass, H. (2017, August 2). Tactical retreat? As seas rise, Louisiana faces hard choices. *Christian Science Monitor*. https://www.csmonitor.com/Environment/Inhabit/2017/0802/Tactical-retreat-As-seas-rise-Louisiana-faces-hard-choices

Hall, L. K. (2008). Strategies of erasure: US colonialism and native Hawaiian feminism. *American Quarterly, 60*(2), 273–280.

Isacoff, R. (2021). Identity and power: How cultural values inform decision-making in climate-based relocation. In I. J. Ajibade & A. R. Siders (Eds.), *Global views on climate relocation and social justice* (pp. 194–208). Routledge.

Jessee, N. (2020). Community resettlement in Louisiana: Learning from histories of horror and hope. In S. Laska (Ed.), *Louisiana's response to extreme weather—A test case for coastal resilience*. Springer.

Jessee, N. (2021). *Tribal leaders raise 'serious concerns' about plans to turn their shrinking Louisiana Island home into a 'sportsman's paradise'*. Desmog. https://www.desmog.com/2021/07/23/isle-de-jean-charles-tribe-louisiana-sportsmans-paradise/

Jessee, N. (2022). Reshaping Louisiana's coastal frontier: Managed retreat as colonial decontextualization. *Journal of Political Ecology, 29*(1). https://doi.org/10.2458/jpe.2835

Kasakove, S. (2019, May 17). The tenants' rights movement is expanding beyond big cities. *The New Republic*. https://newrepublic.com/article/153929/tenants-rights-movement-expanding-beyond-big-cities

Keenan, J. M., & Bradt, J. T. (2020). Underwaterwriting: From theory to empiricism in regional mortgage markets in the US. *Climatic Change, 162*(4), 2043–2067.

Keenan, J. M., Hill, T., & Gumber, A. (2018). Climate gentrification: From theory to empiricism in miami-dade county, florida. *Environmental Research Letters, 13*(5), 054001–054001. https://doi.org/10.1088/1748-9326/aabb32

Knuth, S. (2016). Seeing green in San Francisco: City as resource frontier. *Antipode, 48*(3), 626–644.

Koslov, L. (2016). The case for retreat. *Public Culture, 28*(2), 359–387.

Li, J., & Spidalieri, K. (2021). Home is where the safer ground is: The need to promote affordable housing laws and policies in receiving communities. *Journal of Environmental Studies and Sciences, 11*(4), 682–695.

Louisiana Department of Administration (LDOA). (2019). *Substantial Amendment 5: Introduction of new activities and project narrative clarifications for the utilization of community development block grant funds under the National Disaster Resilience Competition (NDRC) Resettlement of Isle de Jean Charles*. LDOA. https://www.doa.la.gov/media/3wwj2iyx/ndr_idjc_substantial_amendment_5-hud-approved.pdf

Maldonado, J. K., Wang, I. F. C., Eningowuk, F., Lesley, I., Lascurain, A., Lazrus, H., Naquin, C. A., Naquin, J. R., Nogueras-Vidal, K. M., Peterson, K., Rivera-Collazo, I., Souza, M. K., Stege, M., & Thomas, B. (2021). Addressing the challenges of climate-driven community-led resettlement and site expansion: Knowledge sharing, storytelling, healing, and collaborative coalition building. *Journal of Environmental Studies and Sciences, 11*(3), 294–304. https://doi.org/10.1007/s13412-021-00695-0

Maldonado, J. K., & Peterson, K. (2018). A community-based model for resettlement: lessons from coastal louisiana. In R. McLeman, & F. Gemenne, *Routledge handbook of environmental displacement and migration* (pp. 289–299). Routledge.

Mehkeri, Z. A. (2014). Predatory lending: What's race got to do with it. *Public Interest Law Reporter, 20*, 44.

Morris, D. H. (2021). The climate crisis is a housing crisis: Without growth we cannot retreat. In I. J. Ajibade & A. R. Siders (Eds.), *Global views on climate relocation and social justice* (pp. 142–151). Routledge.

Nagle, R. (November 9, 2022). The story of baby O¾ and the case that could gut native sovereignty. *The Nation*. https://www.thenation.com/article/society/icwa-supreme-court-libretti-custody-case/

National Low Income Housing Coalition. (2022). Out of reach: The high cost of housing. https://nlihc.org/sites/default/files/2022_OOR.pdf

Raymond, E. L., Zha, Y., Knight-Scott, E., & Cabrera, L. (2022). Large corporate buyers of residential rental housing during the COVID-19 pandemic in three southeastern metropolitan areas. *Housing Crisis Research Collaborative Research Report*.

Reuveny, R. (2007). Climate change-induced migration and violent conflict. *Political Geography, 26*(6), 656–673.

Shi, L., & Varuzzo, A. M. (2020). Surging seas, rising fiscal stress: Exploring municipal fiscal vulnerability to climate change. *Cities, 100*, 102658.

Siders, A. R. (2018). Social justice implications of US managed retreat buyout programs. *Climatic Change, 152*(2), 239–257.

Taylor, Z. J., & Aalbers, M. B. (2022). Climate gentrification: Risk, rent, and restructuring in Greater Miami. *Annals of the American Association of Geographers, 112*(6), 1685–1701.

Taylor, K.-Y. (2019). *Race for profit: How banks and the real estate industry undermined black homeownership*. UNC Press Books.

Legal References

Uniform Relocation Assistance and Real Property Acquisition Policies Act, 42 U.S.C. § 4601 (1970).

Warnecke, A., Tänzler, D., & Vollmer, R. (2010). *Climate change, migration and conflict: Receiving communities under pressure*? The German Marshall Fund of the United States.

Zonta, M. (2019). Racial disparities in home appreciation. *Center for American Progress*, 15.

CHAPTER 4

Flood Buyout Relocations and Community Action

Introduction

Voluntary buyouts are the primary way that relocation away from climate risk is currently carried out. Within the literature on buyouts, there is widespread consensus that interventions should ideally be conceptualized and administered as a "people-centered," community-based disaster risk reduction strategy, with a focus on supporting populations who have been made vulnerable through unsustainable and inequitable development processes (Rumbach & Kudva, 2011). Scholars and practitioners often note that local communities need to be included in planning processes, to the extent that, ideally, they are meaningfully empowered to assert self-determination and lead program outcomes. What is needed, the argument goes, is integration of community decision-making and action throughout all stages of the buyout process, complementing the local government choices of initiating a buyout program, and the household choice of accepting it. Community needs to have a say in program design—determining where buyouts are (and are not) implemented—decisions surrounding viable alternatives, planning for recovery and the use of open-space after relocation of homes. Devolution, alone, where

This chapter was written mostly by the esteemed Daniel Devries. The "I" in the chapter is his.

A. Jerolleman et al., *People or Property*,
https://doi.org/10.1007/978-3-031-36872-1_4

city and county governments implement a program instead of FEMA or the state, is not sufficient to guarantee actual control by local community members (De Vries & Fraser, 2012). This means long-term planning, and a move away from post-disaster response strategies is also necessary.

This chapter sets out to demonstrate that narrow frames of what is considered successful disaster risk reduction at the "community level" gloss over some of the challenges of community action expressed within buyouts. A regular mistake in development practice is the idea that communities are homogeneous groups of people, and that finding a "representative" speaking on behalf of the community suffices to integrate a community's "voice." Issues of tribal sovereignty are also implicated in the decisions that are made by outsiders regarding who speaks for a community. Most communities are heterogeneous, often sharply divided political spaces, with many voices. In addition to this, in the cases of buyouts, the extent of "community" tends to be defined based on geographic locality. However, the "whole community" (FEMA, 2011) involved is more than the residents physically or geographically affected—the immediate "at-risk" population—but also includes adjacent communities and people or even groups who are linked to the affected populations and may be able to assist in the process of solving or mitigating the flood problem. Such actors may pre-exist in the civic or public realm in the form of potential stakeholder groups (e.g., church communities or labor unions), each with their own interests, subcultures, and specific expertise, or they may emerge during emergency events in the form of new coalitions (such as food aid groups or shelters).

We investigate disaster policy, planning practice, and how different peoples' sense of community is implicated in buyout processes in ways masked by the focus on narrow geographies of at-risk property. The chapter interprets experiences and layers of meaning people attribute to bought out places, properties, and people through a case study of the City of Kinston in North Carolina. As this chapter describes, individual property buyouts have frequently targeted low-income property owners, disregarding the importance of existing local social institutions, and frequently leaving individual families at equal or greater risk. The data used in this chapter is based on the work of one of the authors, Daniel de Vries, who conducted extensive research in Kinston after Hurricane Floyd in 1999 (De Vries, 2008). The focus of this specific research was the way in which history and memory influenced floodplain resident's risk perceptions and consequent decisions to relocate. All first-person references are from the vantage point of de Vries. All quotes are from ethnographic interviews conducted as part of this research.

Vacant Lots

It is the summer of 2002. I walk alone on a grid of empty streets connecting vacant lots. Trees are growing where houses used to be. There is rubble at the curbs. It is hot, humid. Nobody seems to be here. In the distance, I hear the urban sounds of the small City of Kinston in eastern North Carolina. Maintenance-type crews drive around in trucks, apparently ready to cut down some trees. There is a street sign laying on the ground. Thrown flat on its back by the unprecedented flood of water which rushed through these streets in the fall of 1999. The sign reads "Dead End" —a seemingly symbolic message. The remnants of habitation—the paved streets, curbs, and fire hydrants, the empty lots, the office desk standing straight up on its legs in an empty field—are haunting. Some homes still stand. Piles of debris surrounds every one of them. Behind overgrown grass and bushes, a white, wooden structure remains. The home is empty, and "Jesus loves" is graffitied across the shed standing to its side. A "NOTICE" from the City of Kinston hangs on the door:

> Dear property owner, based on damage assessment inspection and the best available information, the structure located at [...] suffered significant damage as a result of the recent flood and is classified as "SUBSTANTIALLY DAMAGED" as defined in the City of Kinston Unified Development Ordinance and/or "CONDEMNED" under North Carolina General Statute 160A-426 and is unsafe to occupy in its present conditions.

Inside the smell of mold is overwhelming. The walls and floors are covered with algae. Children's toys are piled in the middle of what seems to have been the living room. Tables, chairs, a moldy couch upside down. Clothing, books, curtains, bedding, laundry baskets heaped on the floor. All kitchen drawers and cabinets open. Once a family lived here, playing, crying, laughing, cooking, being. I notice a young man standing in a yard.

> See the birds? Those are my gifts. God gave the gift to me. I am taking care of them too. Yeah. I am doing okay. I talk to the birds. They come

to me, anyway. I am taking care of them. Lots of birds now. Less people. They are more friendly. They are more friendly than the people.

He appears to be one of the boys staying in a group-home nearby. I also meet nurse Williams, a staff person, in her fifties and graying, her white, uncontaminated nursing outfit a stark contrast against the moldy, algae filled empty home I just visited. She explains to me that the owner of the group home building simply replaced the deck and continued her business. "There were houses everywhere. It was a nice neighborhood," she says mournfully. "Really pretty over here. Until the flood came. Now they are tearing everything down. They tore quite a few down already. And all back on Holloway Drive, have you been there?" I nod. A local official had driven me around earlier and had shown me some of the worst flooded places. Afterwards the official had told me I better not go this way: "Why would you," he had said to me half-jokingly, "unless you want to buy crack" (Fig. 4.1).

The official had been a key player in the federally and state sponsored acquisition and relocation program, which had bought out over 400 Kinston properties (3,6% of the total number of Kinston households) after they were declared substantially damaged. The buyout of Kinston was one of the largest buyouts in the pre-Katrina history of FEMA sponsored mitigation programs. It bought out all the homes which made up the prominent, historical, black neighborhood called "Lincoln City" by Kinston locals, a neighborhood that had now ceased to exist. Or almost. According to nurse Williams, the owner of the group home declined to participate in the buyout program because the City—the project manager—did not offer her enough for the property. "It is sad," she said, "people lost everything they had. Some people now, they still don't have any place to go. They have these little FEMA trailers. It was really bad. Really bad."

The Political Ecology of Success

"They are all dying out now," the buyout manager told me when I saw him again in 2005, four years after he showed me around the town. "Every time I open the paper and see the obituaries there is a name I recognize." The official expressed a deep affinity for the people and the town, having lived in Kinston for many years. He mentioned two elderly Lincoln City residents I tried in vain to contact for an interview after

Fig. 4.1 Dead End sign amidst remnants of habitation. Photo by Danny de Vries, 2002

one of them had gotten very ill. "He used to teach me," he said, "they died within one week of each other." In a somewhat jarring turn from the mourning of buyout participants, the official then spoke about how great their FEMA funded buyout program has been, how successful: "Our program was so good, that once we did twelve of them, or so, the word came out and they all went." And: "when I first came to talk to them about the buyout and talked about what we had to offer, they looked at each other like 'this is too good to be true!'"

As is often the case within hazard mitigation and community planning programs, participation was cast as the most evident measure of success. Ninety-five percent of the property owners relocated because of the program, a remarkable success for any mitigation program. Planning students at UNC-Chapel Hill documented at length the self-congratulatory rhetoric of City Officials and other Kinston stakeholders (Olivera McCan, 2006). The State of North Carolina included Kinston as one of the examples of their "Hazard Mitigation Successes" (NCDEM, 1999). FEMA put out a CD-ROM detailing the amazing story of Kinston which integrated Geographic Information Systems into a model floodplain management program (FEMA, 2003).

Yet, a FEMA funded buyout survey conducted by De Vries and colleagues in several localities including Kinston only partly confirmed this imagined reality of success (Fraser et al., 2003). Results showed that 36% of the 86 respondents answered "yes" to the question "Would you have stayed and rebuilt if you had been given a chance?" Only 20% said they were provided with choices other than a buyout. When asked what these alternative choices were, 20% answered "eminent domain," "get nothing," or "sue the city." Thirty one percent thought buyout information was not very clear. Thirty six percent felt participation was not voluntary, and 21% mentioned they felt "some" to "a great deal" of pressure to accept the buyout offer. Twenty-five percent did not trust the people doing the buyout. Thirty-two percent were "not very" to "not at all" confident that the local managers had the best interest of the neighborhood in mind. Forty-one percent noted "some" to "a great deal" of opposition to the buyout. Thirty one percent mentioned that the price offered for their home was "not very" to "not at all" fair. Overall, 17% said they were "not at all" satisfied with the way the buyout went overall. Most striking was the observation that a sizable minority—more than thirty percent of the 149 respondents in both Greenville and Kinston—indicated that they felt participation was not voluntary. This feeling of involuntary dispossession harkens back to the contradictions around which this book is framed.

The results would not have shocked participants in the program. The reality behind the troubled Kinston buyout is no secret among the community involved. For example, Mr. and Ms. Spurlock relocated to a new home in 2001, a house situated on a hill. They had lived together on Shine Street, at the edge of Lincoln City, where they had bought a house adjacent to the Adkins canal, a tributary to the Neuse River. Recurring flooding had damaged the foundation of their old house, but with Mr. Spurlock being a carpenter, it could hold and looked fine. After Hurricane Fran in 1996 (three years before the floods of Hurricane Floyd), they chose to participate in the first federal buy-out program designed to move properties out of the floodplain. To their dismay, the city did not want to move their old house to a safer place. Instead, it was burned down as a means of demolition. Many people in the neighborhood did not understand why. It was a perfect house. They told me they missed the house and the community of Lincoln City. They were born there, grew up there, met each other there, and bought a house there. Now it is all gone. Lincoln City is gone. "There is a lot of bitterness in the community," Mr. Spurlock tells me. He explained:

> Many people lived there for years and years and years. After Fran [1996], of course, a lot of those people, they did not want to sell. They wanted to really just have their homes redone and they wanted to stay there. We were on the first flood, Fran. So that made a big difference. You did not have that many people, you know, involved with it, because people made the decision not to sell, even though they gave them opportunity.

Three years later, Hurricane Floyd ended up making people sell. According to Mr. Spurlock, the general sentiment was that if you would stay and the floods would come again, you would not get any assistance, even when you would elevate your home on poles. "We could stay! They could stay! But what was made clear, if you choose to stay, you were on your own." According to the Spurlocks, for many, the buyout money was a way out of an impoverished situation and to avoid worry about flood waters, but it also reflected a lack of assistance and money for continuity and collective futures. Now everybody is gone due to more than simply flooding. A vulnerable population does not have a lot of choice (Fig. 4.2).

How unique are these buyout stories? What do they tell us about the role of community in buyout programs and their evaluation? What is a buyout "community" anyway? How does the community figure in our evaluation if a buyout was successful? How, if at all, are people able to act communally? In our buyout study, there were three additional field sites, one nearby site in the City of Greenville, North Carolina, a neighborhood in Grand Forks, North Dakota, and one in San Antonio, Texas. What these sites have in common is a similar FEMA funded and locally administered buyout and acquisition program, around the same period, and roughly equal buyout sizes of several hundred. At the same time, we see very different histories and political ecologies. Kinston and San

Fig. 4.2 Bought out lots of Lincoln City, North Carolina. Photo by Danny de Vries, 2002

Antonio are low-income neighborhoods, but they differed in flood histories, the role of housing counselors, and government relationships in the buyout process. The City of Greenville has a college rental economy, while Grand Forks had a higher level of local community capacity leading to contestation of structural mitigation and a replacement subdivision. More people owed money on their homes in San Antonio and Grand Forks relative to the two North Carolina communities, resulting in the need to pay off mortgages with some buyout funds. Experienced closeness of the neighborhood and neighborhood satisfaction appears highest in Grand Forks followed by Kinston (Lincoln City), and lower in Greenville and San Antonio. Interestingly, Grand Forks and Kinston also had experienced the highest number of floods prior to the flood event which triggered the buyout offer from FEMA. Considering these site-specific differences, it is striking to find that buyout program "success" rates continue to be defined across many reports and academic studies simply as the percentage of households who accepted an offer and relocated, regardless of their individual outcomes (Manda et. al., forthcoming). An unintended outcome of that logic, is that one might conceive the best buyout strategy as being one led by an authoritative and trusted buyout team who leads participants to believe that the choice of participation is not voluntary, provides as little opportunity for input as possible, minimizes the importance of opinions of family members, neighbors, and community staff, and tries to keep people away from their homes to avoid repairs. While this strategy is closer to reality than we may admit, it clearly goes against ethics of good governance and voluntary participation (De Vries & Fraser, 2012).

What then *is* success? An increasingly suggested answer to this challenge is to think less about numbers and more about reducing vulnerabilities and increasing community resilience (Jerolleman, 2019). Unfortunately, Greer and Binder (2017) document in an excellent historical review of buyouts implemented in the United States that policy learning related to buyouts has been, at best, limited. This has meant that the classical view of the "hazard-centered behavioral response approach" (Binder et al., 2019; White, 1945) which typically translated to top-down government flood control initiatives and individual or household-level interventions to adjust proper risk perception and action has continued to remain dominant. Missing here has been the level in between government and individual households, namely the resilience of the community. Acknowledging this, we have seen an increasing call to integrate a community-based disaster risk reduction (CBDRR) in an integrated floodplain planning strategy that includes a social multi-party process based on long-term thinking, careful planning, true community engagement, and a focus on equity (Freudenberg Calvin Tolkoff & Brawley, 2016; Greer & Binder, 2017; Siders, 2018; Braamskamp & Penning-Rowsell, 2018). This might include listening to resident desires and concerns, providing real alternatives, and identifying additional considerations that will come to bear on outcomes.

Six Ways to Frame What a Buyout "Community" Is Anyway

It is important to recognize that the way in which we frame what a buyout "is" and how this framing relates to notions of community, individual action, and property ownership influences what is seen as success, constraining and influencing relocation possibilities (Herrmann, 2017; Jessee, 2020). Framing encourages certain interpretations and discourages others and as such has political implications (Goffman, 1974). The framing of what buyout communities "are" as such also presents facts to implicate a problem that requires a solution. It influences how policymakers, government planners or involved households think about the origins, importance, and the unfolding of the buyout process, indirectly defining the communication and agenda-setting around this topic. Using the literature on buyouts and our own experiences, we have drawn out six frames.

Neighborhood That Emerged Out of Historical Necessity

Lincoln city is an example of a buyout community that has a strong historical identity and emerged out of necessity. Much of the swampy land just south of the City of Kinston near the Neuse River had remained thick forests until 1898 when Lincoln Barnett, a black, educated man from the area saw an opportunity to buy three acres of land around the turn of the century (USGENWEB, 2007). Barnette, a son of two preachers, cleared the land of trees and started building a place of spiritual and recreational needs for the black community, including a "bush" church and park area. Soon, many of the labor workers who used to live near the City's harbor area—one of the ways of making a living for freed slaves before the civil war (Kinston Daily Free Press, 1976)—began to buy lots. The Black community which developed out of these forest clearings was one which provided a unique opportunity for Black, urban homeownership in the segregated south. The land was officially located outside the city limits in the countryside, even though its land directly bordered white City neighborhoods. As one of its elderly residents explained:

> The people loved each other, they fed each other, clothed each other, and they took care of each other's children. It was a nurturing kind of community. And a very religious community.

Throughout the years, Lincoln City became spatially known to be bounded by Bright Street to the north, Queen Street to the west, Holloway Drive to the east, and the Peach Tree Wastewater treatment plant to the south near the river. The location of Lincoln City included several water features, including the nearby Neuse River, but also the

Adkins Branch and a creek following the railway. Elderly Lincoln City residents consistently referred to Lincoln City as the "bottoms" or "lowlands" and "water always stood out there." Flooding was a recurring problem coming with the seasons inundating the neighborhood and blocking one of the entrances. Accustomed to avoiding the floods, people moved in and out to higher grounds. Residents also indicated that some of Lincoln City's landscape was kept undeveloped for the grazing of livestock. However, the floodplain properties of the landscape were commonly not a top issue of concern for new buyers. People in charge of selling land knew these were flood properties, but because of the rare opportunity to find affordable lands where they could buy, the issue was a moot one. As a former resident explained:

> We weren't offered better land... Naturally, when the floods came, we had to live with it...Because when you are living in a segregated society you know you have a white in one area and blacks in another, and where we was living, this was the only place that we could live. Cause you couldn't go to a white area and buy a house. That was a *no no*.

Drainage ditches—originally dug to contain malaria—littered the Lincoln City landscape and their functionality for flood mitigation was locally enhanced by residents, who built retaining walls and other protective structures around them to protect their homes. Many learned to not plant too many gardens, because they knew they would lose it. When residents knew a big rain would come, they automatically went into their flood preparations, moving garbage cans from one location to another, elevating furniture on bricks, moving their animals to higher ground. Not too much was said about it: acceptance and resignation prevailed. This attitude was part of daily life, with a nod of mutual understanding.

Neighborhoods That Should Not Have Been There in the First Place

To outside planners looking at the land as an environmental risk, Lincoln City—which is exemplary for many similar minority-owned communities across the southern United States—was not seen as a historical necessity, but a neighborhood that should not have been there in the first place. As with many similar floodplain neighborhoods, regulations regarding wetlands protection and responsible building standards only developed much later, in the 1980s (in the USA). Floodplain neighborhoods developed because of general housing shortages and population pressures, combined with governments turning a blind eye to developers building in vulnerable locations. Studies on the buyout processes after Hurricane Sandy in the New York area illustrate how local officials actively encouraged commercial development in floodplains in exchange for political support, while potential buyers were misinformed about flood insurance requirements and the flood zone was very rarely a consideration (Braamskamp & Penning-Rowsell, 2018). In this context, residents felt an inevitable lack of control over development unsolvable by education: "you can educate them all you want, but when it comes to money, it is not going to make a difference."

Relatively Affordable Places to House More Socially Vulnerable Populations

Buyout communities are also often framed as relatively affordable places to live because homes in high-risk areas tend to be relatively cheaper (Bolin & Stanford, 1991; Fothergill & Peek, 2004; Mach et al., 2019; McGhee, 2017). What this also implies is that residents may be at risk of losing their community or ownership relation to property when they relocate through a buyout program, because they may not be able to afford to purchase a home, or a home of comparable value, in a less hazardous area nearby, in proximity to each other. This was, for example, the case for residents in New York's Oakwood Beach (Binder & Greer, 2017). Further, some analyses have found that in racially diverse neighborhoods, buyout may be accepted more by white residents leading to white flight from racially integrated neighborhoods leaving the remaining residents at risk (Robinson et al., 2018; Loughran et al., 2019). However, other studies have found that although white privilege may play a role in the likelihood of being offered a buyout, it can also increase the feeling of voluntariness (Elliott et al., 2020).

In addition, in the buyout process, home value is determined by appraisals that varied due to the discretionary power of the appraisers. Buyout participants not uncommonly question the validity of this process: "They just showed up one day to check how many square feet your house was, and we'll pay you by the square footage. But that's not true, because the houses across the street are the same, and they got more money" (Baker et al., 2018, 465). If disagreements exist, residents often have limited recourse other than hiring a private appraiser, to counter the state's offer which increases the stress and cost of recovery beyond what many residents felt they could manage. Furthermore, even if residents could afford to hire an appraiser, appraisal practices devalue communities of color (Howell & Korver-Glenn, 2021).

Similarly subjective appears to be the substantial damage declaration for homes that are calculated to have damages totaling more than 50% of their property value. Because lower value homes for a given flood severity have relatively more damage, lower-income households are more likely to be offered a buyout (Siders, 2019). Appraisers have been found to give a helping hand in assessments by steering values toward what homeowners desire or need (De Vries & Fraser, 2012). While this might help lower-income residents if they want to pursue a buyout, it could also make them more likely to be displaced if the buyout is perceived as involuntary (Kraan, 2021). A substantial damage declaration can also render a homeowner unable to remain if the cost of coming into compliance with elevation requirements is too high. This is yet another way that accepting a buyout can be rendered involuntary when there are no other alternatives.

Diffused and Ambiguously Bounded Social Networks with Impacts Beyond

Buyout communities are also recognized as having diffused and uncertain boundaries. There often is little certainty as to who is included in the "buyout community." For example, the boundaries of the buyout zone in New York's Oakwood Beach, which designated which households were and were not eligible to participate in the program, shifted over time (Baker et al., 2018). These decisions were contentious. Several communities within New York City that vocally and actively pursued inclusion in the State's buyout, for example, were ultimately excluded from the program (Rizzi, 2014). Cardwell (2021) also describes how many people living close to Charlotte's (NC) buyout areas are still waiting for their chance to participate in the program: "I'm on some sort of a list. It's a bit like purgatory, I keep waiting for the county to contact me" (p. 8). Also in Pointe Gatineau, Quebec Canada, gaps in program eligibility and implementation left homeowners excluded from the process in the Special Intervention Zones (Cottar, 2021). In addition to cost–benefit calculations, government mitigation managers also look at considerations such as the depth of previous flooding, proximity to existing open spaces, number of rental units, or previously purchased buyout properties (Binder et al., 2020).

There are also many complex neighborhood connections extending beyond the designated buyout zone. There has been little study on how buyouts affect communities not selected for participation or communities located near buyout zones (Binder et al., 2020). We know that in some peripheral communities (those located next to buyout areas), residents experienced considerable losses in their sense of safety, perceived government support, self-reported general health, and satisfaction with life (Barile et al., 2020). These negative impacts also extend to communities that unsuccessfully advocate for inclusion in a buyout. Atoba et al. (2020) have noted that intentional inclusion of post-buyout land use plans in the initial selection and prioritization of buyout properties may impact quality-of-life outcomes for peripheral communities.

Spaces with Constrained Choice

Buyout communities may also be framed in terms of a shared sense of constrained freedom of choice, as many increasingly recognize the ways in which the involuntary/voluntary buyout frame does not adequately capture the limited self-determination within relocation processes or the production of space. In our buyout study, respondents who indicated that they felt participation was *not* voluntary mentioned a mixture between the sentiment that people were forced by environmental conditions and programmatic challenges, such as financial constraints, insistence from program officials, or limitations (moratoria) placed on rebuilding damaged homes or construction, and use of the substantially damaged declaration (Binder & Greer, 2016; De Vries & Fraser, 2012; Green & Olshansky, 2012; Greer & Binder, 2017; Kraan, 2021). Baker et al. (2018) describe how nearly half of their survey participants indicated that they felt that they had no real choice but to take the buyout. In retrospect, some participants described the buyout as a foregone conclusion almost from the time that the program was announced: "I think deep down we knew… This can't be that 90% of these people are moving and we're going to stay. It can't be." (p. 469). Participation is certainly not voluntary for renters and some mobile home park residents, who may be effectively evicted when property owners or landowners agree to a buyout (Greer & Binder, 2017; Rumbach et al., 2020) (see also Chapter 6).

Experiences and Attachments to Place

A final framing of "buyout community" common in the literature is that of people who share an experience-based attachment to place. The influence of sense of place or place attachment is an often-cited reason for households not to participate in buyout programs (Binder et al., 2015; Greer et al., 2021; Henry, 2013; Kick et al., 2011; Lynn, 2017; Nelson, 2014; Robinson et al., 2018; Shriver & Kennedy, 2005). This is the result of the many positive effects which home or community attachments have on feelings of security and psychological well-being. The home is both a material and emotional object that fulfills important human needs in tangible and intangible ways (Blunt & Dowling, 2006). Attachment to home and community together form a "place"-based construct that together provide strong motivation to stay in place (Kick et al., 2011), or if possible, preserve the attachment to community by moving together, or by relocating entire homes. In our buyout study of Kinston, we found factors of influence to include having ancestors living on the same piece of property for generations, having grown up in the area, enjoying what the area offers, having raised a family in a particular neighborhood, knowing all the neighbors and having children move close by.

From Housing Counselors to Community-Led Buyouts

In qualitative interviews with buyout managers reflecting on the Greenville and Kinston programs, it was clear that managers from both cities were aware that in the aftermath of a disaster homeowners of flooded houses are extremely vulnerable. As one manager put it:

> I don't know if mistrust is the word… I think many of the people were so confused, dazed, and uncertain that they didn't know who to trust. And so weren't making a judgment as to did or didn't trust anyone. They were really looking for help. I mean it was kind of like the wondering. Particularly, those whose homes were destroyed. (Buyout manager)

In this context, homeowner decision-making ability is vulnerable to succumb to pressures to give in to any bureaucratic local government agenda, unless alternative support structures existed to advocate for their needs or suggest alternative options (De Vries, 2011). An important innovation here is to assign households in a buyout zone an experienced community liaison or case manager who can guide homeowners through the process, or have the local government create and manage an online community where residents can ask questions about the process and engage in discussions with each other and the government planners (Baker et al., 2018). In our study of the Kinston and Greenville buyout programs, such roles had also been requested by the State government in the form of housing counselors. The cities' mitigation agenda was the removal of populations and property from harm and a reduction of costs by ensuring all property owners leave, and several officials were openly condescending to us about the attitude of property owners who would not accept the buyout, in their eyes "abusing the system" by not immediately acquiescing to offers.

The housing counselors, for their part, found themselves navigating the difficult tasks of both advocating for residents' rights as well as recruiting these very people to participate in the buyout programs. Unfortunately, these tensions were escalated by historical and ongoing racism and class-based antagonisms. Housing counselors were part of existing Community Development Corporations (CDCs) that represented low-income African Americans on a range of issues beyond disaster mitigation. The cities begrudgingly contracted with them to work with flooded homeowners. Managers saw the CDCs as lacking professionalism and being "uppity" by advocating for the rights of low-income minority groups to stay when their virtually all-white counterparts in the city were telling the CDCs to follow the city agenda of getting these people out of the flood plain. City officials spoke disparagingly about the fact that these housing counselors were advocating for residents. The infighting between the local government officials and the CDCs increased confusion and stress for flooded residents instead of empowering residents to address their concerns effectively and efficiently.

Clearly then, the effort of community engagement revolves around the success of longer-term histories of civic engagement, including the ability to mobilize community members, negotiate power structures in order to find consensus (Braamskamp & Penning-Rowsell, 2018; Siders, 2013). Not every local government or every community has the capacity or opportunity to deliver or facilitate such processes. In fact, in the history of the City of Kinston, government and community relationships remained hostile even after the buyout was completed (De Vries, 2017). Furthermore, while government-appointed housing advocates open communication, this type of engagement is still often conducted in a one way, top-down attitude mostly geared to providing accurate information and addressing rumors on behalf of the implementing agency to the community. It helps here to see the engagement process on a continuum, instead of an all or nothing approach. This continuum moves from involvement of community-based partners and at-risk communities in the exchange of risk information to the gradual development of longer-term partnerships with shared decision-making that can address a wider range of social, economic, political, and environmental issues relating to health (McCloskey et al., 2011).

To move beyond the precarious position of a kind of housing counselor, buyout programs could consider more participatory community involvement moving toward involvement and collaboration and must redistribute power and resources more substantially at multiple levels of government. Scholars have also pointed out that equitable and transformative climate adaptation requires much greater allocation of funding and a coordination across levels of government that has not been consistently valued at the federal level where the funding could exist (Shi & Moser, 2021). Oulahen and Doberstein (2012) outline a process for soliciting community feedback on possible mitigation measures, starting with public information community meetings, distributing surveys and comment forms at these meetings to ensure broader participation, and conducting door-to-door interviews with residents and business owners. Taking it even further, in a study conducted in several location across the USA on repetitively flooded property owners (Kick et al., 2011), many informants and mitigation managers called for the involvement of an even broader set of community actors including local institutions, foundations, non-profit organizations, churches, or others. All these people and organizations were useful in identifying and helping to supply the resources needed to eliminate roadblocks to mitigation decisions that are favorable and inclusive of the affected and wider community. However, since resources can be limited and histories of civil relationships differ, not all local governments can afford the same level of engagement, and views will differ on how much decision-making an officially mandated authority is willing and able to devolve (De Weger, 2018).

A Predetermined Redevelopment Strategy

In the aftermath of Lincoln City's buyout, conversations with residents revealed that what seemed to be lacking in general was any public or official City acknowledgment that alternative flood mitigation strategies—home elevation, for example—might have preserved a historic neighborhood. Residents were given few alternatives to the buyout, framing the buyout community as one with constrained choice, yet existing out of historical necessity. The buyout effort was a top-down, strategically imposed relocation effort catching a population during a crisis (De Vries, 2011). The Kinston buyout was part of a predetermined redevelopment strategy by the City that did not include continued habitation in the neighborhood, which had its origin in the framing of a community that should not have been there in the first place and which existed of socially vulnerable people in city areas that were seen as "blighted," in need of redevelopment, and therefore appropriate targets for intervention. This attitude was reaffirmed at higher governance levels. In 2003, FEMA and State officials also appeared unwilling to consider alternative forms of mitigation. One informant who had worked all over North Carolina administering FEMA's Hazard Mitigation Grant Programs for many localities explained:

The only thing I would want to say in retrospect on the state's response to all these things is that in Floyd they should have had a little bit more open minded to the elevation alternative in areas where it already had been approved as an effective treatment. But really, we had only been elevating for about a year, effectively, when Floyd came around. It was a lot of back and forth between me and my clients and the state agency about elevation, how you do it, the engineering analysis, and why we were doing substandard homes. Ultimately, they were resolved, but they were not resolved in 1999. Some of the State's response might have been, well… they are working on it, but we got such a huge problem here we are just going to focus on acquisition. It obviously is a lot easier to just acquire 400 homes in Kinston than to elevate 200 and acquire 200.

Interviews with mitigation managers in several States conducted as part of the next repetitive loss study a few years later (Kick et al., 2011) illustrated additional tensions across the several layers of program management from FEMA down to the local government level. Discomfort existed regarding an experienced disconnect between FEMA federal policy and program implementation at the local level. In the context of devolved political programs, accountability for program success as well as failures appeared to be pushed down the chain of command with everyone avoiding liability at their own levels. One [local-level?] mitigation manager explained it like this:

> All we are doing is just passing down the money, we don't want any problem, we are just passing down the money, wasn't our responsibility to make sure it was done properly. So, then they throw all the responsibility on the local community, which they are smart to do it. But I know from being an auditor that is what you do. I mean, attorneys from the government they are smart, because whose got bigger purse strings, the federal government, or a local community? The federal government. I understand why they do what they do, but what they do is they put the local community in a very, very, very bad spot, a very bad spot.

Managers suggested that more involvement on the part of FEMA in understanding local planning priorities would benefit the mitigation and assistance programs. All mitigation managers also mentioned how increased ability to set mitigation policies locally would benefit the effectiveness and efficiency of their work. This included increased local ability to decide which homes make the mitigation list, input in how the benefit–cost equation is derived, and the need for localities to propose alternative forms of mitigation. Mitigation managers also seemed unanimous that the restrictions on buyout lands proved to be a burden on local governments' budget in terms of upkeep and lack of revenues, arguing for more local flexibility to use these lands according to appropriate, up-to-code land use forms. Of course, what the outcome of such devolution means in practice, and here we return to the core theme of this chapter, depends to a large extent on the resilience, capacity, and negotiating power of the community impacted. As long as buyout programs remain institutionally focused on individualized household decision-making, community-wide advocacy is curtailed and voices representing other framings of their lived reality are likely to remain unheard.

A Case for Healing and Memory

Healing and memory can be key issues in buyouts, and are closely tied to notions of reparative justice. One couple told us that they aimed to revitalize the area, to help give voice to concerns many others have expressed by memorializing Lincoln City:

> Once they demolished everything, if you never know there was something there, you'd never know. We were trying to raise money to put a memorial back there, just in remembrance for the first families that started here and all the families that lived in this area. I am still working on it. I feel I am like a one man show in that.

Her sentiment was shared by many others. A local Pastor mentioned that what he thought should happen to the area, was something like a museum.

> Where people that are away can come back. I have seen people come back here and cry. People from New York, and from across the street. Unless something is preserved it will eventually just die. Something like a museum that will help people to remember. Recently we had citizen to die that belonged to a church in another area but was born here, the last thing she wanted is to be brought back into this area. We had this funeral, that day that you came by. Just the memories of sending her from this area. People get out walking looking, taking pictures, a lot of them weeping. I used to play here. My aunt lived there. My granddad's place. Now they torn down most of the houses.

One elderly man remarked that he felt that 80% of the community of Lincoln City was gone. He said that the only thing that is holding Lincoln City together now is Lincoln Street. When asked how he felt about that he was clear:

> Hurt. People drive through who used to live here. You don't feel too good about it. That was God's business. You can't question him. What makes it even harder, with the houses being demolished, is that the grass and weeds come back. If the city would cut some, it would look like there is some hope, but now it just looks like it has been abandoned. Gives you a very bad feeling.

Conclusion

To close, for Lincoln City, attention to the long-term outcomes of the community would have gone a long way to fill the void between individual household decision-making and government imposed flood control measures. While a mitigation success when the number of properties relocated or demolished are counted, and when framed as a neighborhood that should not have been there in the first place, the Kinston buyout for many participants provided them with a communal sense of loss and forgottenness, including the eradication of a piece of important black identity and history, a community identity.

As outlined, during the buyout process, participants' level of choice was constrained in several ways that added non-voluntary dimensions, and their sense of control over their lives was low (Barile et al., 2020). While this sounds like a call for choice among households to participate or not in a buyout, homeowners are not entirely free to make this choice, and rather may desire guidance and legal advice to help them actualize their own plans for the future. To achieve this, we need to acknowledge that the *community* level in flood buyout situations is one needing attention, which goes beyond mere participation in the buyout process. It also requires creating opportunities for communal actions and decision-making, not just individuals. We need to urgently redefine what "success" is, or rather, start seeing success not as a definable outcome, but as a process, an attitude of practical tinkering, of attentive experimentation, of doing good in practice, of empathizing with suffering and pain, yet have the goal to lighten what is heavy. If this happens, with care, then people living in floodplain areas will not have their agency and volition constrained as much in this process.

References

Atoba, K. O., Brody, S. D., Highfield, W. E., Shepard, C. C., & Verdone, L. N. (2020). Strategic property buyouts to enhance flood resilience: A multi-criteria spatial approach for incorporating ecological values into the selection process. *Environmental Hazards*, 1–19. https://doi.org/10.1080/17477891.2020.1771251

Baker, C. K., Binder, S. B., Greer, A., Weir, P., & Gates, K. (2018). Integrating community concerns and recommendations into home buyout and relocation policy. *Risk, Hazards & Crisis in Public Policy, 9*(4), 455–479. https://doi.org/10.1002/rhc3.12144

Binder, S. B., Baker, C. K., & Barile, J. P. (2015). Rebuild or relocate? Resilience and postdisaster decision-making after Hurricane Sandy. *American Journal of Community Psychology, 56*(1–2), 180–196.

Binder, S. B., Barile, J. P., Baker, C. K., & Kulp, B. (2019). Home buyouts and household recovery: Neighborhood differences three years after Hurricane Sandy. *Environmental Hazards, 18* (2), 127–145.

Binder, S. B., & Greer, A. (2016). The devil is in the details: Linking home buyout policy, practice, and experience after Hurricane Sandy. *Politics and Governance, 4*(4), 97–106.

Binder, S. B., Greer, A., & Zavar, E. (2020). Home buyouts: A tool for mitigation or recovery? *Disaster Prevention and Management, 29*(4), 497–510. https://doi.org/10.1108/DPM-09-2019-0298

Blunt, A., & Dowling, R. (2006). *Home*. Routledge.

Bolin, R. C., & Stanford, L. (1991). Shelter, housing and recovery: A comparison of U.S. disasters. *Disasters, 15*(1), 24–34.

Braamskamp, A., & Penning-Rowsell, E. C. (2018). Managed retreat: A rare and paradoxical success, but yielding a dismal prognosis. *Environmental Management and Sustainable Development, 7*(2), 108–136. https://doi.org/10.5296/emsd.v7i2.12851

Cardwell, J. (2021). Community perceptions of a floodplain buyout program in Charlotte, North Carolina. *Natural Hazards, 115*, 2141–2160.

Cottar, S., Doberstein, B., Henstra, D., & Henstra, D. (2021). Evaluating property buyouts and disaster recovery assistance (Rebuild) options in Canada: A comparative analysis of Constance Bay, Ontario and Pointe Gatineau, Quebec. *Natural Hazards, 109*, 201–220. https://doi.org/10.1007/s11069-021-04832-4

De Vries, D. H. (2008). *Temporal vulnerability: Historical ecologies of monitoring, memory, and meaning in changing United States floodplain landscapes* (Publication No. 3304420) (Doctoral dissertation). University of North Carolina at Chapel Hill. ProQuest.

De Vries, D. H. (2011). Temporal vulnerability to flood hazards: Recurrence, risk and referentiality along the eastern North Carolina Neuse River. *Global Environmental Change, 21*(1), 154–164. https://doi.org/10.1016/j.gloenvcha.2010.09.006

De Vries, D. H. (2017). Historical waterscape trajectories that need care: The unwanted refurbished flood homes of Kinston's devolved disaster mitigation program. *Journal of Political Ecology, 24*, 931–950.

De Vries, D. H., & Fraser, J. C. (2012). Citizenship rights and voluntary decision making in post disaster U.S. floodplain buyout mitigation programs. *International Journal of Mass Emergencies and Disasters, 30*(1), 1–33.

De Weger, E, Van Vooren, N., Luijkx, K. G., Baan, C. A., & Drewes, H. W. (2018). Achieving successful community engagement: A rapid realist review. *BMC Health Services Research, 18*(285).
Elliott, J. R., Brown, P. L., & Loughran, K. (2020). Racial inequities in the federal buyout of flood-prone homes: A nationwide assessment of environmental adaptation. *Socius, 6.*
FEMA. (2003). *Innovative floodplain management case studies: Kinston, North Carolina. Mitigation case studies.* https://www.fema.gov/pdf/casestudys/kinston_cs.pdf
FEMA. (2011, December). A whole community approach to emergency management: principles, themes, and pathways for action. (FDOC 104-008-1) https://www.fema.gov/sites/default/files/2020-07/whole_community_dec2011__2.pdf
Fothergill, A., & Peek, L. A. (2004). Poverty and disasters in the United States: A review of recent sociological findings. *Natural Hazards, 32*, 89–110.
Fraser, J., Elmore, R., Godshalk, D., & Rohe, W. (2003). *Implementing floodplain land acquisition programs in urban localities.* University of North Carolina at Chapel Hill.
Freudenberg, R., Calvin, E., Tolkoff, L., & Brawley, D. (2016). *Buy-in for buyouts: The case for managed retreat from flood zones.* Lincoln Institute of Land Policy report. https://www.lincolninst.edu/publications/policy-focus-reports/buy-in-for-buyouts
Goffman, E. (1974). *Frame analysis: An essay on the organization of experience.* Harvard University Press.
Herrmann, V. (2017). America's first climate change refugees: Victimization, distancing, and disempowerment in journalistic storytelling. *Energy Research & Social Science, 31*, 205–214.
Green, T. F., & Olshansky, R. B. (2012). Rebuilding housing in New Orleans: The Road Home Program after the Hurricane Katrina disaster. *Housing Policy Debate, 22*(1), 75–99.
Greer, A., & Binder, S. B. (2017). A historical assessment of home buyout policy: Are we learning or just failing? *Housing Policy Debate, 27*(3), 372–392. https://doi.org/10.1080/10511482.2016.1245209
Greer, A., Sherri B. B. & Zavar, E. (2021). From hazard mitigation to climate adaptation: A review of home buyout program literature. *Housing Policy Debate.* https://doi.org/10.1080/10511482.2021.1931930
Henry, J. (2013). Return or relocate? An inductive analysis of decision-making in a disaster. *Disasters, 37*(2), 293–316. https://doi.org/10.1111/j.1467-7717.2012.01303.x
Howell, J., & Korver-Glenn, E. (2021, November). The increasing effect of neighborhood racial composition on housing values, 1980–2015. *Social Problems, 68*(4), 1051–1071. https://doi.org/10.1093/socpro/spaa033

Jerolleman, A. (2019). *Disaster recovery through the lens of justice*. Springer.
Jessee, N. (2020). Community resettlement in Louisiana: Learning from histories of horror and hope. In S. Laska (Ed.), *Louisiana's response to extreme weather—A test case for coastal resilience*. Springer.
Kick, E. L., Fraser, J. C., Fulkerson, G. M., McKinney, L. A., & De Vries, D. H. (2011). Repetitive flood victims and acceptance of FEMA mitigation offers: An analysis with community–system policy implications. *Disasters, 35*(3), 510–539.
Kinston Daily Free Press. (1976). Historical Highlight. Kinston Daily Free Press, Sunday July 4th, by Miriam Maynard.
Kraan, C. M., Hino, M., Niemann, J., Siders, A. R., & Mach, K. J. (2021). Promoting equity in retreat through voluntary property buyout programs. *Journal of Environmental Studies and Sciences, 11*(3), 481–492. https://doi.org/10.1007/s13412-021-00688-z
Loughran, K., Elliott, J. R., & Kennedy, S. W. (2019). Urban ecology in the time of climate change: Houston, flooding, and the case of federal buyouts. *Social Currents, 6*(2), 121–140.
Lynn, K. A. (2017). Who defines "whole": An urban political ecology of flood control and community relocation in Houston, Texas. *Journal of Political Ecology, 24*(1), 951.
Mach K. J., Kraan C. M., Hino M., Siders A. R., Johnston E. M., & Field C. B. (2019, October 9). Managed retreat through voluntary buyouts of flood-prone properties. *Science Advances, 5*(10). https://doi.org/10.1126/sciadv.aax8995
McCloskey, D. J., McDonald, M. A., Cook, J., Heurtin Roberts, S., Updegrove, S., Sampson, D., Gutter, S., & Milton, (M.) E. (2011). Community engagement: Definitions and organizing concepts from the literature. In D. J. McCloskey, S. Aguilar-Gaxiola, & J. L. Michener (Eds.), *Principles of community engagement. Clinical and translational science awards consortium community engagement key function committee task force on the principles of community engagement* (2nd ed.). NIH Publication No. 11-7782. Retrieved July 15, 2022, from https://www.atsdr.cdc.gov/communityengagement/pce_intro.html
McGhee, D. (2017). *Were the post-Sandy Staten Island buyouts successful in reducing national vulnerability?* (Master's Project). Duke University. Retrieved July 13, 2022, from https://hdl.handle.net/10161/14168
Nelson, M. (2014). Using land swaps to concentrate redevelopment and expand resettlement options in post-Hurricane Katrina New Orleans. *Journal of the American Planning Association, 80*(4), 426–437.

NCDEM. (1999). *Hazard mitigation in North Carolina: Measuring success: Sustainable housing, sustainable business, sustainable infrastructure, sustainable environment*. Division of Emergency Management & Federal Emergency Management Agency. https://digital.ncdcr.gov/digital/collection/p249901coll22/id/638829

Olivera McCan, M. (2006). *case study of floodplain acquisition/relocation in Kinston, NC after Hurricane Fran (1996) and Floyd (1999)* (Master's thesis). University of North Carolina at Chapel Hill. https://doi.org/10.17615/rhp8-te06

Oulahen, G., & Doberstein, B. (2012). Citizen participation in post-disaster flood hazard mitigation planning in Peterborough, Ontario, Canada. *Risks, Hazards, and Crisis in Public Policy, 3*(1), 1–26. https://doi.org/10.1515/1944-4079.1098

Rizzi, N. (2014, April 11). State won't add any more neighborhoods to Sandy buyout program. *DNAinfo*. Retrieved July 16, 2022, from https://www.dnainfo.com/new-york/20140411/new-dorp-beach/state-will-add-no-more-neighborhoods-sandy-buyout-program/

Robinson, C. S., Davidson, R. A., Trainor, J. E., Kruse, J. L., & Nozick, L. K. (2018). Homeowner acceptance of voluntary property acquisition offers. *International Journal of Disaster Risk Reduction, 31*, 234–242. https://doi.org/10.1016/j.ijdrr.2018.05.002

Rumbach, A. J., & Kudva, N. (2011). Putting people at the center of climate change adaptation plans: A vulnerability approach. *Risks, Hazards, and Crisis in Public Policy, 2*(4), 1–23. https://doi.org/10.2202/1944-4079.1096

Rumbach, A., Sullivan, E., & Makarewicz, C. (2020). Mobile home parks and disasters: Understanding risk to the third housing type in the United States. *Natural Hazards Review, 21*(2).

Shi, L., & Moser, S. (2021). Transformative climate adaptation in the United States: Trends and prospects. *Science, 372*(6549), eabc8054.

Shriver, T. E., & Kennedy, D. K. (2005). Contested environmental hazards and community conflict over relocation. *Rural Sociology, 70*(4), 491–513.

Siders, A. (2013). *Managed coastal retreat: A legal handbook on shifting development away from vulnerable areas* (Columbia Public Law Research Paper, 14-365).

Siders, A. R. (2018). Social justice implications of US managed retreat buyout programs. *Climatic Change, 152*(2), 239–257.

Siders, A. R. (2019). Social justice implications of US managed retreat buyout programs. *Climatic Change, 152*(2), 239–257. https://doi.org/10.1007/s10584-018-2272-5

USGENWEB. (2007). *Vertical File Bell 02433-5. Original copy found at Heritage Place*. Lenoir County Community College, Kinston, NC. Retrieved

December 2007, from http://ftp.rootsweb.com/pub/usgenweb/nc/lenoir/bios/jamcdaniel.txt

White, G. F. (1945). *Human adjustment to floods* (Research Paper no. 29, Doctoral dissertation). The University of Chicago. https://biotech.law.lsu.edu/climate/docs/Human_Adj_Floods_White.pdf

CHAPTER 5

Displacing a Right to Act Communally Within Community Relocation

Introduction

Despite the widely proclaimed principle of "community-led" processes within climate adaptation discourse, individuals' assertion of a right to act communally is often undercut by the law, the application of the law, and planning conventions. The previous chapter emphasized some of the profound challenges associated with individual choice and community action during the administration of buyout programs. In Kinston, North Carolina, ill-conceived framings of the buyout community, local officials' myopic exploitative quest for participation, and the goal of claiming success ultimately displaced possibilities for local collective self-determination, critique from participants, and adaptation in place. This chapter elaborates on these kinds of barriers to local community action within relocation planning by bringing readers' attention back to community resettlement planning on Louisiana's Gulf Coast.

As a reminder to readers, Jean Charles Choctaw Nation leaders have worked to plan and advocate for their Tribal community resettlement since 2002. That year, their traditional homelands were excluded from planned regional hurricane protection by the U.S. Army Corps of Engineers. After continued advocacy and planning and forging multiple partnerships, including with a local non-profit, The Lowlander Center. The Lowlander Center, in 2010 and the state of Louisiana's Office of Community Development Office of Community Development (OCD) in 2014. In 2016, the state was awarded $48.3 million of Department of

A. Jerolleman et al., *People or Property*,
https://doi.org/10.1007/978-3-031-36872-1_5

Housing and Urban Development (HUD) funds through the National Disaster Resilience Competition National Disaster Resilience Competition (NDRC) to advance the Tribe's plans. This chapter describes some of the ways that power-laden notions of "community" clashed during the planning process and how OCD officials relied on ambiguities of the term to undercut the Tribe's collective action once federal funding was allocated. For fifteen years prior to state and federal involvement in the resettlement, the Tribe centered their efforts on the aim of reunifying kinship-linked families who constituted a "Tribal community" and restoring cultural lifeways (Maldonado, 2019). Once state officials began to administer the HUD funds, however, the state imposed a divisive planning process that contested the meaning of community to instead emphasize individuals who remained on the Island as distinct from the Tribe as a whole, eliminating the option to choose to act communally and prioritizing individual property ownership instead.

This chapter explores the relationship between a so-called "community-led" resettlement and recognition of community as an entity with rights, including legal rights, and the challenges individuals face in acting communally. Narrow notions of risk often emphasize physical exposure to hazards over social dimensions of vulnerability or adaptive aspirations (Marino & Faas, 2020). In doing so, "community" is aligned with geographic locations or jurisdictions in environmental governance (see Clipp et al., 2017). Ambiguities in the meaning of community became a tool that state officials leveraged in refusing the Tribe's assertion of sovereignty and collective self-determination, reflecting their inconsistent and incoherent approach to recognizing the existence and rights of Indigenous peoples (Jessee, 2020). Definitions of community wielded in this resettlement were varied and dynamic. Some of the ways it was operationalized by Tribal leaders, planners, and local officials included, but were not limited to, community as a tribe, community as geographic location, community as a shared relation to coastal flooding, community as collection of disparate stakeholders, and community as a group that lacks conflict. At times within the planning process, these notions overlapped and at other times they were pitted against each other, implicating vastly different programmatic and political possibilities and constraints. Ultimately, tracking community and community action throughout the encounters produced during the resettlement indicate that despite the existence of possibilities for collective ownership and stewardship of land, including those—like community land trusts—increasingly embraced within movements for housing and land justice and anti-displacement struggles, the application of the law in the United States is subject to the weight of convention and pressures to capitalize on land and thus may discourage possibilities even when they are desired by local resettlement advocates. Moreover, this context demonstrates how community and community engagement, as well as individually focused legal land transactions, might be weaponized to further undercut some forms of community action within resettlement planning.

Legal Definitions of Community

Definitions of community vary and often conflict in their usage. The sociological and anthropological literature in which community features as a key point of analysis is vast, and for nearly a century, scholars point to the divergent conceptualizations of the term (Bryson & Mowbray 1981; Gold, 2005; Titz et al., 2018; Williams, 2002, 2014). As Michael Watts described in his brief summation of the role of community within political ecology:

> The community is important because it is typically seen as: a locus of knowledge, a site of regulation and management, a source of identity (a repository of "tradition"), an institutional nexus of power, authority, governance, and accountability, an object of state control, and a theater of resistance and struggle (of social movement, and potentially of alternate visions of development). (2003, 266)

Within U.S. law, scholars have also debated the meaning of community and the legal implications of influential conceptualizations (Schragger, 2001; Weintraub, 1994). However, our search for a strictly legal *definition* across federal statutes or in case law came up fruitless.

One of the most consequential forms of community, though, has been realized through the history of municipal incorporation. The number of incorporated places in the United States has grown to approximately 19,500 by the year 2020 (census), many of which were formalized in the twentieth century (Jackson, 1985). After massive municipal annexations throughout the nineteenth century, town and village incorporation became more widespread as a result of states passing laws allowing "home-rule" charters and improving suburban infrastructure funded by new financial mechanisms and World War I (Freund, 2007, 47–48; Jackson, 1985, 150). Perhaps most influential was the racist drive for "moral control" among white suburban dwellers. According to Jackson:

> With the vast increase in immigration in the late nineteenth century, the core city increasingly became the home of penniless immigrants from Southern and Eastern Europe. And of course, in the early years of the twentieth century increasing numbers of Southern blacks forsook their miserable tenant farms for a place where, they hoped, "a man was a man." In the view of most middle-class, white suburbanites, these newcomers were associated with and were often regarded as the cause of intemperance, vice, urban bossism, crime, and radicalism of all kinds. And as the central city increasingly became the home of the disadvantaged, the number of white commuters rose markedly. These recent escapees from the central city were anxious to insulate their neighborhoods from the "liquor power" and other pernicious urban influences. An independent community offered the exciting promise of moral control. (Jackson, 1985, 150–151)

The history of incorporation is thus in large part a story of white community action for racial exclusion. In the book, *Colored Property,* historian David Freund tracked the ways that incorporation and subsequent zoning throughout the mid-twentieth century, transformed constructions of race and racism via white elites' embrace of euphemistic language around property values and market dynamics to describe, rationalize, and institutionalize racialized exclusion (Freund, 2007). According to Freund, by the early twentieth century, zoning became a driver of incorporation (ibid., 48). Freund writes, "As of 1931, only 800 cities had adopted ordinances, compared with 6,880 in 1968—and land-use restriction became the central focus of local politics in most suburban municipalities" (2007, 36).

Despite the history of municipal jurisdiction as an expression of white racist community action, it is a version of community that is most legible within the regulatory state. The U.S. Department of Housing and Urban Development's Community Development Block Grant (CDBG) program allocates funds to county or parish and local governments, for example, as grantees. Then, grantees can provide a sub-grant to non-profit or for-profit subrecipients to implement funded community development activities in accordance with program goals and the Housing and Community Development Act of 1974. However, subrecipients must meet certain requirements, including administrative capacity and a history of success with similar grants or quantities of money. Specific initiatives like the CDBG-Disaster Recovery (CDBG-DR) or CDBG-Mitigation (CDBG-MIT) programs may include guidance specific to them that evoke slightly different notions of community pertinent to the allocation of funds. For example, the initial Federal Registrar announcement of the CDBG-DR-sponsored National Disaster Resilience Competition (NDRC) that funded the Isle de Jean Charles resettlement included a "Waiver And Alternative Requirement for Distribution to CDBG Metropolitan Cities and Urban Counties—Applicable to State Grantees Only," which stated:

> Section 5302(a)(7) of 42 U.S.C. (definition of "nonentitlement area") and provisions of 24 CFR part 570 that would prohibit or restrict a State from distributing CDBG funds to entitlement communities and Indian tribes under the CDBG program, are waived, including 24 CFR 570.480(a) and 570.486(c) (revised April 23, 2012). Instead, the State may distribute funds to local governments and Indian tribes. (Federal Register/Vol. 81, No. 109/Tuesday, June 7, 2016/Notices 36573)

In other words, it seems as though normal regulatory restrictions that would prevent the distribution of funds to the Tribe did not apply within the implementation of National Disaster Resilience Competition funds. The burden to figure out and likewise the ultimate discretion on how that language or its implications, like for example, may relate to needs in a specific context, largely falls on the grantee, in this case the state.

The U.S. Federal Emergency Management Agency (FEMA) also typically links community to local governments. Since 1990, FEMA has overseen the Community Rating System (CRS) to incentivize local floodplain management. The program encourages municipal mitigation measures by offering residents of those that do, and who are in "Special Flood Hazard Areas" up to 45% discounts on flood insurance premiums (FEMA CRS, 2017). Participation is typically available to U.S. jurisdictions that exceed the minimum requirements of the National Flood Insurance Program (NFIP)". According to the program's website, "Over 1,500 communities participate nationwide" (ibid.). The current database of CRS "eligible communities" lists over 1,700 towns, cities, villages, boroughs, municipalities, counties/parishes, and, notably, two Indigenous nations: the Lummi Nation and the Lower Elwha/Klallam Tribe (FEMA CRS, 2023). FEMA's notion of "Whole Community," referenced in the previous chapter, advances a stakeholder model of community whereby differently positioned actors within a jurisdiction are encouraged to come together and build consensus around plans (FEMA, 2011). The CRS gestures to this broader sense of community by giving some credit for public information efforts and participatory hazard mitigation planning. However, smaller communities and those lacking staff capacity for floodplain management are often unable to participate in such initiatives.

More recently, FEMA's 2020 Building Resilient Infrastructure and Communities (BRIC) pre-disaster mitigation grant program provided eligibility to "Small Impoverished Communities" as subapplicants. A "small, impoverished community" for pre-disaster hazard mitigation means "a community of 3,000 or fewer individuals that is economically disadvantaged, as determined by the State in which the community is located and based on criteria established by the President" (CFR 42 USC § 5133(a). According to BRIC's technical criteria, a grantee's application is awarded additional points if subapplicants can prove that they are an Economically Disadvantaged Rural Community (EDRC) or:

> A community of 3,000 or fewer individuals, as identified and validated by the applicant in the project subapplication, that is economically disadvantaged; meaning that residents have an average per capita annual income that does not exceed 80% of the national per capita income, based on best available data. 2 A state, territory, or federally recognized tribal government serving as a subapplicant must document the Economically Disadvantaged Rural Community status of the community in which the project is planned to receive the point allotment for this criterion. (FEMA BRIC, 2021, 7)

The contours of community within disaster regulations therefore come to bear on the possibility of securing funds, the cost-sharing ratio between the local jurisdiction, state, and federal governments, and the flow of funds locally—even where these are loosely defined.

Within some federal programs, community is inferred through census tracts. For example, in the administration of new market tax credits, "low-income community" refers to any population census tract if—"(A) the poverty rate for such tract is at least 20%, or (B) (i) in the case of a tract not located within a metropolitan area, the median family income for such tract does not exceed 80% of statewide median family income, or (ii) in the case of a tract located within a metropolitan area, the median family income for such tract does not exceed 80% of the greater of statewide median family income or the metropolitan area median family income. Subparagraph (B) shall be applied using possession wide median family income in the case of census tracts located within a possession of the United States" (26 USC § 45D(e)(1). The Biden administration's White House Council on Environmental Quality (CEQ)'s recent Justice40 Initiative, aimed at coordinating environmental and climate justice investments, also uses census tracts and an analysis of over twenty variables reflecting environmental and health conditions to determine "disadvantaged communities" (CEQ, 2021). The Interim Implementation Guidance for the initiative drew on the CEQ's 1997 National Environmental Policy Act environmental justice guidance: "Either a group of individuals living in geographic proximity to one another, or a geographically dispersed set of individuals (such as migrant workers or Native Americans), where either type of group experiences common conditions" (Young et al. 2023). Justice40 has been criticized for not accounting for race within its operationalization of "disadvantaged community" despite the reality that race is a predictor for the siting of toxic polluting facilities and exposure to hazards associated with the climate crisis (Chemnick, 2022).

The process for U.S. acknowledgment of federally recognized Indigenous nations also involves a specific notion of community. For federal recognition, a petitioning Tribe must satisfy seven criteria, one of which is the expectation that the nation "comprises a distinct community and demonstrates that it existed as a community from 1900 until the present." Importantly, the criteria for federal recognition are imposed and rooted in racist colonial ideologies rather than the diverse experiences, expressions of sovereignty or political philosophies, and social institutions created and sustained by Indigenous peoples (Barker, 2011). According to 25 CFR § 83.11(b) though, "Distinct community means an entity with consistent interactions and significant social relationships within its membership and whose members are differentiated from and distinct from nonmembers. Distinct community must be understood flexibly in the context of the history, geography, culture, and social organization of the entity. The petitioner may demonstrate that it meets this criterion by providing evidence for known adult members or by providing evidence of relationships of a reliable, statistically significant sample of known adult members."

Constructions of community, both as local government jurisdiction and as physical geographic location, came to bear on Jean Charles Choctaw Nation as their resettlement plans garnered funding through the NDRC. In the federal competition, the state of Louisiana was the grantee, and the Jean Charles Choctaw Nation—then referred to as the Isle de Jean Charles Band of Biloxi-Chitimacha-Choctaw Tribe—was framed in HUD materials and state plans as the beneficiaries as a "historically-contextual community" (HUD, 2016, 7). While we have been unable to find a regulatory or legal definition of historically-contextual community, the term seemed appropriate to Tribal leaders who had worked on the application at the time. Once the funding was allocated to Louisiana's OCD, however, state officials began articulating a definition of community that departed from that advanced by Tribal leaders and initially embraced by both state and federal agencies. As the next section describes, state officials relied on ambiguities of the meaning of community to sideline community action as expressed by the Tribal leaders' long-standing efforts that led to the funding in the first place and in doing so erased the very notion of a tribal community with rights within the resettlement planning process. The tribe's ability to act as a non-profit entity was also undercut due to the small annual budget and lack of full-time staff capacity which did not permit IDJC to serve as a traditional sub-grantee.

Undermining Community Action While Administering Community Resettlement Funds

Ethnographic description of the Isle de Jean Charles resettlement planning process may help build an analysis of how ambiguities surrounding the notion of community are at times exploited to undercut collective action. On June 16, 2016, nearly five months after the NDRC award announcement, Jean Charles Choctaw Tribal Leaders and their partners with the Lowlander Center met OCD officials and state subcontractors that included Pan American Engineers, Chicago Bridge & Iron Company, and Concordia Architecture. Not long into the meeting it became clear that, rather than advancing the original Tribal community resettlement plans, the state agency would reduce their commitments to the Tribal Council and Tribal community.

Early in the meeting, a contractor from Concordia pointed to a copy of a 2015 resettlement prospectus that was co-produced by the Tribe's partners and OCD during the application phases of the NDRC. "We have read the report. There is a lot of good information," she assured, before adding, "There are two points: We are committed to the community as the beneficiary. The people in this room have a lot of expertise and know a lot, but I think HUD would want us to speak with every family unit and find out what they think." The statement indicated a divergence from likely expectations and a new approach to community that prioritized contractor engagement with households on the Island individually. The statement also seemed to set up a dichotomy between the "community as the beneficiary" and "the people in this room" which included numerous Tribal leaders who were from the Island themselves but had moved off and who are close family to those who remained living there.

The husband of one Tribal citizen responded, "We need to define family, structures, and community. The families remaining on the Island do not constitute a community." Recognizing the importance of the social networks that exist between on and off Island tribal members and the capacity of Tribal leadership, one of the scholars from the Lowlander Center confirmed the conceptualization of community used throughout the Tribal resettlement planning process up to that point: "We must agree that the community is the entire Tribe, and not just those who remain on the Island." Louisiana's Resilience Policy and Program Administrator responded, "What I would say is we have remnants of community that are somewhat left behind. We have thirty-one households." The director of the OCD added, "We know that the community is as depleted as the land it grows on." Using the Island's land mass as a metaphor, the official asserted his perception that those who remain on the Island are depleted, though not specifying what, and focused on a frame of the community as a location-specific designation. Moreover, the focus on vulnerability as a characteristic of Island residents ignored the capacity, social capital, and possibilities that the Tribal leadership and off-Island Tribal social infrastructure have long contributed to the Island.

After the meeting, OCD began a "Data Gathering and Engagement" process that elaborated a notion of community in opposition of the Jean Charles Choctaw Nation. First, state planners and subcontractors assessed land use and physical infrastructure on the Island and conducted surveys with some Island residents. Additionally, surveys in the engagement process prioritized remaining island residents. The resulting report's description of methodology is opaque at best, or worse, intentionally confusing. Descriptions of sampling, for example, lack consideration of its representativeness of Island residents. While surveys with individuals from 10 of 26 households lasted 60–90 minutes during organized meetings, others were reportedly brief, and at least some Island residents declined to participate, indicating the possibility of a sampling bias (LDOA, 2017,

6). Moreover, data from respondents are presented in brief summarizing sentence fragments rather than direct quotes, potentially removing context and reflecting assumptions by the planners. This routine planning convention obscured social complexity, locally meaningful notions of community, and what ideal processes for acting communally might entail.

Surveyors prioritized questioning Island residents' existing knowledge of pre-NDRC Tribal-driven planning (ibid., 6). According to the report, 16 of 20 people who responded knew about the Tribe's planning, but 12 of them reportedly "did not participate" in those efforts (ibid., 21). However, it is unclear how surveyors probed explanations of residents' knowledge of and participation in Tribal planning. In the documentation, the survey used the term "previous visioning efforts," a phrase that reflects the state's early unwillingness to call Tribal planning "planning" and which may have confused respondents as it is not a phrase used by the Tribe. During one of the Tribe's meetings, a Tribal leader suggested that the language mattered, because while most Island residents were involved in the planning overall, they may not have distinguished the NDRC from other grants that the Tribe had pursued. While the report briefly acknowledged Tribal leaders' contributions to the NDRC application and confirmed that all those surveyed approved of Tribal-driven resettlement plans, authors also diminished pre-award Tribe's planning as "rumors" (ibid., 4).

Additionally, the report presents unsubstantiated claims about political and communal relations on the Island, deemphasizing Tribal affiliation. Authors of the report thus acknowledge their lack of understanding of local meanings, the Tribe or community's social organization, and the possibility that respondents were unwilling to share with them, but nonetheless established a tension between Tribal affiliation and "each other as family and neighbors." The state thus deployed the common conjecture that authentic communities lack conflict to delegitimize a community to whom they did not wish to be beholden. This reductive process of imposing a particular frame for community highlights the reality of multiple overlapping communities and the state's insistence on embellishing one that accorded with the state's own vision, assumptions, and priorities for the resettlement. Contradictory representations of the meaning of family, Tribal affiliation, neighbors, and community pervade the report. According to Appendix A, for example, OCD asked, "How do you interact with your neighbors?" (LDOA, 2017, C-3). Fifteen responses were recorded as bullet-point fragments, with neither direct quotes nor contextualization: “Doesn’t really get together with neighbors much,” “Seems like family visit them (had two family member’s (sic) drop by during our interview,” and “Knows and talks to everyone” (ibid.). Authors point out that “family members” visited during the encounter, but do not indicate whether these family members were also current Island residents. Out of the fifteen responses, eight described interactions with neighbors, but only four, according to the authors, indicated extensive interaction. Four responses described no interaction at all. Two respondents described Chief Naquin’s visits in response to this question about neighbors despite his not living on the Island since the 1970s. Moreover, the relationships between off-Island Tribal leaders and remaining Island residents include many close kinship relations—brothers, sons, nieces, cousins, and grandchildren. The survey also asked respondents how they would define “community” to which there were sixteen responses (ibid.). Ten of them were “family” while four were listed by authors as “other” (ibid.).

The Data Gathering and Engagement phase concluded with a public meeting organized by the state on the morning of October 8, 2016, during which many of the underlying tensions from this process erupted. The meeting, held under the elevated Island home of a Tribal elder, began with a presentation about land use on the Island. Following this, one of the state’s subcontractors reported on the results from the data gathering and engagement process. Pointing to a series of posters with pie charts and data visualizations, they broke down the number of households on the Island, the number of people they spoke with who hoped to resettle, the number of people still unsure, and the number of those who did not plan to move, summing up their effort as follows: “We really wanted to find out what is important to you. We know that there was previous work that was done and some people on the Island participated in that. I’m happy to say and not surprised that when we had the conversations on the Island most people really shared the same sentiments that came across in the earlier work that was done.” The contractors acknowledged that the findings confirmed the values and vision that emerged from the Jean Charles Choctaw Tribal-driven process conducted during the application phases but rearticulated a distinction between the people on the Island and the earlier work that was done.

An OCD representative subsequently established a hierarchy of aims that devalued the Tribe’s most fundamental resettlement goals of reuniting their Tribal citizens and ensuring their cultural survival: “So the

HUD grant and the primary function of this project is to move people out of harm's way." He then rearticulated a distinction between the Jean Charles Choctaw Nation leadership and those who remain on the Island:

> Now, I will add the caveat and say we work for you, the people we intend to benefit, those of you who currently live on the Island especially. If you tell us that you want us to work through the Tribe, that you don't want us to talk to you, and that your input is best served through Chief Albert and his council or whomever, we have to be responsive to what you tell us. But I will say that that is not what we heard when we sat in your living rooms. The information that we got from you all was that, yea, Chief Albert and his folks have developed a vision and generally speaking you all liked the vision but almost none of you said that you had any input on it. So again, you have to tell us what's important to you and how you would like us to move forward.

The planner referenced the findings of the Report on Data Gathering and Engagement that call into question the Tribal Council's previous engagement with remaining Island residents.

The Tribal Council were thus placed in a difficult position in which they had to negotiate multiple dynamics simultaneously. Chief Naquin responded:

> I guess my gripe is you know, the Tribal leaders and the Council must be respected. In other words, the Tribal leadership has been part of our culture. They just said that if somebody doesn't want to move with the community, they will find something for them, but in our plan, we had everybody taken care of. I do believe that if we stay together and move to one location eventually those that say they don't want to go, will eventually come with us too. I believe in that whole-heartedly. If not, the Tribe is being broken up.

Tribal leaders continued to advocate that a Tribal community resettlement was the right path for the future of the Tribe and tried to maintain authority throughout the planning process despite the deepening involvement of state planners in the process. Chief Naquin continued, "'Divide and conquer' is what I'm seeing at the moment," to which the subcontractor from Concordia responded, "Well, that is certainly not the intent, Chief, and we would encourage people to move as a community… but we also believe that this is a democracy and people have the right to make a choice." The contractor's response framed the complex and uneven process of resettlement planning and decision-making as a tension between the Island heritage and individual choice and democracy.

In the months that followed, a developer subcontracted by the state and state planners floated the idea of incorporating the new site. Incorporation would, according to them, give a degree of local control while ensuring that regulatory and legal expectations and conventions were adhered to. Skeptical, Tribal leaders, and their allies worried that incorporation would not ensure the kind of continuity or reunification that the Tribe's plans prioritized. During meetings at the time, the subcontractor assured Tribal leaders and their allies repeatedly, "We can get 90% of what you want." After one meeting with Parish officials, when asked about social continuity, he explained, "Well, that is the 10% that we cannot figure out." For him, the problem was a matter of law, including the Fair Housing Act as discussed in Chapter Three, but also of Tribal community capacity. As the contractor mused on multiple occasions, "Who is going to mow the lawn?" Incorporation would, in theory, provide financial and organizational means legible to the developer, for political authority and economic development. The idea that the Tribal community lacked capacity, though, was seen by Tribal leaders as an affront to their history of self-sufficiency, success in planning the resettlement with no funding, and a racist colonial trope of the Indigenous nations who could not cultivate the land. According to one Tribal citizen:

> They take us for ignorant people, just like the man said, 'Our tribe can't mow the lawn or run the land.' We're smart people... All we need is opportunity, and that is what this land is. [...] We are a tribe with a lot of smart people, and we got a lot of smart people helping this tribe. [...] Let me break this down. We had the master plan. We had the land picked out—the same land that they're going to buy. We had the layout made [...] But we can't run this place? For real? To me, it's just they don't want to see Indians succeed.

Several themes were evident from the community engagement process described above. Most important to Tribal leaders was that state planners and their consultants made clear that they were not interested in understanding the collective needs of the beneficiaries as a tribal community described in the initial OCD co-authored resettlement prospectus, the successful National Disaster Resilience Competition application, and subsequent action plans—the entire Jean Charles Choctaw Nation. Second, planners refused to recognize the Tribal leaderships initiative and multi-faceted work on the resettlement as planning or development. Also, multiple references to the Coastal Master Plan and planners self-identifying as "experts" beg the question as to the politics of expertise in development processes and the technocratic encounters of climate adaptation. The repeated references to the "best science available" while discussing the impending disappearance of the Island and conducting land use surveys to extend state control of land also seem comparable to formations of inevitability of settler colonial development that drove manifest destiny in the 19th Century.

Consequences of Redefining Community

Two and half years later, in 2019, state officials drew upon the fraught engagement process as they defended the euphemistically termed "narrative clarification" substantial amendment request to HUD, which intended to dispel previous commitments to the Tribe from the resettlement plan officially. The substantial amendment proposal to HUD stated: Subsequent to the state's submission of its application to the National Disaster Resilience Competition, the state has worked closely with leaders and residents of Isle de Jean Charles and the surrounding communities, national resettlement and Native American subject matter experts and other nonprofit organizations to better understand the intricate complexities faced by a diverse set of stakeholders (LDOA, 2019, 1).

The state reported that they had come to understand the resettlement's "multiple stakeholders and the diversity of potential program participants" by way of the "Data Gathering and Engagement" phase described above, raising questions about the rules for changing beneficiaries. According to NDR guidelines, "the following modifications will constitute a substantial amendment requiring HUD prior approval: a change in program benefit, beneficiaries, or eligibility criteria; the allocation or re-allocation of more than $1 million; or the addition or deletion of an activity" (Federal Register/Vol. 81, No. 109, 36561). What constitutes a change in beneficiaries for HUD? Would including non-Tribal "stakeholders" or creating barriers for Tribal citizens who once lived on the Island constitute a change in beneficiaries? If so, should the substantial amendment not have come immediately after the Data Collection and Engagement process and before moving on to "Phase 2: Site Selection, Acquisition, and Master Planning" and subsequent phases? The state was exercising its discretion in interpreting what constituted a substantial amendment and when it had taken place, notably submitting the amendment request after the divisive planning process, after the transition between the Obama and Trump HUD administrations, and after the state purchased the land with the HUD funds. In part due to their existing interpersonal relationships to the continuing decision-makers within HUD, state administrators were able to use bureaucratic processes to support what they had already done.

There were also broader social impacts to transforming the operationalization of community within the planning process, as the perception that the state was engaged in a "divide and conquer" campaign persisted. According to one middle-aged father who grew up on the Island and moved a couple miles up the bayou in the early 1990s:

> What do I see? I see we got a battle on our hands, a long battle. The Tribal Council are going to have a long battle with the government as far as them dividing us and trying to get what they want and more importantly what they deserve. We can want a lot of things, but what we deserve is better treatment than what we are getting. We have to keep fighting to keep us together. If we split, we're done. We are over with... The Island always kept their community. The Chief always kept outsiders out and look at what's happening. They got us. They broke it. They were able to get people from the outside in, now they got us scattered, now what are they going to do with us? My ancestors are rolling in their grave big time right now. Y'all just don't know the tears that come rolling down these eyes when I see that. If my grandpa was still alive, today he would be furious. The problem is this government guy going down, and I understand they are trying to do good, but all he is doing is dividing, dividing the community.

Another person, who lived just a few miles from the Island and whose sister lived on their family home on the Island, recounted:

> Will it happen at all? I think it will, but not to the level that we expected and that we would like. Everyone in the same community? No, I think they're going to keep our people split up, and that will not be a community like what we had down there.

As a result of the state's divisive planning process, Tribal leadership became increasingly concerned about not only whether those who used to live on the Island would be excluded from the new site but also that the resettlement would be a place for the state to relocate anyone living in a location deemed "at risk" to future coastal flooding. "They don't care about a historically contextual community at all," one Councilperson emphasized:

> They just want to move the Island residents. We just going to have a big old subdivision. It ain't going to be a community. What we had; we were rebuilding the Island with this move. That was the resettlement. We could have a church, a store, community center, day care center, and a deal for the elderly. That would have been the whole community. As far as resettlement, now it is going to be a regular subdivision. That's how it's going to be. They just want a place to dump all us 'climate refugees.' The next thing you know they say anybody can go to this here resettlement community. It is not a Tribal community anymore, so these people over here need a home. They are going in there too. It is not going to be the Island community.

Conclusions

Groups planning resettlements, as well as their allies, have observed that there is currently no legal or policy framework in place to manage community-led resettlement in response to climate change (Pettus, 2019). Instead, individual buyouts are often used in floodplains and those trying to relocate as a group struggle to do so and have their efforts hampered by a confusing mass of conflicting agency regulations (Bronen & Chapin, 2013). In some cases, governing agencies may express a commitment to community, shared culture, or heritage but then rely on individual households as "units of administration" when conducting planning activities (Wilmsen & Webber, 2015). All too often planners treat the concept of "community-driven" or "community-led" as nothing more than a process which allows for multiple stakeholders of a region to share opinions on plans or processes, while decisions are made by jurisdictional leaders and the meaning of community goes ill-defined or contested. At best, community is romanticized in grant narratives, but ignored in practice.

Critical development and disaster scholars have become increasingly skeptical about the notion of community due to its use in masking within-group conflict, discrimination, and violence (Guijt & Shah, 1998; Titz et al., 2018). Michael Watts described the underlying assumption of singularity: "[Community] is often invoked as a unity, as an undifferentiated entity with intrinsic powers, which speaks with a single voice to the state, to transnational NGOs or the World Court. Communities, of course, are nothing of the sort" (2003, 266–267). Anthropologists have argued that constructions of community are linked to broader political economy and struggles for justice. In *Practicing Community*, anthropologist Rhoda Halperin described how community can be seen as an action, the "day to day, ongoing, often invisible practices" that are "connected but not confined to place" (1998, 5). For Halperin, community is both a "dynamic, changing, and at times tumultuous and dangerous process" and yet one that also can engender a sense of "peace and well-being" (ibid.). Halperin's work describes the myriad of ways community is practiced in response to class conflict, racism, colonialism, and gentrification in the East End in Cincinnati, Ohio. Similarly, Jeff Maskovsky (2006) described how community in neighborhood planning meetings expressed ahistorical and race-avoidant approaches to urban governance that engendered renewed resistance among African American residents in their struggle against gentrification. Melissa Checker (2011) also observed the ways community was used rhetorically within planning meetings to encourage Harlem residents "to accommodate a technocratic compromise that shunned politics as unseemly and counter-productive" (225). These analyses demonstrate some of the ways that the social construction of community brings together conflict over self-determination, the allocation of resources, place-making, and redress for ongoing legacies of historical social injustices.

The version of public community advanced by local officials was wielded in opposition to the existing concept of a Tribal community used by Jean Charles Choctaw Nation leaders. Resilience administrators utilized individual discretion, though also constrained by legal formations of community, liberal planning conventions, and inter-governmental and inter-agency relationships in their approach. The engagement process was at times a violent exercise that reduced the social process of acting communally into an imagined form that contorted to widespread notions of legal community and reduced the relationship with a community partner to a relationship with one among many stakeholders. The particular notion of a public community advanced by local officials was also wielded in opposition to Tribal community action, functioning as what Alyosha Goldstein (2014) refers to as a settler colonial formation, drawing on the work of Stoler and McGranahan (2007) who observed that "imperial formations are polities of dislocation, processes of dispersion, appropriation, and displacement" (2007, 8). Ambiguities around the meaning of community prompted and embellished by state planners enabled them to align the resettlement more directly with broader regional redevelopment aims on the Island and at the inland location. In part, this established conditions to transform Tribal members' kinship-based land tenure on the Island into individualized property relations at the new site and creating confusion regarding land use and new inequities among Indigenous people resettling and non-Indigenous property owners and campers on the Island. Moreover, representations of community, community meetings, and reports on those community meetings that advance co-opted notions of community were key sites for fabricating consent to state-driven processes, casting assimilation into the U.S. property regime as climate adaptation, and re-territorializing land in accord with capitalist redevelopment (Jessee, 2022). Reducing resettlement to little more than a series of individual land transactions, as is the case when property acquisition is, or is viewed as, the only viable (or most desirable) policy vehicle (or outcome), risks excluding people and undercutting collaboration and collective healing.

References

Barker, J. (2011). *Native acts: Law, recognition, and cultural authenticity*. Duke University Press.

Bronen, R., & Chapin, F. S., III. (2013). Adaptive governance and institutional strategies for climate-induced community relocations in Alaska. *Proceedings of the National Academy of Sciences, 110*(23), 9320–9325.

Bryson, L., & Mowbray, M. (1981). 'Community': The spray-on solution. *Australian Journal of Social Issues, 16*(4), 255–267.

CEQ. (2021). Executive Order 14008: Tackling the Climate Crisis at Home and Abroad (January 27, 2021).

Checker, M. (2011). Wiped out by the "greenwave": Environmental gentrification and the paradoxical politics of urban sustainability. *City & Society, 23*(2), 210–229.

Chemnick, J. (2022, June 1). *Experts to "White House: EJ screening tool should consider race"*. E&E News, ClimateWire. https://www.eenews.net/articles/experts-to-white-house-ej-screening-tool-should-consider-race/

Clipp, A., Gentile, B., Green, M., Galinski, A., Harlan, R., Rosen, Z., & Saucier, M. (2017). *2017 coastal master plan. Appendix B. People and the landscape*. Coastal Protection and Restoration Authority. http://coastal.la.gov/wp-content/uploads/2017/04/Appendix-B_People-and-the-Landscape_FINAL.pdf

FEMA. (2011, December). *A whole community approach to emergency management: Principles, themes, and pathways for action* (FDOC 104-008-1). https://www.fema.gov/sites/default/files/2020-07/whole_community_dec2011__2.pdf

FEMA BRIC. (2021). https://www.fema.gov/sites/default/files/documents/fema_fy21-bric-technical-criteria-psm_111521.pdf

FEMA CRS. (2017). Community rating system coordinators manual. https://www.fema.gov/sites/default/files/documents/fema_community-rating-system_coordinators-manual_2017.pdf

FEMA CRS. (2023). Eligible communities database. https://www.fema.gov/sites/default/files/documents/fema_crs_eligible-communities_oct-2023.pdf

Freund, D. M. P. (2007). *Colored property: State policy and white racial politics in suburban America*. University of Chicago Press.

Gold, A. G. (2005, May). *Conceptualizing community: Anthropological reflections*. Brown University. Retrieved July 14, 2022, from https://www.brown.edu/research/research-ethics/conceptualizing-community-anthropological-reflections

Goldstein, A. (2014).*Formations of United States Colonialism*. Duke University Press

Guijt, I., & Shah, M. K. (1998). *The myth of community: Gender issues in participatory development*. Intermediate Technology Publications.

Halperin, R. H. (1998). *Practicing community: Class culture and power in an urban neighborhood*. University of Texas Press.

Jackson, K. T. (1985). *Crabgrass frontier: The suburbanization of the United States*. Oxford University Press.

Jessee, N. (2020). Community resettlement in Louisiana: Learning from histories of horror and hope. In S. Laska (Ed.), *Louisiana's response to extreme weather—A test case for coastal resilience*. Springer.

Jessee, N. (2022). Reshaping Louisiana's coastal frontier: Managed retreat as colonial decontextualization. *Journal of Political Ecology, 29*(1). https://doi.org/10.2458/jpe.2835

Louisiana Department of Administration (LDOA). (2017). *The resettlement of Isle de Jean Charles: Report on data gathering and engagement phase*. Louisiana Department of Administration. http://isledejeancharles.la.gov/sites/default/files/public/IDJC-Final-Report-Update.pdf

Louisiana Department of Administration (LDOA). (2019). *Substantial Amendment 5: Introduction of new activities and project narrative clarifications for the utilization of community development block grant funds under the National Disaster Resilience Competition (NDRC) Resettlement of Isle de Jean Charles*. LDOA. https://www.doa.la.gov/media/3wwj2iyx/ndr_idjc_substantial_amendment_5-hud-approved.pdf

Maldonado, J. K. (2019). *Seeking justice in an energy sacrifice zone: Standing on vanishing land in coastal Louisiana*. Routledge.

Marino, E. K., & Faas, A. J. (2020). Is vulnerability an outdated concept? After subjects and spaces. *Annals of Anthropological Practice, 44*(1), 33–46.

Maskovsky, J. (2006). Governing the "new hometowns": Race, power, and neighborhood participation in the new inner city. *Identities: Global Studies in Culture and Power, 13*(1), 73–99.

Pettus, K. (2019). The first American climate refugees and the need for proactive relocation. *The George Washington Law Review, 87*(1), 172.

Schragger, R. C. (2001). The limits of localism. *Michigan Law Review, 100*(2), 371–472. https://doi.org/10.2307/1290541

Young, S. D. Brenda, M., & Ali, Z. (2023) "Memorandum for the Heads of Executive Departments and Agencies (M-23-09)" (memorandum, Executive Office of the President, 2023), https://www.whitehouse.gov/wp-content/uploads/2023/01/M-23- 09_Signed_CEQ_CPO.pdf, 1.

Stoler, A. L., & McGranahan, C. (2007). Introduction: Refiguring imperial terrains. In A. L. Stoler, C. McGranahan, & P. C. Perdue (Eds.), *Imperial formations* (pp. 3–42). SAR Press.

Titz, A., Cannon, T., & Krüger, F. (2018). Uncovering 'community': Challenging an elusive concept in development and disaster related work. *Societies, 8*(3), 71.

United States Department of Housing and Urban Development (HUD). (2016). *National disaster resilience competition grantee profiles*. https://www.hud.gov/sites/documents/NDRCGRANTPROFILES.PDF

Watts, M. (2003). Alternative modern—Development as cultural geography. In K. Anderson, M. Domosh, & S. Pile (Eds.), *Handbook of cultural geography* (pp. 433–454). Sage. https://doi.org/10.4135/9781848608252.n31

Weintraub, B. A. (1994). Environmental security, environmental management, and environmental justice. *Pace Environmental Law Review, 12*, 533.

Williams, B. (2002). The concept of community. *Reviews in Anthropology, 31*, 339–350.

Williams, R. (2014; orig. 1976). *Keywords: A vocabulary of culture and society*. Oxford University Press.

Wilmsen, B., & Webber, M. (2015). What can we learn from the practice of development-forced displacement and resettlement for organized resettlements in response to climate change? *Geoforum, 58*, 76–85.

CHAPTER 6

Precarious Possessors and "the Right to (Rebuilding) the City"

Introduction: A Right to Rebuilding the City

This chapter focuses on communities, groups, neighborhoods, individuals, classes of individuals, and families who have a precarious relationship with property. Here, we discuss the ways in which that relationship structures rights to imagine, access, and rebuild infrastructure and social life after a disaster and during processes of relocation as an adaptation to climate change—rights we collectively describe as "the right to rebuilding the city." Over the last four decades, the language of "the right to the city" (Harvey, 2008; Lefebvre, 1974) has become a powerful rallying cry for social movements such as the Right To The City Alliance, formed in the years after Hurricane Katrina (Greenberg, 2013; righttothecity.org/). The "right to the city," which we do not view as limited to metropolitan areas (Angelo & Wachsmuth, 2015), is conceived as both a right to access public goods, such as housing, or public spaces, and a right to participate in their planning, governance, and transformation (Cohen, 2018; Weinstein & Ren, 2009). This may consist of policies and practices that delineate rights of realistic accessibility to non-property owners, or promote self-organizing communities acting in resistance to, or in the absence of, policies and the imposition of formal property law (for a contemporary example, and a critique of property law as neocolonial and settler colonial logic, see Grandinetti, 2019). In contrast to liberal conceptions of individual rights resting on private property ownership, the right to the city invokes the collective human rights of those

A. Jerolleman et al., *People or Property*,
https://doi.org/10.1007/978-3-031-36872-1_6

excluded from such "paradigms of propertied citizenship" (Roy, 2003). This compels us to ask how property structures access to planning a city, the accessibility of the city, collective feelings of efficacy in space, and the symbolic construction of "place" across different epistemological understandings of "land." It also compels us to inquire how community members make "claims and appropriations that do not fit neatly into the ownership model of property" (Roy, 2005); in our case, during and after hazardous events and in relation to resettlement, where questions of who has a right to be included are often related to understandings of ownership and participation.

There are a set of assumptions we, the authors, make about justice, and the "right to the city" with regard to those we are calling precarious possessors, disaster, and relocation. The first is that we assume all people, regardless of their status as a legally recognized property owner, have a right to recover after a disaster and not to be further entrenched in risk. This is particularly important when we think about long-term outcomes and risk distribution. We assume that non-property owners should not be increasingly exposed to risk while property owners are not in the aftermath of a hazardous event. Second, we assume that recovery should be possible in one's home community, or at least, that property ownership should not determine a community, household, or individual's "right to return" (Ansfield, 2015). In instances where relocation is preferred, or necessary, we assume that renters and other precarious possessors should have power and voice in deciding how relocation occurs, where to, whether community rebuilding or restructuring is possible, and the option to live in the relocation site.

These assumptions produce a set of questions: If there are decades of writing and organizing dedicated to the "right to the city," how can we translate that work into the right to imagine what a new city, a new community, a relocated future will look like in the context of climate change—what DuPuis and Greenberg (2019) query as the "Right to the *Resilient* City?" How does a hazardous event and the ensuing response jostle people and communities such that they are in a position, or not in a position, to participate in the reimagining, reconstructing, and relocation of a community? Given that low-income renters are especially vulnerable to displacement by disasters, as well as housing recovery and buyout processes as currently practiced (Lee & Van Zandt, 2019), what can we do to ensure that their rights of participation and return are upheld as a new community is being imagined and created? And, given that precarious relationships to property are the norm rather than the exception (Blomley, 2020), what possibilities exist for disaster and climate policy and activism to rework or dismantle, rather than reproduce, the dominant systems of property that produce widespread vulnerability, all the more so under conditions of disaster and climate change?

This chapter will explore precarious possession, disaster events, and the policies around post-disaster relocation for non-property owners. First, we discuss the diverse categories of (dis)possession and the rhetorical and material power of conflating property ownership with participation in the body politic, as remains the norm today. Second, we discuss the experience of disaster for renters, and identify renting as a characteristic that predicts exposure to risk under current housing, recovery, and adaptation regimes. Third, we discuss the particular intersection of renting and citizenship status. Fourth, we turn to the policies governing renters under cases of flood disaster where relocation is an adaptation option. Included in this, we highlight the data gaps related to renters and other precarious possessors under conditions of relocation and retreat. Finally, we offer a vision forward, highlighting research needs and policy possibilities. We reflect on how home tenure relates to vulnerability indices, how vulnerability may be even more exacerbated in cases of community-based relocation, and how little researchers actually know about the experiences of precarious possessors in relocation scenarios.

Precarious Possessors: Diverse Categories of Possession/Dispossession

Property ownership has been an organizing category and mode of exclusion for how British and American societies function for at least 300 years, as this book has continuously shown. Early in American political life, property-qualification was a prerequisite to cast a ballot. Contemporarily, research demonstrates that property ownership is still predictive of participation in local politics (Yoder, 2020). In 2003, President Bush made the claim, "it is in our national interest that more people own their own home. After all, if you own your own home, you have a vital stake in the future of our country" (George W. Bush, cited in Yoder, 2020). The historical context of property ownership, and the quote given above, demonstrate the deep assumption that to "own" land or infrastructure under legal title is to enshrine a right to participate in the legal apparatus of the state and to participate in the advancement of an aspirational utopia—to "have a vital stake in the future of our country." If you own a piece of land, you have an assumed principled interest in a community and are afforded greater rights and opportunities to imagine its future, and to realize that vision through participation in planning processes. This harkens back to Alexander's assessment of the role of property in civic life, described at the beginning of the manuscript (1997).

These conscious and unconscious ties between property and participation have intersectional implications across gender, race, ethnicity, and citizenship status. Persistently excluded are those on whose dispossession U.S. property ownership rests: Indigenous people; Black people, formerly construed as property themselves; the poor, and particularly poor women; immigrants uprooted from formerly colonized nations where wealth has been extracted by and to the Global North; and the unhoused, whose "homelessness" renders them "the 'constitutive outside' of propertied citizenship (Kawash, 1998, 329), the alien figure that at once violates and thereby reinforces the norms of citizenship" (Roy, 2003, 464; see also Bhandar, 2018; Blomley, 2020; Harris, 1993; Moreton-Robinson, 2015). U.S. property and the associated rights of citizenship remain concentrated among white men, with the vast majority of agricultural land (98% as of 2002) in the hands of white owners, and the racial homeownership gap recently measured at its highest level in 50 years (Agyeman & Boone, 2020; Gilbert et al., 2002).

From the perspective of the state, property ownership is a dominant way to formalize the relationship among a citizenry and the colonial state—rendering the formal legible and traceable (Scott, 1986). During disasters, legibility, traceability, and deservedness (Jerolleman, 2019; Louis-Charles et al., 2020) are linked to property ownership, which increases access to aid and participation in the rebuilding of communities, neighborhoods, and societies. For example, federal aid is frequently channeled to owners so that they have the capacity to rebuild infrastructure as a tangible outcome, and as a proxy for rebuilding the social functioning of a neighborhood and city. The vast majority of individual assistance from the federal government in a presidentially-declared disaster goes to single-family homeowners when compared to renters, while rental properties are especially slow to be rebuilt, if they are rebuilt at all (Lee & Van Zandt, 2019). After Hurricane Harvey, for example, over 80% of individual assistance went to homeowners, while under 20% went to renters (Dundon &

Camp, 2021). In one sense, this is an obvious split. Homeowners are responsible for rebuilding walls, putting on new roofs, and cleaning up debris associated with their properties. In another sense, if owning a home or property is a prerequisite for participating in the decision-making of how a society, a community, or a city will continue to function post-disaster (and into a utopic future), then more precarious possessors are at a disadvantage in their ability to recover, make demands, and actualize their vision for a post-disaster social life in their home communities.

Individuals who do not own property, and their experiences of relocation following flooding and other hazard events, are notably absent from the literature on "managed retreat" (for exception see Dundon & Camp, 2021). When Valmeyer, Illinois relocated most of their community and infrastructure in the aftermath of flooding of the Mississippi River in the 1990s, it was considered a "successful relocation" by city, state, and federal agencies and governments. However, notably missing from the metrics for success was an indication of where renters had gone. The new community was predicated on homeownership and so those families and individuals who did not purchase land or a home "disappeared" from inclusion even within the notion of *who* and *what* made up Valmeyer's community (Manda et al., 2023).

While the disaster literature frequently compares owners and renters as analytic categories, the lives of people who do not hold formal title to a property or fit neatly into these categories are less frequently described in detail and nuance (for an exception, see Sullivan, 2018).[1] These "precarious possessors" in fact occupy a wide range of engagement with possession and dispossession of land, legibility, and formality (Blomley, 2020; Durst & Wegmann, 2017; Mukhija, 2014), all of which structure the experiences of people during and following a disaster as well as during relocation planning and implementation. Examples include, on-the-books renters; the houseless (in many forms); informal title holders; off-the-books renters; people with "divided tenure;" people living in trailers or mobile homes in formal land-lease agreements (Rumbach et al., 2020); people living in trailers or mobile homes without formal lease agreements; holders of heirs' property (Hardy et al., 2022); people with underwater mortgages; people with historic claims to spaces, despite not formally residing there; and people living in informal settlements; among

[1] Wegmann et al. (2017, 194) describe how housing tenure in the United States is not "a binary variable," though it is often treated as such.

others. All of these possession/dispossession positionalities have implications for the assistance available post-disaster and the capacity to act in a meaningful way during relocation planning and receive support and compensation for one's move. Additionally, as discussed further below, these categories of property non-"ownership" and status are complicated by other intersectional characteristics, most notably race, socio-economic status, citizenship status, gender, and recognition (or not) as a tribal entity.

Disaster Experiences for Renters

Climate disasters will continue to limit the availability of housing nationally. According to New York University's Furman Center, "An average of 15 million people nationwide lived in the 100-year floodplain in 2011–2015" (Furman Center, 2017). Ten percent of all occupied housing was in the combined 100-year and 500-year floodplain (Furman Center, 2017). Nearly 22 million properties remain at moderate to extreme risk to flooding in the 500-year floodplain (First Street Foundation, 2020). Additionally, 104,497 public housing units (9% of total) sit in the floodplain (ibid.). Fleming et al. (2019) found that as many as 180,400 public housing units (13.8% of current total) could see flooding with 7' of sea level rise. And flooding, of course, is not the only climate-related hazard that leads to resettlement as a risk reduction strategy. According to First Street Foundation, 30.4 million properties are currently at moderate to extreme risk to wildfire.

Renters face a variety of forms of social vulnerability to disasters (Lee & Van Zandt, 2019; Tate et al., 2016; Wachtendorf et al., 2013). According to the NYU Furman Center, between the years 2011 and 2015, an estimated 64% of all houses in the United States were owner occupied and 36% were renters. During this period, 38% of all houses in the combined 100 and 500-year floodplain were renter occupied (Furman Center, 2017). Before a storm, renters have less control over taking protective action (i.e., retrofitting their home or apartment to withstand hurricanes or tropical storms) and are instead dependent on landlords to take disaster precautions which they may be unwilling or unable to undertake. After a disaster, renters often end up displaced, leaving many individuals away from social networks, which play an important role in preparedness, response, and recovery capabilities. However, as Weber and Peek (2012) show, reliance on social networks can also be detrimental during catastrophic events when communities are severely disrupted and many network members are displaced simultaneously (Quarantelli, 2006, for a more extensive inquiry into these complexities, see Browne, 2015). For instance, many New Orleans community members had strong social ties to the city prior to Hurricane Katrina in 2005. However, when they were displaced, they suddenly found themselves in new locations, leaving them isolated, and with weakened social support systems, especially considering that those in their networks were also suffering similar losses (Fussell, 2012; Messias et al., 2012). This resulted in severe challenges to accessing housing assistance programs and finding stable and safe housing (Pardee, 2012). Even for those with several social networks, social capital alone was unable to address structural obstacles to recovery, such as discrimination, segregation, and isolation, lack of public transportation, and lack of legal documentation that pose a hindrance to finding housing and present particular barriers for renters (Garza, 2012; Messias et al., 2012).

Compared to owners, renters have less opportunity for public financial assistance after a disaster, and renters in public housing even less so. Recovery programs in the United States are largely tailored to upper- and middle-class single-family homeowners (Jerolleman, 2019; Kamel & Loukaitou-Sideris, 2004; McConnell, 2017; Pastor et al., 2006; Peacock et al., 2015; Sutley & Hamideh, 2020; Zhang & Peacock, 2010). Kamel and Loukaitou-Sideris (2004) found that areas with higher concentrations of multi-family and rental units are less likely to access federal disaster assistance. Consequently, areas with lower access to federal assistance are associated with negative recovery outcomes, such as population loss and increased abandonment of rental units (Kamel & Loukaitou-Sideris, 2004; Zhang & Peacock, 2010). Rental properties also rebuild much slower, which significantly impacts the capacity for renters to return home and rebuild their lives (Peacock et al., 2015; Zhang & Peacock, 2010).

These challenges amplify trauma and impede recovery after a disaster for renters. Post-Katrina, displaced renters or other precarious possessors had limited choices in where they went after the storm. Renters, and specifically poor, Black renters, were less supported or less willing to return to New Orleans. Also, several public housing projects were closed and barred from reopening, with the storm presenting an opportunity for redevelopment projects that displaced tenants from properties that were not directly affected by flooding (tenant displacement also occurs post-disaster when landlords who lose their own houses opt to move into rental properties that they own that did not sustain damage, or when other homeowners chose renting as an alternative to other forms of temporary housing while awaiting repairs and drive up rental rates). As is common following disasters, rents rose. On average, rents rose 40% in New Orleans in the months after Hurricane Katrina (Rodriguez-Dod & Duhart, 2007). In a particularly egregious and eventually unlawful example following Hurricane Katrina, St. Bernard Parish Council approved an ordinance that prohibited all single-family homeowners from renting to anyone except a family member (Rodriguez-Dod & Duhart, 2007). A civil rights complaint was filed against the ordinance, which was eventually overturned due to violation of the Fair Housing Act, but the explicit attempt to exclude renters from an overwhelmingly white community rendered visible the persistent intersection of race, precarious possession, and de facto displacement following a disaster event.

Over the longer term, housing instability continues and compounds for precarious possessors post-disaster. Families displaced to Texas after Katrina were moved into subsidized housing but were later expected to pay market value for rent or to move into regular public housing, which some were unable to do (Lein et al., 2012). Additionally, those who received short-term assistance were not always eligible for long-term assistance in Houston similar to what they received in New Orleans. For instance, many struggled to obtain Section 8 vouchers (Lein et al., 2012), and couldn't always find available units even when they had successfully obtained such vouchers. Many low-income evacuees were evicted from undamaged units or faced rent hikes for failure to pay while evacuated (Pardee, 2012). Renters, and specifically women, faced numerous displacements in the years following Katrina as a result of increased rent and discriminatory barriers to housing stability (Elliot & Howell, 2017).

Precarious Possession and Citizenship Status

Citizenship status and lack of citizenship compound the challenges for renters. For one, immigrant populations tend to be renters. Second, immigrant groups, especially those that are undocumented or living in mixed-status households, often choose not to open bank accounts or sign housing contracts and sometimes receive cash payment for employment "under the table." The "off-the-books" renter, possibly an "under the table" employee, becomes particularly at risk and "invisible" in disaster management. Recovery programs demand burdensome amounts of documentation from applicants, which immigrant populations are usually unable to present due to these efforts to remain under the radar. Third, FEMA assistance is set up for nuclear families and utilizes the one head of household model, excluding non-traditional households (Jerolleman, 2019). Immigrant households often have several families living together in overcrowded conditions due to lack of affordable housing (McConnell, 2017), leaving many in need of assistance with no help. Even for eligible immigrant households, disaster recovery programs are designed using a cost–benefit approach intended to compensate for monetary losses to allocate disaster assistance, privileging higher value properties (Jerolleman, 2019).

Further, immigrants, specifically Latinx immigrants, are often assumed to be undocumented and therefore ineligible for federal assistance (Horton, 2012; Muñiz, 2006; Trujillo-Pagán, 2007). Even in situations where aid is available to anyone regardless of legal status, public employees or volunteer aid-workers still ask for identification from Latinx immigrants based on perceived illegality (Garza, 2012; Horton, 2012; Muñiz, 2006). Even if immigrants know they are eligible for assistance, policies such as the public charge law and the SB4 policy in Texas (Gilman & Steglich, 2017–2018) make immigrants hesitant to seek federal disaster assistance as they fear that accessing such services would tarnish an immigration case (Muñiz, 2006; Trujillo-Pagán, 2007).[2] Fears can extend to undocumented household members, or other family members, even when the primary applicant is eligible for assistance. Difficulties also arise when the eligible applicant is a U.S. born minor, residing with ineligible parents.

Legal status severely adds to the challenges faced by immigrant renters. Immigrant renters are often threatened with deportation or face forced eviction by landlords refusing to provide necessary repairs to rental units. For Garifuna immigrants displaced after Katrina, lack of legal documentation became a hindrance to finding stable housing and led to joblessness (Garza, 2012). A few months after the storm, only those who were documented were back at work (Garza, 2012). Many Garifuna immigrants held non-contractual and temporary jobs prior to Katrina, rendering them

[2] SB4, informally known as the "show-me-your-papers" policy, makes it against the law for local law enforcement and other public institutions in Texas to refuse to work with the federal government on immigration enforcement. It also allows law enforcement to ask about the immigration status of anyone they detain (American Civil Liberties Union, 2018).

vulnerable both before and especially after Katrina (Garza, 2012) and illustrating the intersecting and compounding informalities that affect precarious possessors post-disaster.

Renters and Retreat: Current Policy

The literature on disaster is replete with examples of how precarious possession, or the lack of being a clear, individual title holder, can (1) make immediate housing needs difficult; (2) make long-term recovery difficult; and (3) force displacement away from home communities. Yet renters appear little in the existing literature on managed retreat. When they do, it is as a "forgotten population" (Dundon & Camp, 2021), largely absent from the popular, scholarly, and policy imagination of relocation and resettlement programs designed for property owners (Morris, 2021). As discussed in earlier chapters, in the United States, managed retreat occurs primarily through federally funded home buyout programs, which enable state and local governments to purchase flood-damaged properties and convert them to open space.[3] Buyout programs target "willing sellers," landowners with the interest and capacity to sell their property; renters, if considered at all, are an afterthought in program design and implementation. They are excluded from decision-making processes, provided a minimum set of protections that can prove inadequate in practice, and are defined narrowly in law, policy, and research, rendering many of the most precarious possessors invisible and at increasing risk through the process of climate-linked relocation.

The primary policy governing renters faced with the prospect of managed retreat in the United States is the Uniform Relocation Assistance and Real Property Acquisition Policies Act of 1970 (also known as the Uniform Relocation Act, Uniform Act, or URA).[4] The URA came about as a belated response to the damaging effects of mid-century urban renewal, when government action led to the demolition of millions of homes, displacing many more millions of residents, with Black and low-income communities disproportionately targeted for destruction (Becher,

[3] Federal support for buyouts comes primarily, though not exclusively, from the Federal Emergency Management Agency (FEMA)'s Hazard Mitigation Grant Program (HMGP) and the Department of Housing and Urban Development (HUD)'s Community Development Block Grant—Disaster Recovery (CDBG-DR) funding.

[4] See 42 U.S.C. § 4601 *et seq.* and 49 C.F.R. pt. 24.

2014; Hartman, 1971). For any project that receives federal funding and involves the acquisition, rehabilitation, or demolition of property, the URA stipulates baseline amounts of compensation and relocation assistance for people who are displaced, provided they are found eligible for assistance.[5] In the case of buyouts, renters are classed as "displaced persons" subject to URA policy because they have no power to exercise agency in the buyout process. By contrast, property owners can generally choose whether or not to accept a buyout offer. Though the choices owners make may also be constrained or coerced, as described in Chapter 4, they are legally considered voluntary, meaning URA protections do not apply.[6] Though this is changing, mandatory buyouts are currently happening in Houston, which qualifies buyout recipients for URA protections. Tracing both renter and homeowner experiences during large-scale mandatory buyouts will add critical understanding to the differentiated experiences people have during these processes.

Like other government assistance, including for disaster recovery, URA benefits are subject to stringent eligibility requirements. As the Act sets out, "The term 'displaced person' does not include— (i) a person who has been determined, according to criteria established by the head of the lead agency, to be either in unlawful occupancy of the displacement dwelling or to have occupied such dwelling for the purpose of obtaining assistance..." It also excludes "any person (other than a person who was an occupant of such property at the time it was acquired) who occupies such property on a rental basis for a short term or a period subject to termination when the property is needed for the program or project."[7]

[5] Some states and municipalities have devised similar rules of their own for projects that are not federally funded. See Garnett (2006, 123–124).

[6] Voluntary participation for property owners distinguishes buyouts—also called "voluntary home buyouts"—from eminent domain, in which the government takes or condemns property regardless of consent from owners or occupants. In practice, the distinction is murky (de Vries & Fraser, 2012; Kuo, 2016). Eminent domain may also come to be considered necessary to force retreat for the purposes of flood protection (Flavelle, 2020). On general URA applicability to buyout programs, see: https://www.icf.com/insights/disaster-management/ura-compliance-buyout-programs.

[7] See §4601. The Act does allow for advisory services to adjacent persons who can prove economic injury and to short-term tenants and tenants whose lease terminates on acquisition who are otherwise excluded under §4601. Moreover, under §414 of the Stafford Act, which governs disaster assistance, tenants cannot be found ineligible for URA support if they do not meet occupancy requirements due to disaster damage and displacement. In other words, if a tenant is unable to return to a substantially damaged or destroyed

Immigrants without U.S. citizenship or permanent residence are also excluded from assistance.[8] In sum, many of the precarious possessors we describe above who are disproportionately vulnerable to flooding and related displacement are not protected or compensated under current law. Even renters with legal status and formal leases may struggle to secure the benefits to which they are entitled. Proving one's eligibility for government aid and disaster assistance demands supporting documentation that is time-consuming and often difficult to compile, especially in the aftermath of a flood that destroys paperwork, computers, photographs, and other personal belongings.

To comply with the URA, buyout programs for their part must notify tenants in advance that their homes are being acquired and they may be eligible for benefits. URA benefits to eligible renter recipients include help finding alternative "decent, safe, and sanitary" housing; moving expenses; and payments to cover the difference in rent for 42 months, up to a maximum amount of $7,200, or an equivalent lump sum that can be applied to a down payment should the tenant buy rather than rent. The $7,200 cap, increased from $5,250 in 2012, arguably remains insufficient; eminent domain scholar Becher (2014, 229) calls the URA's compensation limits "appallingly low." In practice, programs can—and often do—pay higher amounts (Garnett, 2006, 122),[9] invoking the URA's "Housing of Last Resort" (HLR) provision, which gives agencies "broad latitude" (see Chapter 10 on discretion) to ensure that eligible displaced

home before it is acquired, the tenant is still eligible for URA assistance under the Stafford Act (see: https://stormrecovery.ny.gov/sites/default/files/crp/community/documents/20210729_BuyoutAcquisition_PolicyManual_7.1_Final_0.pdf, p. 40). Assistance for people who fail to meet the length of occupancy requirements can also be provided under the URA's Housing of Last Resort subpart (49 CFR §24.404).

[8] This exclusion is qualified: "If a displacing agency determines by clear and convincing evidence that a determination of ineligibility of a displaced person [due to their undocumented status]...would result in exceptional and extremely unusual hardship to an individual who is the displaced person's spouse, parent, or child and who is a citizen of the United States or an alien lawfully admitted for permanent residence in the United States, the displacing agency shall provide relocation payments and other assistance to the displaced person under this chapter if the displaced person would be eligible for the assistance but for [their status]" (§4605).

[9] The Department of Housing and Urban Development (HUD)'s URA training module notes, "Paying RHPs [replacement housing payments] in excess of URA statutory limits is authorized and common." (Module 1: URA Overview. Accessed December 21, 2021 at https://www.hudexchange.info/trainings/ura-the-hud-way/).

persons have access to a comparable replacement dwelling. This may entail paying additional compensation on a case-by-case basis, or for an entire program or project if the agency deems it necessary. HLR also authorizes approaches that go beyond sheer compensation, including construction of new replacement housing and purchase of land or housing to sell, lease, or exchange with those displaced (49 CFR §24.404), though it is unclear whether these possibilities are used in practice (see Chapter 7).

Despite the options that agencies have to assist displaced people, support is typically short-lived and inadequate to meet the full spectrum of needs associated with relocation. This is true for all participants, including owners, but is particularly evident in the case of renters. Deborah Morris (2021), who administered New York City's acquisition program after Hurricane Sandy, describes the predicament facing renters who resided in flood-prone homes partly due to their affordability. Moving outside the floodplain entailed paying much higher rents, which the program only helped cover for the period mandated by the URA. Tenants were left with a choice between moving somewhere they would be unable to afford to stay long term, or moving somewhere at similar risk of flooding. In "Our buyout programs," Morris (2021, 148) writes, "did not have the tools to create a different outcome, which would have required providing substantially more than moving expenses and time-limited rent differential." De Vries and Fraser (2017, 934–935) argue the need for a "logic of care" in flood mitigation programs, in which "caregivers do not give up after contractual obligations are over, but instead continue to monitor and engage with individuals and communities in order to address injustices." In a system governed by property markets, however, logics of care are superseded by "logics of choice" that frame people as individual consumers, prioritizing them accordingly based on the power afforded by the resources they possess.

Discussion and Conclusion: A Study in Remembering

In this chapter, we discussed how ethnocentric and metaphorical conflations of property and citizenship/legal visibility become re-problematized when considering precarious possessors in relocation scenarios, and we discuss possible policy solutions (and their embedded assumptions) as a concluding point to the chapter. If there are decades of writing dedicated to the "right to the city," how can we translate that literature into the right to imagine what a new city, a new community, and a relocated future will look like in a warming world? How do we think beyond just urban environments and across various models of community? What can we do to ensure these rights of participation are enshrined and protected in the very minute that a new community is being imagined and created, so that precarious possessors can lay claim to their positions within the community of their choosing?

References

Agyeman, J., & Boone, K. (2020, June 18). *Land loss has plagued black America since emancipation—Is it time to look again at 'black commons' and collective ownership?* The Conversation. https://theconversation.com/land-loss-has-plagued-black-america-since-emancipation-is-it-time-to-look-again-at-black-commons-and-collective-ownership-140514

Alexander, G. S. (1997). *Commodity & propriety: Competing visions of property in American legal thought 1776–1970*. University of Chicago Press.

American Civil Liberties Union. (2018). *ACLU Annual Report 2018*. Retrieved July 7, 2022, from https://www.aclu.org/other/aclu-annual-report-2018

Angelo, H., & Wachsmuth, D. (2015). Urbanizing urban political ecology: A critique of methodological cityism. *International Journal of Urban and Regional Research, 39*(1), 16–27.

Ansfield, B. (2015). Still submerged: The uninhabitability of urban redevelopment. In K. McKittrick (Ed.), *Sylvia Wynter: On being human as praxis* (pp. 124–141). Duke University Press.

Becher, D. (2014). *Private property and public power: Eminent domain in Philadelphia*. Oxford University Press.

Bhandar, B. (2018). *Colonial lives of property: Law, land, and racial regimes of ownership*. Duke University Press.

Blomley, N. (2020). Precarious territory: Property law, housing, and the socio-spatial order. *Antipode, 52*(1), 36–57.

Browne, K. E. (2015). *Standing in the need: Culture, comfort, and coming home after Katrina*. University of Texas Press.

Cohen, D. A. (2018). *Climate justice and the right to the city*. Penn University.

De Vries, D. H., & Fraser, J. C. (2012). Citizenship rights and voluntary decision making in post disaster U.S. floodplain buyout mitigation programs. *International Journal of Mass Emergencies and Disasters, 30*(1), 1–33.

de Vries, D. H., & Fraser, J. C. (2017). Historical waterscape trajectories that need care: the unwanted refurbished flood homes of Kinston's devolved disaster mitigation program. *Journal of Political Ecology, 24*(1), 931–950.

Dundon, L. A., & Camp, J. S. (2021). Climate justice and home-buyout programs: Renters as a forgotten population in managed retreat actions. *Journal of Environmental Studies and Sciences, 11*(3), 420–433. https://doi.org/10.1007/s13412-021-00691-4

DuPuis, E. M., & Greenberg, M. (2019). The right to the resilient city: Progressive politics and the green growth machine in New York City. *Journal of Environmental Studies and Sciences, 9*(3), 352–363.

Durst, N. J., & Wegmann, J. (2017). Informal housing in the United States. *International Journal of Urban and Regional Research, 41*(2), 282–297.

Elliott, J. R., & Howell, J. (2017). Beyond disasters: A longitudinal analysis of natural hazards' unequal impacts on residential instability. *Social Forces, 95*(3), 1181–1207.

Flavelle, C. (2020, March 11). Trump administration presses cities to evict homeowners from flood zones. *The New York Times*.

Fleming, B., Cohen, D. A., Graetz, N., Lample, K., Lillehei, X., McDonald, K., Brave Noisecat, J., Paul, M. (2019). Public housing at risk: Adaptation through a green new deal. https://www.filesforprogress.org/memos/public_housing_at_risk.pdf

Fussell, E. (2012). Help from family, friends, and strangers during Hurricane Katrina: Finding the limits of social networks. In L. Weber & L. Peek (Eds.), *Displaced: Life in the Katrina diaspora* (pp. 150–166). University of Texas Press.

First Street Foundation. (2020). *The First National Flood Risk Assessment Defining America's Growing Risk*. https://assets.firststreet.org/uploads/2020/06/first_street_foundation__first_national_flood_risk_assessment.pdf

Garza, C. M. (2012). Twice Removed: New Orleans Garifuna in the Wake of Hurricane Katrina. In *Displaced: Life in the Katrina Diaspora* (pp. 198–217). University of Texas Press.

Garnett, N. S. (2006). The neglected political economy of eminent domain. *Michigan Law Review, 105*, 101.

Gilbert, J., Wood, S. D., & Sharp, G. (2002). Who owns the land? Agricultural land ownership by race/ethnicity. *Rural America/Rural Development Perspectives, 17*(4), 55–62. https://doi.org/10.22004/ag.econ.289693

Gilman, D., & Steglich, E. (2018). The unending floods. Disaster recovery and immigration policy. *Texas Law Review Online, 96*, 91–101. https://texaslawreview.org/the-unending-floods/

Grandinetti, T. (2019). Urban aloha 'aina: Kaka'ako and a decolonized right to the city. *Settler Colonial Studies, 9*(2), 227–246.

Greenberg, M. (2013). The disaster inside the disaster: Hurricane Sandy and post-crisis redevelopment. *New Labor Forum, 23*(1), 44–52. https://doi.org/10.1177/1095796013513239

Hardy, D., Bailey, M., & Heynen, N. (2022). "We're still here": An abolition ecology blockade of double dispossession of Gullah/Geechee land. *Annals of the American Association of Geographers, 112*(3), 867–876.
Harris, C. I. (1993). Whiteness as property. *Harvard Law Review, 106*(8), 1707–1791.
Hartman, C. W. (1971). Relocation: Illusory promises and no relief. *Virginia Law Review, 57*(5), 745–817.
Harvey, D. (2008). The right to the city. *The City Reader, 6*(1), 23–40.
Horton, L. (2012). Nowhere to turn: Obstacles for immigrants seeking disaster assistance. *National Lawyers Guild Review, 69*, 140–159.
Jerolleman, A. (2019). *Disaster recovery through the lens of justice*. Springer.
Kamel, N. M. O., & Loukaitou-Sideris, A. (2004). Residential assistance and recovery following the Northridge Earthquake. *Urban Studies, 41*(3), 533–562.
Kawash, S. (1998). Bodies at risk: The architecture of reversible destiny. *PAJ: A Journal of Performance and Art, 20*(2), 17–27.
Kuo, S. S., & Means, B. (2016). Collective Coercion. *Boston College Law Review, 57*, 1599.
Lee, J. Y., & Van Zandt, S. (2019). Housing tenure and social vulnerability to disasters: A review of the evidence. *Journal of Planning Literature, 34*(2), 156–170.
Lefebvre, H. (1974). *The production of space*. Wiley-Blackwell.
Lein, L., Angel, R., Beausoleil, J., & Bell, H. (2012). The basement of extreme poverty: Katrina Survivors and poverty programs. In W. Lynn & L. Peek (Eds.), *Displaced: Life in the Katrina diaspora* (pp. 47–62). University of Texas Press.
Louis-Charles, H. M., Howard, R., Remy, L., Nibbs, F., & Turner, G. (2020). Ethical considerations for postdisaster fieldwork and data collection in the Caribbean. *American Behavioral Scientist, 64*(8), 1129–1144.
Manda, S., Jerolleman, A., & Marino, E. (2023). Assumptions and understanding of success in home buyout programs.*International Journal of Disaster Risk Reduction,*103863.
McConnell, E. D. (2017). Rented, crowded, and unaffordable? Social vulnerabilities and the accumulation of precarious housing conditions in Los Angeles. *Housing Policy Debate, 27*(1), 60–79.
Messias, D. K. H., Barrington, C., & Lacy, E. (2012). Latino social network dynamics and the Hurricane Katrina disaster. *Disasters, 36*(1), 101–121.
Moreton-Robinson, A. (2015). *The white possessive: White possession and Indigenous sovereignty matters*. University of Minnesota Press.
Morris, D. H. (2021). The climate crisis is a housing crisis: Without growth we cannot retreat. In I. J. Ajibade & A. R. Siders (Eds.), *Global views on climate relocation and social justice* (pp. 142–151). Routledge.

Muñiz, B. (2006). *In the eye of the storm: How the government and private response to Hurricane Katrina failed Latinos*. National Council of La Raza.

Mukhija, V. (2014). The value of incremental development and design in affordable housing. *Cityscape, 16*(2), 11–20.

NYU Furman Center (2017). Housing in the U.S. Floodplains. https://furmancenter.org/research/publication/housing-in-the-us-floodplains

Pardee, J. W. (2012). Living through displacement: Housing insecurity among low-income evacuees. In L. Weber & L. Peek (Eds.), *Displaced life in the Katrina diaspora* (pp. 63–78). University of Texas Press.

Pastor, M., Bullard, R., Boyce, J. K., Fothergill, A., Morello-Frosch, R., & Wright, B. (2006). Environment, disaster, and race after Katrina. *Race, Poverty & the Environment,13* (1), 21–26.

Peacock, W. G., Van Zandt, S., Zhang, Y., & Highfield, W. E. (2015). Inequities in long-term housing after disaster. *Journal of the American Planning Association, 80*(4), 356–371.

Quarantelli, E. L. (2006). Catastrophes are different from disasters: Some implications for crisis planning and managing drawn from Katrina. *Understanding Katrina: Perspectives from the social sciences*. Chicago.

Right To The City Alliance. (n.d.). Retrieved July 7, 2022, from https://righttothecity.org/

Rodriguez-Dod, E. C., & Duhart, O. (2007). Evaluating Katrina: A snapshot of renters' rights following disasters. *Nova Law Review, 31*(3), 467.

Roy, A. (2003). Paradigms of propertied citizenship: Transnational techniques of analysis. *Urban Affairs Review, 38*(4), 463–491. https://doi.org/10.1177/1078087402250356

Roy, A. (2005). Urban informality: Toward an epistemology of planning. *Journal of the American Planning Association, 71*(2), 147–156.

Rumbach, A., Sullivan, E., & Makarewicz, C. (2020). Mobile home parks and disasters: Understanding risk to the third housing type in the United States. *Natural Hazards Review, 21*(2).

Scott, J. C. (1986). *Seeing like a state: How certain schemes to improve the human condition have failed*. Yale University Press.

Sullivan, E. (2018). *Manufactured insecurity: Mobile home parks and Americans' tenuous right to place*. University of California Press.

Sutley, E. J., & Hamideh, S. (2020). Postdisaster housing stages: A Markov chain approach to model sequences and duration based on social vulnerability. *Risk Analysis, 40*(12), 2675–2695. https://doi.org/10.1111/risa.13576

Tate, E., Strong, A., Kraus, T., & Xiong, H. (2016). Flood recovery and property acquisition in Cedar Rapids, Iowa. *Natural Hazards, 80*(3), 2055–2079.

Trujillo-Pagán, N. (2007). Katrina's Latinos: Vulnerability and disasters in relief and recovery. In K. A. Bates & R. S. Swan (Eds.), *Through the eye of Katrina: Social justice in the United States* (pp. 147–168). Carolina Academic Press.

Wachtendorf, T., Nelan, M. M., & Blinn-Pike, L. (2013). Households and families. In D. S. K. Thomas, B. D. Phillips, W. E. Lovekamp, & A. Fothergill (Eds.), *Social vulnerability to disasters* (pp. 281–310). CRC Press.

Weber, L., & Peek, L. (2012). *Displaced: Life in the Katrina diaspora*. University of Texas Press.

Wegmann, J., Schafran, A., & Pfeiffer, D. (2017). Breaking the double impasse: Securing and supporting diverse housing tenures in the United States. *Housing Policy Debate, 27*(2), 193–216.

Weinstein, L., & Ren, X. (2009). The changing right to the city: Urban renewal and housing rights in globalizing Shanghai and Mumbai. *City & Community, 8*(4), 407–432.

Yoder, J. (2020). Does property ownership lead to participation in local politics? Evidence from property records and meeting minutes. *American Political Science Review, 114*(4), 1213–1229.

Zhang, Y., & Peacock, W. G. (2010). Planning for housing recovery? Lessons learned from Hurricane Andrew. *Journal of the American Planning Association, 76*(1), 5–24.

CHAPTER 7

Interrogating "Just Compensation" and Flexibility: Details on the Inadequacy (and Importance) of Voluntary Buyouts for Relocation in Alaska

Introduction

One premise of this book is that the most prominent federal solution and funding mechanism to support relocations linked to repetitive flooding is the use of voluntary buyouts and acquisitions of at-risk properties. As authors, we have seen a substantial increase in research and political interest in acquisitions and buyouts, which are often discussed as part of an economically sound response to climate change (Salvesen et al., 2018). There is also ongoing scholarship to understand how buyouts interact with the intersectional identities of homeowners and communities (Siders, 2019); though there remains a gap in our knowledge about who agrees to a buyout in proportion to who is offered one; and a lack of governmental transparency about who is offered a buyout in the first place, or how the decisions to offer a buyout (either to a particular property owner or as opposed to other mitigations strategies or nothing at all) are reached (Siders, 2019). The rise in interest in voluntary buyouts and acquisitions are why we make the claim in the introduction that relocation is being mostly carried out as a property transaction agreement between a selling

This chapter was written with Joel Neimeyer and Stacey Fritz.

A. Jerolleman et al., *People or Property*,
https://doi.org/10.1007/978-3-031-36872-1_7

homeowner and purchasing government. The question that this chapter addresses is whether and why these programs are unsuccessful at sufficiently funding relocations in Alaska, and what could improve their fit for the Alaskan context.

Alaska has been foregrounded in scholarship (Bronen & Chapin, 2013; Marino, 2015), journalism (Callison, 2017; Herrmann, 2017; Marino, 2015), and policy analysis (GAO, 2009) related to relocations that have a climate signal. Because Alaska is warming at a faster rate than other areas of the globe; and because many small, rural, Indigenous communities are located along the coast and in riverine environments (Marino, 2015), these communities are increasingly involved in conversations about full or partial relocation or as an adaptation strategy to climate change. In March 2009, the U.S. Army Corps of Engineers (USACE) published an Alaska Baseline Erosion Assessment of rural Alaska communities. Months later, in June 2009, the U.S. Government Accountability Office published Report 09-551 partially based upon the earlier USACE erosion assessment. Report 09-551 identified 31 villages that were at imminent erosion risk. Out of those 31, 12 had "decided" or had expressed a potential desire to relocate (GAO, 2009). At the time, the state focused especially on three communities that seemed most "at risk" and had been proactive at planning and locally organizing support for relocation. These communities were Shishmaref, Newtok, and Kivalina. The GAO also found that over 200 Alaska Native communities were at some risk of flooding and erosion. These numbers indicate that even if full relocation is not needed or preferred in many communities, there are houses and other kinds of infrastructure that will need to be moved so that people throughout the state can sleep knowing that they are safe from imminent flooding and inundation.

In November 2019, the Denali Commission published the Statewide Threat Assessment: Identification of Threats from Erosion, Flooding, and Thawing Permafrost in Remote Alaska Communities. One of the authors of this chapter actively worked on this report. In consultation with GAO staff who prepared Report 09-551, it was recommended that the agency undertake a study of erosion, flooding, permafrost degradation in rural Alaska communities. As with the USACE 2009 erosion efforts, GAO followed up the Denali Commission assessment with a new report on environmentally threatened communities in May 2022. Both the GAO report and Denali Commission report identify over 70 rural

Alaska communities that face significant erosion, flooding, and permafrost degradation risks.

As we write this chapter, the western coast of Alaska has just suffered through the worst storm in 50–70 years. Newtok is a community that has been in a years-long process to relocate to the new site of Mertarvik. According to colleagues in Mertarvik, during the storm, the Newtok airport was cut off, 12 homes flooded with at least one foot of water, one boat was missing, two 5000-gallon empty fuel tanks floated away, one house was knocked off of its foundation, power was knocked out, there was massive erosion of up to 40 feet of riverbank, which flooded the entire village. During the storm, there was no ground to walk on. Now, only 25 feet of shoreline remains to the one remaining community potable water system. Likely the school, which serves as the emergency shelter, will be lost in the next storm or during the high tide processes in which erosion occurs a couple feet at a time. Twenty-two families do not have a home identified for them in Mertarvik, despite decades of effort. While solutions to flooding are complex, the ongoing inundation of homes and infrastructure, the stress and disruption to people's lives and subsistence activities, and the deterioration of landscapes that have been lived with and protected by Indigenous communities since time immemorial should pressure all of us to seek solutions sooner rather than later.

Buyouts in Alaska

Of the communities that are considering relocation, Newtok has made the most substantive strides toward securing a new site and relocating residents and tribal members to the new location. The new community is called Mertarvik, which translates from Yup'ik to English as "getting water from the spring." In 2019, after more than a decade of dedicated organization and planning across local and state agencies and governmental organizations, and after three decades of community-wide discussion (Ristroph, 2021), 140 residents moved into 21 homes in the first stage of relocating the community. According to the 2022 census, one hundred and eighty-one residents, twenty-two families, still remain in the old site.

Part of the funding for the first phase of Newtok's relocation was supported by voluntary buyouts granted by FEMA's Hazard Mitigation Grant Program. FEMA gave $1.7 million to buy out and demolish seven of the most at-risk houses. After appraisals and buyouts were completed, this translated, on average, to \$242,857 per house. For people from Newtok, during the 2019 construction season, building a new, modest, 1,100 square foot home in Mertarvik cost \$600,000 (Ristroph, 2021).

The community of Akiak, Alaska is also in the process of a partial managed retreat to move infrastructure away from Kuskokwim River erosion. As part of this retreat, one of the authors of this chapter helped to organize the acquisition of a home in the community with two residents. The acquisition process started in January 2021 and still remains unfinished 20 months later. The property has multiple owners as a result of being an heir's property—one that is passed after the death of a family member who does not have a will and so is owned by multiple family members. Like in the case of Newtok, and in all buyout processes, the home was appraised and then offered \$85,000 for purchase to be demolished and put into public use as green space. Building a new home in the community to replace this modest house will cost approximately \$475,000.[1]

The discrepancy between the purchase price and replacement price means that buyouts do not automatically create relocation options for Indigenous and rural Alaskan communities. First, buyouts assume that there is a functioning residential real estate market from which homeowners can select a new home of equal value in a safer location. In rural Alaska, there is already a lack of housing stock. Many houses are overcrowded and there are several complex barriers to accessing safe land, funding, and capacity for building homes. This means that when older homes are demolished because they are at-risk, the only option is to build a new home to replace the demolished home, or for the people occupying that house to move hundreds of miles away and out of traditional subsistence territory. For many people the latter is unthinkable.

It is also difficult to establish fair market value for voluntary buyouts in rural Alaska. In the case of Akiak, an appraiser compared home prices from communities that were a plane flight away. A home that sold in the hub community of Bethel, for example, was compared to the price of the home in the much smaller village of Akiak, even though the economic basis for these communities are significantly different. Whether

[1] Infrastructure costs in Alaska are, and since colonial incursion, extremely high. This is due to the cost of shipping (usually barging) materials into communities with no interconnected road system; and the need to insulate and protect in Arctic and Sub-Arctic conditions.

this comparison favors or disadvantages the homeowner is uncertain, but appraisals for market value are suspect, at best, in the relative lack of a real estate market. It is also difficult to do a comparative analysis for an *n of one*. If there is only one home "for sale" in Akiak and a community of people who do not want to leave, the value of the home may be infinite.

Buyouts require that residents vacate homes in 90 days, and that the homes be demolished after purchase by the local project sponsor. Again, in the lack of a functioning residential real estate market, and a rental market of frequently 0% capacity, this is a difficult timeline to adhere to. In Newtok, according to a presentation by the Newtok Planning Commission, yurts had to be purchased as interim housing for families that received a buyout. In Akiak, one of the residents has been offered housing in the infrastructure built for COVID quarantine. The other resident was offered housing in a tribally-owned duplex. The tribe, therefore, has to take on housing responsibilities for community members who take buyouts. This incurred cost to tribes is functionally a taxation that local governments must bear for policies that are ill-fitting to rural communities.

Because buyout funds do not cover the costs of building new homes in rural Alaska, tribes have had to create new and piecemeal ways to offset costs of building new homes. In Newtok, legislative funds helped cover the cost of construction. In Akiak, grant funds from the Bureau of Indian Affairs and other tribal appropriations are being leveraged to build a new house for a homeowner that is presently residing in a home structurally unsound to relocate and that is threatened by riverine erosion. The tribal council's task list for completing the buyout proposal in Akiak, includes getting all heirs to sign an agreement, finding temporary housing, finding additional funding, and eventually holding the loan for the homeowner. This is an overwhelming amount of work in a village of less than 400 people. These tasks, taken on by community members, Alaskans who have family connections to villages, or state agency workers that have dedicated their entire careers to these relocations, are one of the only ways that relocations in Alaska have moved forward.

In the end, we see that the buyout policy, while it has been used in Alaska to facilitate relocations as an adaptation strategy to high water, has failed as a sufficient funding solution. Outside of considerations for renters and non-homeowners that also must relocate, and to whom we dedicated chapter six, buyouts are ill-suited to many situations, including those in Alaska and other rural and tribal areas because of their inability to capture the social and economic forces that make existing homes worth little, and new homes expensive to build.

What Is Just Compensation in Voluntary Buyouts?

As outlined in chapter one, private property is protected from seizure by the government without just compensation in the last clause of the Constitution's Fifth Amendment, known as the Takings Clause. This protection applies during cases of eminent domain, where the government takes a property for public use with or without the property owner's consent. Voluntary buyouts are not cases of eminent domain because they are voluntarily agreed to by the homeowner instead of being a takings, however, the structure of the exchange is similar, including the fact that at-risk properties purchased during FEMA buyouts are turned into green spaces that can act as flood protection for other development and so constitute public use.

The Takings clause fails to define either public use or just compensation and both have been left to the courts to decide. Marisa Fagen and Christopher Serkin contend that disagreements about what constitutes *public use* have been focused on much more as an area of contested and evolving jurisprudence than what constitutes just compensation (Fagen, 2006; Serkin, 2004). Fagen's paper, which we are relying on heavily for our argument here, claims that just compensation remains unsettled in the courts. She points out that the first Takings Case to be brought before the Supreme Court in 1893 stated, "There can, in view of the combination of those two words, be no doubt that the compensation must be a full and perfect equivalent for the property taken" (Monongahela Navigation Co. v. United States).

In that case, the court pointed out that "just" is inserted before "compensation" as a mechanism to ensure fairness to the property owner. Some legal writers have interpreted this notion of "fairness" as "making a homeowner whole again" or a "goal of putting a property owner in as good of a position as if his property had not been taken" (Fagen, 2006). Important to the idea of just compensation is protection of an individual from undue government overreach, and "the court [has] explained that the takings clause is designed to protect individuals from bearing public burdens that should be borne by the public as a whole" (Fagen, 2006, 275).

Generally, legal scholars who critique an equivalency between fair market value and just compensation have argued that, "fair market value excludes, for example, consequential damages and compensation for any of the real but subjective harms suffered by the property owner" (Serkin, 2004). Subjective harm could be considered emotional distress, incidental costs, or, in a theoretical argument rooted in Locke and Hegel, the loss of the self, as personhood is bound up in labor, but also in interactions with material things, such as a house (Radin, 1982). What generally argued is that valuation of loss is more complex than fair market value, and that real property exchanges are frequently inflected by elements outside of what an assessment can locate. Another, perhaps more important critique is the reliance on assessors to "value" a home at what they think is "just" according to the market. Assessors can come to wildly different conclusions about what a home is worth (Serkin, 2004). Real estate markets, for example, are racialized markets, and lower property values can be an outcome of an assessor's subjective inability to see the cultural values in one neighborhood and simultaneously overvalue cultural markers in another. Akiak is on the Kuskokwim River. What is that worth, and to whom?

Some legal scholars have argued that it is replacement value, instead of fair market value, that should be considered "just compensation." Serkin writes that "replacement value will usually exceed any measure of the fair market value of the property, although it is still likely to provide something less than the property's subjective value to its owner" (Serkin, 2004). In other words, the value of the property includes several intangibles such as the connections to the community itself and the memories that might be tied into a home. In the case of Alaska, replacement value might not cover all expenses related to building a new home, but it would arguably be of significantly higher value than the assessed, "fair market" value. Broadly, the idea of replacement better captures the original intent of recreating conditions for the selling owner to have a life and livelihood that is commensurate with the life and livelihood one had before selling property to the government. In the case of voluntary buyouts as a risk reduction strategy in Alaska, replacement costs may be a more realistic exchange for allowing Indigenous community members to stay in traditional territory and maintain social relationships and family bonds. In other words, if rural Alaskans received "replacement" value for a house, this might be equated to what it would cost to rebuild a similarly sized house in their community. Thus "replacement" would be identified as "just compensation" and not just "market value." It seems fairly obvious that it is not "just compensation" to receive funds that, because of their inadequacy, would forcibly relocate families or individuals to outside communities hundreds or thousands of miles outside of traditional homelands.

There is precedent for voluntary buyouts to add incentives for homeowners to accept a buyout, such as additional funds when a family remains in the same county. We encourage FEMA to offer rural Alaskans replacement value as just compensation in cases of voluntary buyouts as a means toward relocation. It is possible that a legal argument could be made to justify such an offer as necessary to maintain the original intent of the law to not put undue burden on a homeowner for selling property to the government. The decision to test the legal status of just compensation may be particularly timely as FEMA, to meet the goals of the Biden administration's "Justice40" initiative, has indicated an increased appetite to prioritize environmental justice into their mission and policies. If just compensation has been undertheorized (Serkin, 2004), it would be interesting for an administration to test it, specifically through incentives or valuations of properties in communities that meet the standards for rural and impoverished.

Flexible Infrastructure and Climate Change: Just Compensation as Repair

This chapter has been considering what it would mean to interpret "just compensation" during voluntary buyouts, as something beyond fair market value. Namely, we have been considering "replacement value" as an alternative. Replacement value would ensure that people whose homes were "bought out" after being appraised at a much lower value than what it would cost to rebuild, would have some measure of protection from displacement. This would be particularly useful in rural communities where housing stock is low. The next section will consider what it would mean to interpret "just" compensation as *justice in compensation*. This interpretation may incur new historical dimensions to voluntary buyouts.

The development (settlement) of communities in Alaska as a result of colonization is relatively recent in Alaska—within the past century in some areas. Forced "emplacement" or sedentarization displaced traditional seasonal movements across the landscape and is one of the many unintended consequences that accompanied colonial occupation of western Alaska. It is important to point out here that this is not an argument against infrastructure development. Communities and their strongest advocates work toward the infrastructure development that would be expected in most places in the lower 48—like health clinics, running water infrastructure, and schools. It is not infrastructure per se that is the problem, but that traditional adaptive strategies to a highly variable coast were not adequately replaced by equivalents as infrastructure developed. Traditional Iñupiat and Yup'ik infrastructure, for example, was flexible to changing coastlines. To have infrastructure that could be moved was an essential component to resilient and strong communities prior to colonization in the state, and this strategy of flexibility has been used continuously since.

Surprisingly to outsiders, but common to Alaskans working on these issues, is that moving infrastructure, particularly homes, has been part of nearly all forced and voluntary relocation scenarios in Alaska and part of adaptation broadly to changing coastlines. In Shishmaref, at least twenty homes have been moved off of their foundations, away from the coast. In Akiak, one of the reasons the house was deemed eligible for a buyout was because it was structurally unable to be moved. The tribe moved six homes that were structurally sound. Whether by a few feet, or across frozen bodies of water during winter, moving homes in rural Alaska occurs, and is part of an overall, mostly informal, strategy of being adaptive to an ultimately changing and changeable world (Davis & Marino, 2023).

This traditional adaptation strategy of flexibility is also increasingly part of formal architectural design, especially by architects living in places that face imminent climate risks. Fairbanks, Alaska-based Cold Climate Housing Research Center (CCHRC), is a non-profit committed to advancing Arctic infrastructure to meet the needs of Arctic communities. Commensurate with this mission, they have begun to prototype building systems that have consistent flexibility as the key criterion for their design.

One adaptable building system being developed at CCHRC is a system-built kit of parts that can be assembled on site without heavy equipment or specialized labor. It is a simple and traditional modified timber frame and panel on frame system. The principle of the system is to develop a standard framing size and connection system to ensure the interoperability of components—the most common analogy is Legos. The system is designed to be expandable without requiring any destruction to the existing structure, so that families can add on or retract as needed. These adaptable homes are also moveable or transportable, and not only in the way modern manufactured homes (previously known as mobile homes) are. A truly adaptable home can be disassembled, moved, and reassembled. Many log cabins meet these criteria and have been moved in this manner. In many situations, a far more manageable and less traumatic retreat can be achieved with houses that can be skidded, sledded, or towed overland with small equipment or off-road/all-terrain vehicles.

The New Orleans-based Buoyant Foundation Project vision also has potential for Alaska. A buoyant foundation is a type of amphibious foundation in which an existing structure is retrofitted to allow it to float as high as necessary during floods while remaining on the ground in normal conditions. In China, this is referred to as a mud anchor: at least one corner of the house is attached to a post in the ground, the house floats up with storm waters and pivots into the current with deflectors on the posted end to shunt debris. Practically, there are still challenges to these emergent infrastructure projects, such as how to ensure that utility connections don't fail and what can be done when there is a large amount of debris. The Buoyant Foundations are not approved to carry flood insurance under the National Flood Insurance Program, for example, creating other risks for homeowners that want to use this technology (English et al., 2017).

Despite these setbacks, however, investment in improved living conditions, and innovative infrastructure, has the potential to provide justice in compensation. This would define just compensation as the creation of homes that are livable and adaptive, and contain the flexibility that proved successful prior to colonial intrusion. Justice in compensation might mean increasing housing stock, or square footage, or hazard mitigation upgrades for people who have been unduly burdened by the risks of rising water and redlining, high winds and colonialism. Climate adaptation and climate justice might be more aligned if a "buyout" was also an opportunity for innovation that facilitated long-term housing needs.

New Infrastructure Technologies Are Not Enough

The politician/community member/academic/practitioner co-authors of this chapter also want to acknowledge that while adequate funding for homes, such as more funding when an individual is offered a buyout, would improve the relocation possibilities in rural Alaska, there is no "magic" solution to complex problems. Other challenges that arise when confronting relocation or housing insecurities are land ownership complexities. As we have described earlier in this book, the Alaska Native Claims Settlement Act (ANCSA) established land holdings for tribes, to be held as corporations. Broadly, there can be a lack of available land for construction, and it can be challenging to finalize conveyances from tribal corporations to individuals for housing. Additionally land swaps for ANCSA corporations to use public land for appropriate building sites require Congressional approval (Nicewonger et al., 2022). In addition, construction in Alaska is complicated by the weather and timing issues that can be underestimated by outside builders. Most materials are barged into communities and must be timed well so that there is adequate time for building during the summer, before freeze-up, and after fuel has been barged into a community to run heavy equipment. These timing complexities have severely delayed many projects (Nicewonger et al., 2022).

Additionally, small tribes and cities generally do not have project management capacity to oversee large construction and management projects such as managed retreats and relocation efforts. Those efforts include, experience drafting contracts, contracting for and incorporating geotechnical assessments, managing contractors, developing design documents, site control, coordinating with relevant groups, and project scheduling and budgeting. Identifying someone who could act as an "owner's representative" to represent the tribal council and administration interests might offer important support toward realizing the tribe's goals on their own terms. While there are frequently multiple agencies and funders involved in relocation, none of these agencies can provide the community funding for an owner's representative, nor can they provide comprehensive project management. The agencies can only provide project management for the specific infrastructure development funded by the agency. In this case, it would be useful for the tribe to have some say over who manages the many agency project managers!

As an example of the overwhelming bureaucratic hurdles communities face, we offer the following. In May 2019, Akiak experienced a new form of riverine erosion when, in two days, 50 to 75 feet of riverbank along 1200 feet of riverfront—in front of the village—was lost. Historically, Akiak experienced mild fall time erosion during storms when a couple of feet of riverbank was lost. No one in the village could recall such a springtime erosion event and there were no stories from the elders of such an erosion event. By July 2019, the community voted for a managed retreat solution. Since that time the tribe has directly managed fourteen separate grants from eight separate agencies for housing improvements, sanitation and power plant improvements, broadband development, roads, and relocating homes. In addition, two non-profit organizations are managing development of new housing and new sanitation infrastructure. Additionally, one state agency completed improvements to the marine fuel header and piping. In short, there is demand locally for available equipment, lodging, and manpower that all must be managed so that all of the projects are completed timely and within budget.

Local capacity is also important as many grant agencies include capacity as a necessary grant scoring element. The result of the capacity scoring rubric is that the tribes with administrative capacity are often the tribes that receive competitive grants. Often, tribes that face greater environmental threats are not able to compete successfully for grants. While the agencies can defend this approach to outside inquiry as ensuring they are good stewards of public funding, some of the communities with the greatest needs are unserved. These communities face years of effort to improve capacity and associated measurements (i.e., clean audits, track record of timely grant reporting, etc.) before they can compete for grants to support relocation solutions. This need has been recognized by the new federal hazard mitigation competition, and the Building Resilience Infrastructure and Communities (BRIC) program does make allowances for technical assistance prior to application—but this is limited to one grant, not the suite of grants that tribes apply for. Additionally, technical assistance is only offered to a select number of communities and is not a guarantee of future funding.

Finally, the Hazard Mitigation Plans (HMP) that FEMA requires in order for a community to be eligible to seek disaster resilience funds are currently completed by every tribe individually in Alaska. Over half of the rural Alaska local governments lack an approved HMP. Additionally, any HMPs that have lapsed are no longer useful. This is well known within FEMA and the Alaska Division of Homeland Security and Emergency Management and both agencies are taking steps to address this issue. In the event of a disaster, the Governor can declare a disaster declaration, and in larger disasters, the President can declare a disaster. However, lacking an approved HMP document, local priorities for disaster response, recovery, and resilience can easily go unheard. The value of the HMP document is therefore two-fold: it allows the local community to compete for disaster resilience funding from both FEMA and the State and, equally important, it can serve as a blueprint for agencies to follow after a disaster event occurs with the knowledge that the priority solutions identified in the HMP document are locally approved.

So far as the authors can tell, there does not appear to be any regional HMP documents for rural Alaska communities that have ever been drafted, although FEMA regulations allow for this (CFR 44.201.7(a)(3)). One reason may be that the Stafford Act allows FEMA to work directly with states and tribes. Regional tribal organizations can serve as sub-recipients to states and tribes, but do not represent tribes directly with FEMA. However, in Indian Country, tribes are comfortable working with tribal organizations that represent their interests directly with federal agencies (NCAI Resolution #SAC-21–037). Tribal organizations have a long-standing history of working with the U.S. Department of Housing and Urban Development (i.e., tribally designated housing entities), Indian Health Service (Title I and Title V contractors through 25 USC 46), and the Bureau of Indian Affairs (Title I and Title V contractors) on behalf of their tribes. Tribal organizations often provide the project management services described above. Lacking authority in the Stafford Act for a tribal organization to represent tribes on disaster resilience matters, existing tribal organizations are limited in serving tribes in developing disaster resilience projects, drafting a regional HMP and a host of other pre-disaster tasks that can overwhelm a small tribe with limited capacity. While there may be some tribes who prefer to act independently, regional considerations are important and should be supported by legislation.

Conclusion: From One House to Regional Solutions

This chapter is dedicated to thinking through challenges of relocation planning in Alaska. We have focused especially on how buyouts are interpreted; what new home construction could look like, and how regional planning may facilitate capacity issues in extremely small tribes and communities. The other concern, of course, is what rights people have, and can exercise, to stay within their home community when threatened with repetitive flooding. Broadly what this chapter shows is that solutions that are possible if interpretations of the law are broadened so as to be useful to people who need to move because of flooding. Environmental injustice often implicates broad swaths of decision-making and long histories of oppression; but environmental justice may sometimes, in part, be found in a new interpretation of the law.

References

Bronen, R., & Chapin, F. S., III. (2013). Adaptive governance and institutional strategies for climate-induced community relocations in Alaska. *Proceedings of the National Academy of Sciences, 110*(23), 9320–9325.

Callison, C. (2017). Climate change communication and indigenous publics. In M. Nisbet (Ed.), *The Oxford encyclopedia of climate change communication.* Oxford University Press.

Dennis, D., & Elizabeth, M. (2023). Representation and Luck: Reflections on Climate and Collaboration in Shishmaref, Alaska. In S. Crate & M. Nuttall (Eds.), *Anthropology and Climate Change* (3. 1). Routledge.

English, E. C., Friedland, C. J., & Orooji, F. (2017). Combined flood and wind mitigation for hurricane damage prevention: Case for amphibious construction. *Journal of Structural Engineering*, *143*(6), 06017001.

Fagen, P. W. (2006). *Remittances in conflict and crises: How remittances sustain livelihoods in war, crises and transitions to peace.* International Peace Institute.

GAO. (2009). *Alaska native villages: Limited progress has been made on relocating villages threatened by flooding and erosion.* Government Accountability Office Report GAO-09-551.

Herrmann, V. (2017). America's first climate change refugees: Victimization, distancing, and disempowerment in journalistic storytelling. *Energy Research & Social Science, 31*, 205–214.

Marino, E. (2015). *Fierce climate, sacred ground: An ethnography of climate change in Shishmaref*. University of Alaska Press.

Nicewonger, T., Fritz, S., & Mcnair, L. (2022, January). Complexities in Alaskan Housing: Critical reflections on social forces shaping cold climate building projects. In *Proceedings of the American Society of Engineering Education 2022 Annual Conference & Exposition.*

Radin, M. J. (1982). Property and personhood. *Stanford Law Review*, 957–1015.

Ristroph, E. B. (2021). Navigating climate change adaptation assistance for communities: A case study of Newtok Village, Alaska. *Journal of Environmental Studies and Sciences, 11*(3), 329–340.

Salvesen, D., BenDor, T. K., Kamrath, C., & Ganser, B. (2018). *Are floodplain buyouts a smart investment for local governments.* Final Report for the UNC Policy Collaboratory.

Serkin, C. (2004). The meaning of value: Assessing just compensation for regulatory takings. *Nw. UL Rev.*, 99, 677.

Siders, A. R. (2019). Social justice implications of US managed retreat buyout programs. *Climatic Change, 152*(2), 239–257. https://doi.org/10.1007/s10584-018-2272-5

PART III

The Legal Framework

CHAPTER 8

A Primer of Laws, Legal Concepts, and Tools That Structure Relocation and Novel Ways of Utilizing the Law

> Most of the laws you see written lack respect, and the biggest thing they lack is love. (Chief Shirell Parfait-Dardar)

> We have to ask how someone can say an entire community is not feasible or the cost-benefit ratio is not large enough to protect? I truly believe this is what colonialism and capitalism really give us, a means to judge a community's worth. (Chantel Cormardelle)

Throughout this book, we suggest that understanding the law, particularly the law as it pertains to property, is important for pursuing justice within the context of relocation planning linked to climate change. As described in the previous chapters, communities inevitably confront and work within legal structures that frame relocation processes. These engagements with the law can be "successful" in carrying out physical relocation, but they can also be divisive, tiring, obfuscating, and lead to unsatisfactory and inequitable outcomes. All relocations are informed by community histories and interactions with government and legal structures. In the case of the Isle de Jean Charles resettlement, Jean Charles Choctaw Nation leaders were pushed out of planning processes in part through legal justifications of particular notions of Indigeneity and fairness, planners' drifting operationalization of community, and the state's imposition of individual property ownership structures at the expense of Tribal development. In Alaska, legal definitions of just compensation have

A. Jerolleman et al., *People or Property*,
https://doi.org/10.1007/978-3-031-36872-1_8

limited options for buyouts and resettlement. In the case of Kinston, North Carolina, it is unclear whether hazard mitigation options, like elevation, could have prevented relocation and would have been preferable to residents. All of these scenarios are created and conditioned by the interplay of laws, legal tools, regulations, and the interpretation and use of these structures by the many actors involved.

This chapter explores and explains some of what we view as the most critical legal structures that frame relocation possibilities and some under-explored legal possibilities that may give rise to increased options for relocating communities. While we see many academics and practitioners entering discussions of relocation, few have a working understanding of all these legal structures that shape or could shape relocation and resettlement discussions and processes. This is understandable. In fact, relocations and resettlements implicate an almost inexhaustible set of legal structures; including property law, administrative law, Indian law, corporate law, torts, environmental law, and tax law, among others. Addressing all of these is impossible. There are also key concepts in property law itself that are barely explored in this chapter, such as squatter rights or laws related to lessors that merit further exploration. Despite these limitations, there are areas of the law which have a particular relevance for relocation and resettlement and the property transactions that occur therein. There is growing support among those working on relocation as adaptation for the recreation of a New Deal-style federal resettlement agency that would coordinate resources, most importantly financial but also including legal knowledge, to support communities who are planning their relocations. On its own, such an agency is not enough if it must still operate within existing regulatory boundaries. Ultimately, though, those of us working with communities facing or embracing resettlement must also learn what is currently possible, so this is an effort to contribute to a broad ongoing query as to whether existing law and policy can be utilized in support of communities facing increasing disaster risks and relocation.

Land Use, Building Codes, and Zoning as Hazard Mitigation

The suffering felt in communities around the country each year as a result of erosion, sea level rise, and increased flooding in coastal and riverine areas demands regional-scale risk reduction measures. One way to reduce risk of infrastructure flooding is by broadly regulating land use.

Land use regulations are primarily a local function, stemming from police power that is held by states and enforced locally. Land use management and regulation can be achieved through a broad suite of mechanisms, but three of the most used and relevant for relocation and resettlement are: (1) the enforcement of stricter building codes, such as requiring a minimum lowest floor elevation, which can drive relocation but also increase the safety of new communities; (2) blight ordinances, that can drive redevelopment; or (3) zoning regulations, such as limiting development in risk-prone areas or create setbacks. Generally, land use planning and building codes are seen as critical tools for hazard mitigation to disasters that stem from climate change (Berke et al., 2014; FEMA, 2021).

Hazard mitigation via zoning and building code regulations rearrange risk and safety on the coast. They can exacerbate inequity under certain conditions, and create the areas that look economically efficient to "buy out." For example, when local jurisdictions want to implement higher standards via building codes, such as higher elevation requirements, those higher standards are applied to either new construction, or are required to permit construction on existing structures that will be substantially improved or are substantially damaged. These latter designations mean that either a structure is being improved to over 50% of the home's value (substantially improved), or the damage to the home that needs repair totaled over 50% of its value (substantially damaged).

Elevating infrastructure is expensive and not everyone can afford the cost. Local jurisdictions can offer subsidies toward the cost of retrofitting current structures to meet new building codes, utilizing elevation grants via hazard mitigation funding. This can happen either in advance of a disaster or following a disaster. Hazard mitigation grants through FEMA are primarily available via annual appropriations to programs such as BRIC (Building Resilient Infrastructure and Communities) or following a disaster, through programs such as HMGP (Hazard Mitigation Grant Program). Local jurisdictions can apply to FEMA for money to aid homeowners in elevating their homes, provided that eligibility criteria are met and that grants are available. In practice, this means that local governments set criteria that identify which homes and homeowners to reach out to for elevation grants, and whether elevation or another strategy, such as buyouts, make sense within their jurisdictions. In some cases, particular neighborhoods or families actively seek such grants; but it is more frequently local officials who begin these processes. When funding is available, mitigation grants are competitive among jurisdictions and applicants must demonstrate to the federal government that projects are cost-beneficial. If there is insufficient grant funding, it is not enough to meet a basic cost–benefit threshold (every dollar spent on the risk reduction measure prevents one dollar of losses in the future), but it is also necessary to be even more cost-beneficial than other projects. Older structures, often in areas where there has been a disinvestment in infrastructure and a reduction in population, are less suited to cost–benefit calculations (Frank, 2022a), leaving these areas further neglected. The outcome may be that low-income neighborhoods are ineligible for hazard mitigation, such as elevation or armorment, and in turn they are more exposed to flooding and subsequently seem like neighborhoods that should be bought out.

In addition, hazard mitigation grants from the federal government often require a local match of 10 or 25% that is borne either by the local jurisdiction or by the individual homeowners. If municipalities are dependent on property taxes to meet match requirements for federal mitigation grants, it may be impossible for a municipality to apply for federal aid if/when property values (and therefore property taxes) are low because they may be unable to fund the match. Additionally, reduced property taxes after a buyout can have negative impacts on the provision of municipal services. Frequently, homeowners must pay the price of matching requirements themselves, predisposing wealthier communities to be able to make this investment, which is heavily subsidized by federal aid. Wealthier and larger communities may also have an advantage over less wealthy and smaller communities in terms of staff capacity to manage grants, as was described in Chapter 7 for Akiak, Alaska. As a result of these socio-economic constraints, local jurisdictions make decisions regarding where to focus mitigation efforts. Those decisions are rife with socio-political and economic considerations. Hazard mitigation, therefore, is not deployed as a risk reduction strategy to high water and ecological conditions alone. Subsequent socio-political and market-driven flooding, therefore, makes neighborhoods that failed to elevate seem like likely candidates for relocation. Wealthier neighborhoods supported through mitigation subsidies can thus withstand flooding and may not become candidates for relocation.

The poor, and communities of color, may be more likely targeted by local jurisdictions for buyouts. As described in previous chapters, race and class has long structured land use planning in the United States and relocation and buyouts are intimately tied to longer trends in local or regional forms of social exclusion, built environment, and regional planning. This includes how zoning and land use structure risk. An analysis by A. R. Siders and Jesse Keenan found that while risk exposure to flooding was linked to all methods of hazard mitigation among risk-prone neighborhoods in North Carolina, socio-economic features were inversely correlated to which mitigation strategies were implemented. In their analysis, "median home value correlates positively with shoreline armoring and negatively with the occurrence of buyouts." More expensive homes were armored via hazard mitigation, less expensive homes were bought out. Likewise, "the percent of the population that identifies as people of color correlates positively with buyouts and negatively with shoreline armoring" (Siders & Keenan, 2020). Similarly, a recent analysis of FEMA's home elevation grants found that in many states grants had the unintended effect of turning wealthier and more white areas into more resilient neighborhoods with rising property values. In fact, many recipients of elevation grants benefited from reductions in insurance costs and increased property values, in some cases selling their newly elevated homes at a substantial profit (Frank, 2022a). In twelve of the states analyzed by Frank, over half of the elevation grants had gone to wealthy and/or mostly white communities. Two exceptions were North Carolina and Virginia, both of which had met match requirements for homeowners and therefore eliminated a tremendous impediment for lower-income grant recipients (Frank, 2022a). This illustrates the ways in which purposeful consideration of these barriers, coupled with government action, can in fact render these programs more equitable.

Zoning ordinances are discussed contemporarily as a promising hazard mitigation solution to climate change, such as permitting or not-permitting development in the floodplain or requiring minimum elevation levels. Often left unmentioned in these narratives is that the concept of zoning has a violent history. Zoning emerged from intellectual conceptualizations of the best economic use of a property, and has ties to the eugenics movement and scientific racism (Freund, 2007). Urban historian David Freund has argued that zoning and racial covenants originally shared a similar rationale (2007). Between 1910 and 1948, as many as 85% of new developments had racial covenants, legally contractual prohibitions on use, purchase, or occupancy by Black Americans. These racial covenants were later replaced with zoning regulations, such as minimum lot size, single-family housing requirements, or expensive building codes that ostensibly had the same exclusionary intent and effect. Racial zoning was ruled illegal in the 1917 Buchanan v. Warley ruling and racial covenants were eventually deemed unenforceable in 1948; but, in practice, socio-economic exclusion continued to be legal. Following the 1926 Supreme Court holding in Euclid v. Ambler, municipal zoning was considered valid if designed to promote "general welfare," which functionally replaced racial covenants, though they accomplished similar ends. The federal district court opinion that preceded the Supreme Court holding in 1926 and was overturned, had directly expressed concern that the zoning ordinance discriminated against renters and people of modest income, classifying and segregating people based on race, wealth, and housing status (Freund, 2007).

Relocation after climate change-fueled extreme weather can also be seen as a form of forced displacement of people who cannot afford to meet new building codes. Zoning also continues to be used as a means of attempting to delimit the users of property. As discussed in Chapter 6, after Hurricane Katrina made landfall in 2005 and the subsequent floods due to levee failure, a proposed St. Bernard Parish regulation prohibited renters that were not family members as a means of preventing an influx of African American renters, was struck down due to a Civil Rights complaint (Rodriguez-Dod & Duhart, 2007). Over the last two decades, costs associated with federal and local elevation requirements may be segregating the coast along these same socio-economic and racialized lines. Those who are able to meet the requirements and maintain flood insurance are better able to rebuild after storms, others move in the aftermath and sell land to those who can rebuild above minimum flood requirements.

In 2021, FEMA released a guidance document called the "Guide to Expanding Mitigation: Making the Connection to Codes and Standards" (FEMA, 2021). In it, FEMA explicitly calls for stricter building codes and zoning regulations as a measure of promoting disaster mitigation. The guide makes the claim that "such codes can provide insurance benefits for residents and improve a community's applications for federal mitigation grant funding." The 11-page guide to implementing codes and land use standards, including zoning, does not explicitly refer to the racialized histories outlined above; or the difficulties in benefit/cost, federal-cost matches, or competition that may accompany "applications for federal mitigation grant funding." However, it does state that, "At its worst, code enforcement gives privilege to those who make complaints, sends more resources to those with the loudest voices, and neglects those with the most need" (FEMA, 2021). The solution to this "worst scenario" is to develop regular procedures and mechanisms that ensure that those with the loudest voices (or racist voices) are not given as much or more standing in urban governance as the poor. While true, this is unenforceable advice. Some practical solutions are that municipal governments could offer owners who need them low-interest loans or, better yet, grants for mitigation. It is not clear the extent to which municipalities have these mechanisms or the funding to promote equity in hazard mitigation—or if FEMA is monitoring these outcomes.

Using and Better Understanding Land Use, Building Codes, and Zoning

We believe that land use zoning and higher building standards can and should be utilized to ensure greater safety of housing, including for renters; and to limit irresponsible development. However, extreme care is needed to avoid simply displacing those who cannot afford to meet a higher standard. And even more care is needed to prevent the unequal application of hazard mitigation in favor of those who have greater resources and ability to navigate the resulting regulatory systems. A more robust understanding of who benefits from stricter building codes is critical. Frank's analysis of elevation grants demonstrates that when matching requirements are met by the state, greater equity in hazard mitigation follows. An approach to hazard mitigation that has been called for by several community allies is for the federal government to eliminate the cost match in hazard mitigation grants for rural and impoverished communities, or for individuals who meet identified economic thresholds. The 10–25% matching requirement of a buyout, elevation project, community protection, or other hazard investment is unable to be met by some portion of the population, and by many municipal governments. This results in inequities in the distribution of adaptation and mitigation resources, but also creates an inability to remain in compliance with increased codes and standards that are intended to provide protection. Property owners inequitably affected and injured by land management, zoning, and other hazard mitigation strategies. Because FEMA has certain civil rights obligations, it would be interesting to see if inequitable grant distribution may incur liability. However, the courts accord great deference to agency decisions, and it can be quite difficult to hold an agency accountable in court.

The National Flood Insurance Program (NFIP) and ongoing proposed changes to the program (Teirstein, 2022) will also have an impact on land management in floodplains, including the current administration's proposals to not issue flood insurance to businesses in the floodplain or to new construction. Efforts at using flood insurance pricing to drive individual decisions regarding investments in hazard mitigation, or relocation, through efforts such as Risk Rating 2.0 seek to eliminate the false market signals that subsidized rates offer. It is clear to us that this will disproportionately injure those who cannot afford the substantially higher premiums and also cannot afford to, or do not want to, leave the floodplain. Increasing insurance costs can simply result in even further reduced levels of insurance coverage and greater impacts to communities and families after a flood. A substantial drop in insurance coverage has already been occurring following rising rates under Risk Rating 2.0 (Frank, 2022b). Although we realize that flood insurance has been a driver of unsafe development, we also recognize that many of the communities most impacted by rising rates are individuals who were either inadequately informed of their risk or whose presence predates the NFIP and the current levels of flood risk. Again, a robust impact analysis of these decisions is necessary. While it is beyond the scope of this book to analyze the NFIP, a continuing concern is that hazard mitigation will essentially lead to gentrification of the coast, and that the burden of past policy decisions is being placed upon families and not upon the larger systemic actors that drive risk. Current policy proposals fail to differentiate between those who willingly take on risk and those upon whom flood risk has been imposed. They also fail to differentiate between those who may be unwilling to take on the burden of higher premiums and those who are unable to do so. After all, the federal government itself owns many properties in the floodplain, and state actors continue to directly permit and encourage floodplain development when it suits their economic interests.

Restricting Development

Although land use and zoning can be used to restrict development, and are discussed above, it is worthwhile to separately discuss the role that restricting development can play and the challenges that such efforts face.

There is a tension between developing coastal properties, which are seen as valuable—and emptying coastal areas that are seen as vulnerable. Land use management reflects a tension between requiring or encouraging land to be left in its "natural" undeveloped condition as a mitigation decision, and permitting development as an economic decision. Broadly, this tension has been "solved" through a property regime that privileges economic utilization of land (Platt, 1999a; Sprankling, 1996). For example, the right of property owners to develop their land for economic gain is consistently privileged above a collective right to safety. In the "Guide to Expanding Mitigation" mentioned above, FEMA explicitly addresses the issue of when codes are seen as obstructive, not to current residents—which we find likely to be injured by such codes—but to *development*. The document states, "Many communities avoid adopting current codes or choose to adopt older versions because people think more strict requirements may limit development and increase building costs" (FEMA, 2021). This argument continues to focus on the needs and desires of developers and not on the concerns of existing residents, and highlights the same misalignments Isle de Jean Charles residents faced when confronting state logics of economic development.

Again, in coastal Louisiana, in the town of Dulac, Chief Shirell Parfait-Dardar of the Grand Caillou Band of Biloxi-Chitimacha-Choctaw, consistently sees tribal members be unable to rebuild following a disaster due to the high cost of home elevation, the limited availability of federal grants that can be used to offset the costs of meeting rebuilding requirements, and the barriers of matching requirements (Chief Shirell interview). Developers take advantage of this situation, purchasing property at low cost from residents (who often cannot afford property elsewhere), and then subdividing the property to develop for recreational users. The presence of recreational users, who bring political clout, higher home values, and the increase in income for municipal governments, can lead local governments to invest in protection mechanisms that were previously not considered cost-beneficial. This subdividing can be perceived as an overall net-benefit in economic terms; while investing government funds in damaged houses without insurance can be understood as "wasting" government funds on people who "need to relocate," or whose neighborhoods, "shouldn't have been there in the first place." These conditions have led tribal leaders like Chief Parfait-Dardar to point out, "So you couldn't assist the community residents that live their entire lives and are stewards of that land. But now you can make exceptions for anybody that wants to move in there that has money and wants to turn it into camps?" A 2020 complaint to the United Nations, submitted on behalf of five Tribes in Alaska and Louisiana references this dynamic as leading to the forced economic displacement of Grand Caillou Dulac Band of Biloxi-Chitimacha-Choctaw citizens and discusses the catastrophic consequences such displacement has for social relations, culture, and livelihoods (Alaska Institute for Justice, 2020).

While rarely used, there are mechanisms available to address the economic interest of current land holders while not sacrificing the safety of future owners. Two mechanisms are worth a brief discussion: Transferable Development Rights (TDRs) and Conservation Easements. TDRs are a mechanism by which there is a payment for the extinguishment (or transfer to an inland area) of development rights (Georgetown, 2020). Could a community that already wishes to maintain its property in an undeveloped state, sell these rights to support its conservation, or relocation, efforts? Several scholars and policymakers have looked toward transfer of development rights (TDR) mechanisms as a possible way in which to defray the economic impacts of restrictions on economic development (Dyca et al., 2020; Robb et al., 2020). A TDR treats the right to develop as only one stick in the bundle, and allows it to be severed and traded (Siders, 2013). Of course, the success of such a mechanism depends upon the existence of a marketplace in which such rights can be traded. While controversial, the carbon market does provide an example for which climate mitigation is funded by swapping use and voluntary disuse. Attempts have also been made to create markets for urban drainage rights. Could climate adaptation via a TDR mechanism be another such market?

Another tool that could potentially fund a lack of development is a conservation easement, which gives power to either a land trust or a government entity to limit development on a particular parcel. The sale of this right becomes attached to the land and impacts even future owners. Here, a landowner is also compensated for the loss of development rights. Conservation easements have been used successfully to protect ecosystem services, watersheds, and promote long-term recreational uses (Wuerthner, 2020). Although there are also criticisms of their use, we ask if there could be compensation given to people who self-select to not rebuild following a storm, or to give up development rights. For our purposes, we also wonder if these existing mechanisms could provide funding for communities to advance a dignified and locally-led relocation.

Takings Jurisprudence

As authors concerned with the scope of issues related to climate justice, we are particularly curious about how development along the coasts can co-occur with some neighborhoods and families feeling regulatory and economic pressures to abandon or relocate from the coast. In other words, as schools close in the bayous of Louisiana (Setyawan, 2021) and mandatory buyouts are implemented in Harris County (Project Recovery, 2023), how does new development simultaneously come into existence in nearly these same spaces? Regulating land use and limiting development, as we've seen, is a strategy for hazard mitigation; but this strategy has multiple obstacles. Most simply, municipal governments sense future losses in tax revenues on potential development, and are hesitant to limit this development. This can happen simultaneously to buyouts and resettlement because of the hazard mitigation and risk creation outlined above. More challenging to limiting development, structurally, is that limiting development as a hazard mitigation strategy is complicated by the widespread interpretation of property rights championed among conservative and libertarian advocates that call for unrestricted freedom of property owners to make their development decisions unencumbered by the government (Douglas & Lord, 2017). Mentioned in Chapter 2, property rights are linked to Takings Jurisprudence, which is derived from the Fifth Amendment and guarantees an owner the right to just compensation if property is taken for public use. A conservative interpretation of property law can mean that by "downzoning" an area from developable, to less developable, a municipal government can be threatened with a "per se taking," meaning the municipal government may be threatened by having to pay the property owner the value *potentially* lost by not developing due to changes in regulations. In this case, changes in regulations would be interpreted as a taking of use rights (in the property bundle) from the owner, for the public. Although the specter of takings is raised far more often than may be merited, takings jurisprudence is unsettled, meaning that there is a fluctuating set of parameters utilized by courts over time. Those parameters are likely to be continually challenged as coastlines face repetitive floods and potentially incur additional development restrictions.

Despite the challenges of adequately summarizing an unsettled and changing area of the law, some legal scholars have attempted to create a typology of takings jurisprudence. One such attempt at summarizing case law was completed by Robin Kundis Craig who suggested that the Supreme Court has recognized three categories of takings: physical takings, partial takings where there is the loss of some uses or value, and regulatory takings, including per se takings (Craig, 2011). Physical takings occur when the land is literally taken from the owner, such as when highways were built in the 1950s, and neighborhoods demolished for urban renewal. These types of takings always require compensation and are the easiest to prove, at least when the land is taken from an owner recognized under U.S. law.[1] Physical takings are legally carried out via eminent domain, which we explore later in this chapter. Partial takings arise when the government only needs to expropriate a portion of a property for a public use, such as when a transportation project requires the use of a portion of a larger lot.[2]

Per se regulatory takings occur when the owner has been deprived of all possible economic uses by changes in regulation or law. This concept stems from a 1922 Supreme Court Case, *Pennsylvania Coal Co v. Mahon*, in which the court found that regulations, if they go "too far" in limiting possible uses of a property, can constitute a taking. Because per se takings can mean local governments are culpable for economic loss of potential development, they are a worrisome area of the law when trying to regulate development as hazard mitigation; but how "worrisome" is unsettled. The concept of "too far," for example, has been described as a nearly impossible bar to reach, as regulations rarely deprive owners of any and all uses. Furthermore, the owner has to have had a reasonable expectation of those uses, and there is no taking when the rights that are being claimed were never part of the owner's title as understood by the confines of state law (Craig, 2011; Meltz, 2007). This is one of several examples of where state constitutions and laws are critical and making comparisons between states can be challenging.

Courts have also found governmental actions which take away essential elements of property ownership, such as the right to exclude others from

[1] This law does not apply to loss of Indigenous lands since the Supreme Court in its Tee-Hit-Ton decision (1955), held that Aboriginal title, title based on status as the first and original inhabitants of the land is not property within the meaning of the Fifth Amendment (Shoemaker, 2020).

[2] These types of takings can create many different challenges for government and the courts, including the question of how exactly to assess the value of the expropriated portion when the reduction in lot size may decrease the value of the property as a whole or may even leave it unusable (Bell & Parchomovsky, 2017).

your property, to be a takings in some cases (Ely, 2008). For example, requirements that a recreational walking trail be permitted have been found to impinge upon property owners' rights and thus constitute a taking. In cases like these, litigation usually focuses on whether or not compensation should be provided, and less on whether the regulation itself is permissible (Fitzpatrick, 2006). If municipalities incur compensation burdens for taking essential elements from property as a zoning strategy, for example requiring a setback from the water that limits access, it may limit what is financially feasible as hazard mitigation.

Cases in which the courts have found that there was *not* a per se regulatory taking also have implications for resettlement, relocation, and development in the floodplain. In 1978, the Supreme Court held in *Penn Central Transportation Co. v. City of New York* that the state could exclude persons from developing the air space above the Grand Central Terminal into a multistory office building without incurring an obligation to pay compensation. In its holding, the court provided a three-part test that looked at the economic impacts of the regulation, the existence of investment-backed expectations, and the character of the regulation and found that there was no taking. This is consistent with other cases that demonstrate when zoning regulations serve a beneficial public interest, a takings has not occurred and no compensation is warranted.

In a similar case, but with the opposite outcome, Supreme Court Case, *Lucas v. South Carolina Coastal Council*, in 1992, the Supreme Court noted that the *Mahon* ruling had left ambiguity about what would constitute "too far." In this case, the landowner had purchased empty lots two years prior to the passage of a law which prohibited development on that site. The Supreme Court found that Lucas had been deprived of all economically beneficial uses, that there had been a taking,[3] and the owner was owed compensation. It is worth pointing out, however, that the Court did note that: "...the property owner necessarily expects the uses of his property to be restricted, from time to time..." (Lucas, 1027). It is also worth noting that the economic value of the lots in question was

[3] The court provided an analysis for whether a total taking had occurred which looked at: (1) the degree of harm to public lands and resources, or adjacent private property, posed by the claimant's proposed activities, (2) the social value of the claimant's activities and their suitability to the locality in question, and (3) the relative ease with which the alleged harm can be avoided through measures taken by the claimant and the government (or adjacent private landowners).

not a product of a free market, but of governmental interventions such as flood insurance that subsidize and even promote at-risk development (Connolly, 2003). However, the court did not question the free market that it allegedly was protecting (Connolly, 2003).

Another case which is frequently cited as an example of takings law impeding regulations is *Dolan v. City of Tigard*, in 1999, in which the plaintiff sued the City after being told that they would need to dedicate a portion of their property to the city to be used for a bike path in order to enlarge their store. The portion of the property in question was in the floodplain, and the City was not offering compensation. The Court held that there must be "rough proportionality" between the burden placed on the property owner and the harm to be avoided (Platt, 1999a, 1999b). According to Platt's analysis, this act was held to be a taking because the land was going to be used for an amenity and not just to reduce harm: "Harmful hazards can be regulated without compensation through the police power, while public benefits, such as parks, or open space, must be acquired through governmental purchase or condemnation" (Platt, 1999a, 1999b, 158). In essence, the legal challenge was not due to the floodplain element, but to the use to which the property would be put.

These cases help outline when zoning can limit development without being a takings and when zoning will incur compensation burdens.[4] These legal boundaries remain unsettled; but are critically important. Municipal governments already lose potential tax revenue when limiting development; if they must also pay compensation to land owners, the bar for hazard mitigation through regulation becomes very high. With compensation, governments may impose restrictions on development or physically take private property, but both actions must, at least theoretically, serve legitimate public interests. The definition of "public interest" has been fluid and contested over time; but was broadened in the *Kelo v. City of New London* (2005) ruling. Here, in a controversial decision, the Supreme Court concluded that private property could be taken to promote economic development, which it considered in the public interest. Many legal scholars and planners have theorized about the implications of the *Kelo* ruling, as it appears to open the door to wholesale efforts at turning over land use from lower-income residential properties

[4] The cases described are only a subset of the cases that relate to property rights and the Fifth Amendment. There is also substantial jurisprudence related to due process that is beyond the scope of this manuscript.

to larger-scale commercial properties. However, its application has thus far been limited.[5] There is possible concern here for climate resettlement, however, if lower-valued homes were purchased and owners relocated to protect commercial or higher value properties, this could legally be considered in the public interest.

Novel Uses of Takings Jurisprudence

One question that we had is whether takings law could support communities who need to relocate. As described above, the specter of takings is more commonly used to prevent regulations that would limit development, and not in support of climate adaptation or hazard mitigation. However, the long history of takings jurisprudence has done much to define the extent of property rights, the components of the metaphorical bundle, and the ways in which property rights can be threatened by state actions. Is this a space where the law can address the needs of relocating communities by drilling down into their rights as property owners?

One potential strategy to support resettlement, may be to consider the possibility of passive takings. Christopher Serkin has suggested that takings liability might apply in cases of regulatory *inaction* by government that exacerbates risk or might be thought of as neglect (Serkin, 2014). Serkin notes that the Constitution is "typically thought to create only negative rights—rights that constrain the government from acting in certain prescribed ways" (Serkin, 2014, 346). Thus, regulatory takings are typically conceived of as compensation that is owed when regulations or policies limit property development or use. However, Serkin argues that because the government is already so enmeshed in regulating coastal areas and because local and state jurisdictions can purposefully avoid taking action due to liability concerns, it is possible to use the

[5] One test for the existence of a legitimate public interest is whether or not the burden on the owner, from the regulation, is proportional to the public benefit, and whether the regulatory burden serves the same purpose that simply denying a permit would serve (Fitzpatrick, 2006). For example, the public benefits of an amenity that only serves a small number of persons are different than those accrued through the construction of a facility such as a hospital with public health implications. A regulation that provides a blanket exclusion might also be more likely to be treated as a taking, rather than a process in which permits are denied or provided based upon a more nuanced understanding of the particulars.

same legal theory to argue that *inaction* by the government to regulate development or protect property may constitute Takings liability. In this case, inaction is seen as negligence in a government that is already acting within the context of development regulations and disaster mitigation. Serkins takes the example from tort law concerning the difference between negligence in the case of a passerby who neglects to throw a rope to a drowning person (who is not liable), versus a driver who neglects to turn the wheel when a person is in the road (who may be liable). "While both involve *inaction*, there is a critical difference: the driver, by getting into the car, has created the conditions giving rise to the ultimate injury" (Serkin, 2014: 348). Claiming the state is already involved in coastal regulation, Serkin likens government liability to be more akin to the driver, rather than the passerby. This thinking goes beyond most legal theorists' interpretations of liability, but these speculative claims on the role of government to protect property may continue to be tested in courts.

At this point in time, there is little case law to support the possibility of a passive taking (CLF, 2018), and there is often a wide gulf between the speculation of legal scholars and the decisions that take place within courts. For example, in a 1982 case, Allain-Lebreton Co. v. Dept. of Army, etc. the Court of Appeals found that the decision by the USACE to not locate a levee on property owner's lands was not a taking. The Court indicated in its decision that simply leaving property alone did not constitute a taking, and that the sovereign must only pay for what it takes and not for lost opportunities. However, one case in which the Fifth District held that a governmental inaction in the face of an affirmative duty to act could constitute inverse condemnation. *Jordan v. St. John's County*, involved a road that the county had ceased maintenance upon. The court stated that the County could follow its formal abandonment procedures; but could not just stop maintaining the road, and therefore limiting the access of property owners. It could, however, go through the appropriate public process leading to the same result without abandoning its duties in the interim. On appeal, the Appellate Court held that the trial court should be left to determine what constitutes an appropriate level of maintenance, leaving this question of whether inaction could constitute a takings, unsettled.

Eminent Domain

The previous section asked when a regulation could be considered a taking, but a more direct example of takings is the exercise of eminent domain. When the government exercises its right to take property from a private owner in order to serve the public good, with compensation, it is exercising its right to eminent domain. There is a long history of urban renewal policies disproportionately taking homes from racialized minorities and leading to a net loss of low-income housing as well as the decimation of thriving African American neighborhoods (Rothstein, 2017). Likewise, the use of eminent domain as a response to blight has been used in some cities to penalize owners who could not afford to maintain properties and to accelerate gentrification. The Uniform Relocation Act, described in Chapter 6 was created, in part, as a response to this history of displacement.

Therefore, it may be justified to be concerned when eminent domain begins to be a tool of forcing buyouts and resettlement. Currently in Harris County primarily Latinx communities are in the middle of a "mandatory buyout" sponsored by HUD after FEMA voluntary buyouts did not remove a substantial portion of homeowners out of the floodplain (Ahmed, 2022). While the program appears to be attempting to ensure buyout participants a comparable home outside of the floodplain, some unknown portion of the population is also upset by the policy (Ahmed, 2022). In addition to the HUD funded mandatory buyouts, the U.S. Army Corps of Engineers also formally "acknowledges the requirement for a complete plan includes retaining the use of eminent domain, if necessary, for acquisition, relocation, and permanent evacuation of the floodplain" (USACE, 2018). In other words, the USACE is requiring local and state jurisdictions to agree to using eminent domain, "if necessary" if large-scale relocations are part of hazard mitigation planning. Most acquisition programs done as a flood mitigations strategy, to date, have been voluntary, but this recent shift in USACE policy, and the use of mandatory buyouts in Houston, has been seen as a cause for alarm by some local jurisdictions (and causes concern among the author team). It's too early to tell what the scale of mandatory buyouts will be; and whom these plans will target. It is also worth inquiring whether the guarantee of a comparable home might not have been sufficient for many homeowners.

Eminent domain and blight ordinances have historically been weaponized against Indigenous and marginalized populations, but recent perceptions of and opportunities within eminent domain may not be as overwhelmingly negative as many legal theorists have speculated. A study on the use of eminent domain in Philadelphia found that residents expected the government to protect property as an investment, and were only opposed to the use of eminent domain when the property was in active use. The use of eminent domain when a property was abandoned, or otherwise seemingly outside of active use, did not engender opposition (Becher, 2014). When properties are in active use, eminent domain also triggers the Uniform Relocation Act, possibly allowing for moving costs associated with relocation. In other words, unlike voluntary buyouts, use of eminent domain could trigger additional financial and administrative support for relocating individuals, families, and communities.

In a more novel approach to eminent domain, we consider what happens to properties that have been previously taken and are now owned by local government. Municipalities across the United States have acquired vacant properties, as a result of blight ordinances, abandonment related to previous housing crises, etc., and in some cases have left them unused in the hopes of a future sale and profit. This in essence creates unaccounted for surplus capital within municipal systems. Sheila Foster has argued that land which has become the property of the state should be considered a public property and therefore subject to the public trust (2022). If so, at least in some states, being part of the public trust might put limits on the transfer or sale of that land for purposes outside of the public good. She has questioned whether the state has a responsibility to place these properties into productive use, such as allowing neighbors to use land for food production, or simply utilizing them to house residents who lack basic housing. According to her analysis of state laws, some have used the public trust doctrine to prevent the sale of public parks or streets, for example (Foster, 2022). Adopting such an approach to publicly held lands could create a source of land within and around receiving communities which could be utilized to house relocating communities. One key challenge faced by communities trying to relocate together is not only the high cost of lands further inland, but also the increases in prices that result when landowners become aware that a large tract of land is being sought. Putting previously seized blighted lands into use as receiving parcels seems to us like a gracious legal response to people in difficult situations.

The use of eminent domain in relocation and resettlement scenarios, to date, remains worrisome to the author team. As we've discussed throughout this book, forced relocation is part of some of the worst episodes of U.S. history. Most importantly we urge climate activists and policymakers not to consider forced relocation out of an at-risk area as climate adaptation. We feel compelled to point out, however, that use of eminent domain does ensure compensation. Compensation is mostly equated to fair market value, which we have discussed extensively in Chapter 7. We point out again here that appraisals may be the outcome of racialized and cultural bias. For example, there is indication that appraisers may select lower value comps when appraising a property owned by a black family (Kamin, 2022). This problem has risen to national interest, and the Biden administration has created a Task Force on Property Appraisal and Valuation Equity, in order to evaluate the causes of appraisal bias. Even without bias, prices frequently hold historical legacies of disinvestment in communities or racialized housing practices. Environmental justice advocates, such as Rachel Godsil, have suggested that damage awards for nuisance claims for pollution in minority communities need to set the replacement cost of a home to that of a similar home, in a nearby non-segregated community and not to fair market value (2005). Similarly, in Chapter 7, we argue for replacement cost to replace fair market value in some instances of buyouts or when eminent domain is used in cases of relocation as an outcome of flooding risk or hazard mitigation.

While we worry about the use of eminent domain in relocation scenarios, and the problems with fair market value and appraisal, we also worry about abandonment. If no mechanism for resettlement exists, and environmental degradation renders continued habitation impossible, there may be no requirement for the government to compensate those persons with no recourse other than to leave. Abandonment and/or property seizure may be defended by the government using the doctrines of public trust and public necessity.

Public Trust and Public Necessity

Two commonly used defenses that can be applicable to a physical, partial, or per se takings claim, are the public trust doctrine and public necessity, both of which may come to bear on resettlement. The public trust doctrine, which varies slightly from state to state, is intended to protect submerged and submersible lands for the purpose of navigation, fishing, and recreation (Moore & Acker, 2018). It dates back to Roman law, and was brought to the colonies and later codified via state and national legislation, such as the 1953 United States Submerged Lands Act. The doctrine holds that waters of the state are a public resource, held in trust, which should be managed on behalf of the public and to which all citizens should have access (Siders, 2013). A recent case, *Murr v. Wisconsin*, decided in 2017 by the Supreme Court, noted that when the challenged land use limitations are inherent in background principles of state law, then there cannot be a taking (Murr v. Wisconsin, 2017). In other words, this delimits the holding in *Lucas* to cases where the proposed regulation is not directly related to state law. This allows the public trust, as defined by the state, to play a larger role in the decisions regarding what constitutes a taking.

The public trust doctrine allows the state to defeat a takings claim when the infringement on another's property was for the purpose of protecting coastal and tidal waters, including their usage (Craig, 2011). As a result, the Public Trust doctrine is often used as a defense for coastal regulation and protection activities that impinge on property rights (Craig, 2011). This is the case with regard to larger infrastructure projects, for example. There is some variability from state to state regarding how expansively the public trust is imagined. For example, there is a great deal of variability regarding the definition of submerged lands, with some states using a high water mark, while others use the mean low water or even the first line of vegetation (Peloso & Caldwell, 2011) The state's role with regulating submerged lands is an important consideration in the face of sea level rise, because the rights that property owners have within an at-risk community may change as it becomes submerged. In many states, ownership can actually be lost when lands meet the classification of water due to repeat submerging, or changes in tides. It is unclear what this means for communities that are becoming submerged. Peloso and Caldwell have speculated that the public trust might actually require limiting development in order to protect future interests and prevent waste (2011). Full understanding of this doctrine, therefore, becomes critical as sea levels rise.

Public necessity is a defense which the government may invoke in times of emergency. Like the public trust doctrine, public necessity depends upon the state statutes and constitution, including how they define an emergency. Although the origins of public necessity focused more on immediate emergencies, such as urban fire, there have been more recent expansions of the concept. In Louisiana, for example, coastal protection is included under the umbrella of public necessity and the destruction of oyster leases for coastal restoration has not been found to be a taking (Craig, 2011).

Public use doctrine and public necessity may be legal tools that can limit development without incurring compensation for owners who are denied future development costs. However, in the context of resettlement, a state could also lean on public use as a means to avoid compensating property owners for the loss of their property. In essence, this creates a particular set of circumstances where uncompensated takings of property can be legal. This is a frightening possibility, as protections for homeowners who wish to remain in place may potentially be lost as the land erodes away; if the state decides it is necessary due to emergency or comes under state jurisdiction as submerged land.

Alternatives to Individual Property Exchange as a Relocation Solution

Existing Communal Relocation Mechanisms

One of the main questions we had as authors is whether legal mechanisms existed that would allow a community to act, and be funded, collectively, as opposed to individually, when planning for relocation. This could include how to organize collectively to recreate a community in a different location, and how to leverage state or federal funds to develop new community-based infrastructure as well as homes. These questions become particularly relevant for tribes, racialized minorities (Phillips et al., 2012, 410), and communities with strong social ties, and may apply to communities who wish to recreate community-centric or livelihood continuity after relocation events.

Articulating options for collective organization and action may provide some protective bargaining power against a state that has its own goals. Given the problematic history of how eminent domain was used to disrupt Black and BIPOC communities for highway development, and the challenges that may accompany coercive migration as a result of land management and zoning, we were interested in national and international examples of collective property decision-making structures and legal co-ownership organization. The creation of collective property rights can also increase community stability, create wealth, and even slow gentrification (Lamb et al., 2022). There are many forms of community associations across the United States, including condominiums, cooperatives, and homeowners associations (Foundation for Community Association Research, 2021). In 2021, 29% of the U.S. population occupied a housing unit in such a community association (Foundation for Community Association Research, 2021). Many of these associations are very limited in purpose, restricting certain types of development or paying for a shared amenity such as a community center. In and of themselves, they don't serve the desired purposes articulated here, but they do show that communal ownership is more common than most might assume. This is in addition to land trusts and other mechanisms described below.

It is worth interrogating whether communities who wish to collectively relocate could, working with trusted partners, utilize under-exploited existing legal mechanisms in order to serve their needs. This may or may not occur in conjunction with state enabling legislation and support from regulatory agencies. This section is not a set of recommendations—but rather a series of thought experiments in identifying options that, so far as we know, have not been thoroughly explored as possibilities for relocation adaptation strategies. These possibilities each have drawbacks and will differ based on the local context in which they are being implemented and who is implementing them. The detrimental aspects should be considered along with the hopeful. We also recognize that there are additional alternatives not considered here, and that many more possibilities might be imagined.

Community Land Trusts

The first potential mechanism that we think could be used by retreating communities is the property institution known as the Community Land Trust (or CLT). The first CLTs in the United States emerged in marginalized rural communities in the late 1960s and 1970s to combat depopulation and absentee land ownership and to give poor rural people a chance to own their own homes (Lovett, 2020a, 2020b). CLTs spread to urban communities in the 1980s as a tool to promote resiliency and create more affordable housing options in communities hit hard by deindustrialization or facing threats of gentrification (Lovett, 2020a, 2020b).

Although the CLT model can be adapted to any community's particular context and goals, five key design features typically distinguish a CLT. First, a CLT will usually be housed in a non-profit entity that owns land or buildings and manages that property in the long-term interest of a community (Davis, 2010). Although the size of the geographic or social community served by the non-profit entity can vary widely, the non-profit management structure of the CLT helps guarantee that a CLT's managing board will act in a "trusteeship" or "stewardship" capacity, with its focus on long-term sustainability rather than short-term economic gain (Lovett, 2020a, 2020b; Stein, 2010). The second fundamental feature of a CLT is separation of ownership established through the legal device of a ground lease. Usually, the non-profit entity that establishes the CLT will own land itself or a large building that potentially houses multiple housing units. The CLT will then lease parcels of land or particular units in a large building to individuals, families, businesses, or other persons who then own the improvements constructed on the land or unit, and who acquire a right of exclusive use and control of the improvements (Lovett, 2020a, 2020b). The third and fourth design features of a CLT focus respectively on entrance and exit restrictions. Most CLTs limit who can become a lessee-owner to certain income-qualified households (Davis, 2010). The organizers of a CLT will typically impose these income restrictions voluntarily at the commencement of the CLT in the ground lease. Some states, however, mandate income restrictions for a CLT by statute. In cases of planned resettlement, where the community includes a range of incomes, this may need to be revised.

When an individual or family wants to depart from a CLT community by selling their leasehold interest, the fourth key design feature kicks in—a preemptive right (a right of first refusal) declared in the ground lease itself. This preemptive right will give the CLT the right either to (a) purchase the unit owned by the lessee-resident if it is put on the market, or (b) require the leaseholder to sell the leasehold interest to another income-qualified buyer selected and approved by the CLT (Lovett, 2020a, 2020b). Furthermore, the purchase price that the existing individual or family can realize from the sale of their leasehold interest will be prescribed by a resale formula established in the ground lease. Although there is considerably variety in how CLT resale formulas can be structured, the essential goal of the resale restriction is to allow the departing individual to keep some portion of the increased equity attributable to their contribution to the community, and the physical asset itself, but reserve the remaining portion of the increased market value of the property for the community as a whole (Lovett, 2020a, 2020b). In other words, resale restrictions in a CLT separate the commodity value of an asset from the use value of the asset. The great advantage of these resale restrictions is that they allow the CLT to offer the house or apartment unit to a prospective new owner at a substantial discount from the actual "fair market value" of the property. This helps assure that a new generation of potential residents has access to housing and property ownership at an affordable price and extends the utility of any initial subsidy that may have been granted to the CLT by a government or non-profit funder. The final typical design feature of a CLT relates to the structure of the non-profit entity that establishes and oversees the CLT. Most CLT organizational documents mandate that the board of directors or board of trustees charged with ultimate responsibility for oversight of the CLT be composed of a number of lessee-residents, non-lessee residents of the community, and independent representatives of the broader community or public at large. This diversified, broadly constituted form of community control reinforces the stewardship mission of the CLT and its focus on long-term viability (Lovett, 2020a, 2020b).

What benefits could a CLT model bring? First, the CLT organizational form could reduce the upfront costs to individuals and families who want to relocate along with other community members in a new location. The resale restrictions simultaneously could help preserve affordability for future generations of the relocating community and thus preserve existing social capital and collective efficacy. Second, the reliance on a non-profit, community-led organization that actually owns the underlying land or major improvements in a new location could build trust within the community, as opposed to relying on state actors to organize internal dynamics. Third, the CLT structure could be used, not just as a tool for organizing property ownership and resources in the new location, but also to control land and natural resources left at the site of the discontinued community. In combination with conservation easements, discussed below, a CLT structure could thus help assure guaranteed access to the grounds of the former community if a complete transfer of ownership is not required upon departure. Finally, the inherent flexibility of the CLT structure allows for other economic and social development projects. Some land and resources owned by the CLT might be reserved for non-residential uses and dedicated to other uses, such as agriculture or aquaculture, forestry, environmentally sustainable industries, or recreational or cultural activities. In these cases, one critical feature of a CLT is that highest and best use can be subverted or reinterpreted by community members and the Board of Directors to achieve ends other than greatest overall economic profit.

Land Trusts have been successfully utilized in anti-displacement campaigns (DeFilippis et al., 2019; Jane Place Neighborhood Sustainability Initiative, n.d) and in Land Back and Rematriation struggles by tribes, such as the Ohlone who created the Sogorea Te' Land Trust in what is now known as Oakland, California (Sogorea Te' Land Trust, 2023). The Land Trust is led by Ohlone women and takes an intertribal and multicultural approach focused on the restoration of reciprocal relationships with the land. There is currently no housing on the Land Trust, but it has served as a model for creating communal spaces, as well as a model for funding possibilities as some funding comes directly from donors who wish to make reparations.

Community Development Corporations and Community Housing Development Organizations

The second mechanism that we think could be a model for some retreating communities to achieve community-based goals is the creation of a Community Development Corporation (CDC). A CDC is a non-profit real estate development organization controlled by a community and focused upon the revitalization of a community. CDCs have been successful in redeveloping neighborhoods in a number of urban areas in the United States but, to the best of our knowledge, have yet to be utilized in any climate retreat, relocation, and resettlement initiative. CDCs are supported by several national and regional organizations that can help communities seeking to form a CDC with funding and technical assistance. Although CDCs have traditionally focused on revitalization of an existing community in its current place, the CDC structure could be utilized for a planned community resettlement project if the geographic bounds of an existing community are expanded to include areas further inland with a lesser risk profile; or, if a CDC is created specifically to encompass the land at the new location.

A community that wishes to resettle in another location without a formal designation as an entity may find its efforts hindered because the state has historically interacted with individual homeowners as the decision-makers during buyout processes. By organizing as a CDC, and thus incorporating as a non-profit entity that can interact directly with government agencies and funders, a community composed of individuals and households with a shared community identity, can acquire a recognized legal status to engage with other private, non-governmental, and governmental entities.

A Community Housing Development Organization (CHDO) represents another kind of organizational structure that might assist a community engaged in planned retreat. The Cranston-Gonzalez 1990 National Affordable Housing Act created the HOME Investment Partnership Act to expand the supply of affordable housing. The HOME Act primarily focuses on rental housing for low-income families, but it can also be used for new construction and acquisitions. The HOME Act includes a 15% set aside for CHDOs which are defined as non-profit organizations that (1) include the provision of housing for low-income families as a primary purpose, (2) demonstrate capacity for this kind of work, (3) have a history of serving the community; and (4) have a formal process for community input and control, including a governing board consisting of at least one-third residents of the low-income community. Many CDCs qualify easily as CHDOs, although a CHDO does not have to be a CDC.

Given the fact that so many at-risk communities are also low-income communities, a community engaged in planned retreat could form a CHDO both to attain a recognized legal entity structure and to access a funding pool via the HOME Act. One potential limitation of HOME Act funds, however, is that CHDO must coordinate with local political jurisdictions or the state, and a local jurisdiction may not wish to expend funds for development outside of its juridical boundaries. Thus, the CHDO mechanism may be most useful when a community seeks to resettle close to its current location or at least within its current local government's jurisdictional boundaries.

Community Right-to-Buy

The United States is not alone in grappling with issues surrounding property, communal rights, and what constitutes the best use of land. Although there is limited transferability from nation to nation, some property scholars do look to other national experiments with property and seek to learn from their success or failure. The scope of this manuscript is generally restricted to the U.S. context, but we also recognize that similar conversations are happening in other spaces. As a result, we next turn to a novel legal institution outside the United States for inspiration in equipping communities seeking to engage in planned retreat. The institution is the community right-to-buy established under two innovative pieces of legislation passed by the Scottish Parliament in 2015 and 2016 (Lovett, 2020a, 2020b). Although Scotland's parliament had already given communities a right to register what is a called a "preemptive right" to buy land (a right of first refusal) if a landowner attempted to sell the land, the 2015 and 2016 legislation strengthened the ability of "community bodies," in the words of the Scottish legislation, to actually force landowners to sell land for the purpose of promoting sustainable community development (Lovett, 2020a, 2020b). In particular, the 2015 legislation gives a properly constituted community body the right to force a sale of land that is abandoned, neglected, or causing environmental harm to the community. The 2016 legislation goes further and gives a properly constituted community body the right to force a sale of land for the sole purpose of furthering sustainable development. Both tools also feature prominently in the Scottish government's plans to accomplish one of the principal objectives of its "Land Rights and Responsibilities Statement"—enabling more local communities to own, lease, or use buildings and land to contribute to their well-being and future development. This is a far different approach to that taken in the United States via blight ordinances and other legal mechanisms to address properties that are considered neglected.

While a detailed assessment of all the features of the new community right-to-buy in Scotland is beyond the scope of this book, several community right-to-buy mechanisms could be adapted to aid U.S. communities seeking to accomplish a planned retreat. First, the Scottish legislation allows a *community body*, the legal entity that will undertake to acquire ministerial consent for a forced sale of eligible land, to consist of a wide variety of non-profit organizations, as long as the entity has at least ten members, three quarters of whom are members of the represented community, and as long as these community based members "have control" of the entity (Scottish Government, 2016). For now, the community that is represented by the community body must be a community of place, that is, a community defined by some identifiable geographic boundary, although other Scottish legislation will allow a "community of interest" to request that land or assets owned by the State or some public entity be transferred to a representative community body (Scottish Government, 2016). Like the CDC or CHDO form, a Scottish style "community body" could be a useful organizational model for forming a legal entity with the capacity to act on behalf of a community planning retreat. Such a mechanism permits for a much wider range of communal entities and provides legal visibility.

Next, the new Scottish community right-to-buy legislation addresses the important question of what land is *eligible* for a community right to buy acquisition. Although the Scottish legislation treats this subject in considerable detail, at a basic level, the legislation makes two broad categories of land "eligible" for a compulsory community acquisition. The first category consists of any land, rural or urban, that is "wholly or mainly abandoned or neglected" or any land whose current use or management is causing, directly or indirectly, "harm to the environmental well-being of a relevant community." American readers might instinctively equate this category with what state legislation in the United States often refers to as "blighted" property, a label that some U.S.-based scholars have criticized as being too vague and subject to manipulation by municipal redevelopment agencies eager to acquire private land for urban redevelopment projects likely to benefit private, for-profit developers or wealthy, non-profit organizations like major private universities (Somin, 2011). The Scottish legislation wisely limits these problems, however, by specifying that the environmental harm must be *more than* "negligible," although that concept still leaves room for discretion. Meanwhile, accompanying regulations also limits the scope of abandoned, neglected, or detrimental land to property in some physical state of deterioration that is causing immediate health and safety threats (Lovett, 2020a, 2020b).

The second broad bucket of land "eligible" for a community acquisition to promote sustainable development also includes both rural and urban land and is otherwise unlimited in scope except that the legislation carves out land featuring a building or structure that serves as an individual's home. This exclusion for homes should avoid the kind of controversy sometimes seen in the Unites States when eminent domain is used to acquire residential property for economic development purposes despite the important dignity interests associated with homes and the difficulties that inherently surface when governments or courts are faced with the problem of accounting for the subjective value of residences to homeowners and tenants in just compensation awards (Underkuffler, 2006).

After a community body is formed and eligible land is identified for a potential community acquisition, the community body will then apply to the government (to "Scottish Ministers" in the language of the legislation) for consent to acquire the land (Lovett, 2020a, 2020b). If the ministers grant consent, the landowners must sell the land at a price determined by the ministers, after consultation with third-party appraisers (Lovett, 2020a, 2020b). Once again, the details of the Scottish legislation on this point are well beyond the scope of this book, but the crucial criteria in both pieces of legislation attempt to limit the compulsory, involuntary nature of such acquisitions to make sure that this extraordinary community and governmental power is limited to cases in which there is essentially no other practical or market-based alternative to the proposed involuntary acquisition. In the case of the 2015 legislation focused on abandoned, neglected, or detrimental land, the relevant criteria require the government ministers to determine that the proposed community acquisition is the only way to avert blight or environmental harm. In the case of the 2016 legislation designed to implement community acquisitions for sustainable development, the key criteria focus not just on the likelihood that the particular proposed acquisition will further sustainable development, but also whether it is "in the public interest," "is likely to result in significant benefit to the community," and "is the only practicable, or the most practicable, way of achieving that benefit," and that not granting consent to the proposed acquisition "is likely to result in harm to the community." Although these are inevitably open-textured standards, they do attempt to narrow governmental discretion and require community bodies to prove that they have made significant efforts to achieve their sustainable development goals by first seeking cooperation from landowners or first seeking to acquire land and property on the open market.

Another intriguing feature of the Scottish community right-to-buy legislation is the requirement that before a community acquisition can proceed to the actual transfer stage, a community body must conduct a "community ballot," with at least half of the community members voting, to determine if there is sufficient community support in favor of the proposed acquisition.

Finally, any community acquisition of land for a climate retreat initiative must confront the question of funding. The Scottish community right to buy legislation addresses this question in instructive ways. First, the legislation provides if a community shows that it has tried but is unable to obtain funds on its own the Scottish government can supply to support the community acquisition. Most community acquisitions in Scotland have so far been funded with public grants from the Scottish Land Fund, which in turn is funded directly from the Scottish government and by proceeds from the sale of public lottery tickets. Further, the 2016 Scottish legislation also allows a community body to form a partnership with a "third-party purchaser," which could be either a non-profit funder or a non-profit development entity or perhaps a for-profit private development entity. Although the Scottish legislation provides little guidance on how such partnerships will work, the legislation's allowance of such partnerships is probably a realistic acknowledgment that many community bodies seeking to achieve a community acquisition will need not only technical assistance but also financial support to accomplish their goals. We do not mean to suggest that the Scottish community right-to-buy legislation could simply be copied and transplanted onto American soil wholesale. However, many of its individual features, including its use as an organizational tool against outside developers, could well be adapted and transformed into a workable community-scale relocation mechanism (CSRM) and thus help vulnerable U.S. communities seeking to accomplish a community-wide relocation.

Hazard Mitigation, Adaptation, and Resilience Grant Funding

A great deal has been written about the existing funding mechanisms for hazard mitigation and climate adaptation, including their limitations and biases (citations). Although mechanisms such as the Hazard Mitigation Grant Program (HMGP) have been utilized for community relocation efforts, as is the case in Newtok, Alaska, the limitations of these programs have not permitted the kind of community-led efforts that we describe here. An analysis of the potential changes to be made to these granting mechanisms is beyond the scope of this manuscript, but some key areas of concern include: local match requirements and benefit–cost analysis requirements (which we discussed at the beginning of this chapter) as well as allocation of funds by Congress and state level emergency management agencies, disparate access to resources for grant writing and administration, and the inability to directly fund community-level entities.

Conclusion: Considering Repair as a Legal Solution

Aside from describing the laws, legal concepts, and legal tools that frame relocation, this chapter has suggested uses of present law to further community-led relocations and resettlements. We would like to point out that these uses are speculative. Each community is embedded in socio-historical contexts that we do not know and cannot hypothetically imagine. The author team is not convinced that single track, scalable solutions are the paths toward justice—and we have seen efforts at one-size-fits all solutions cause harm. We are convinced that local contexts and community-desires matter, will differ, and that these specificities are critical to successful climate adaptation.

There are clearly times when the law will fail to provide just solutions, as we have seen occur in the past. Many communities facing relocation today are part of historically overburdened groups that have already borne the burdens of industrialization and racist policies. As we've shown, these previous failures of the law to promote justice are "baked in" to contemporary risk creation (such as when hazard mitigation privileges wealthier communities) and legal solutions to relocation (such as fair market value for houses). Under these conditions, it is necessary to consider reparative solutions as possible legal remedies. Reparations consist of a series of tools that societies can use to provide redress, or relief for past harms, such as mass violence or other forms of historic injustice (Sanders, 2013). Material reparations include financial compensation, such as the direct payment to victims or their immediate descendants; restitution, which includes the return of rights and property; and rehabilitation, such as providing health care or other services.

In the previous section, we highlighted Kinston, North Carolina, Isle de Jean Charles, Louisiana, and rural Indigenous Alaska. In all of these cases, socio-historical circumstances are such that reparative solutions are applicable. If more than market value was available to Kinston residents as a mechanism to repair the harm of segregation and lack of access to less risky land due to racist policies, then perhaps the relocation would not have registered as coercive to some residents. If tribal sovereignty was respected and funding was made available specifically to reconstitute a tribal community that fled to lower bayou landscapes as a retreat from Indian removal and subsequent racism, then perhaps tribal leadership would be satisfied with the outcome. If funding was available for Alaska Native Communities to reconstitute flexibility to fluctuating coastlines as a reparative strategy for colonial intrusion, then new, Arctic-specific infrastructure would not be so challenging to develop and implement.

Climate reparations are politically divisive, as are most reparations claims. In these cases, we argue, the Constitutional Amendment that frames takings, buyouts, and eminent domain—all applicable to relocation scenarios—do allow for just compensation. A feasible interpretation of this clause could mean that justice can come through compensation; and justice in these communities includes repairing historical harm. This decision, as in so many other applications and interpretations of the laws we have laid out in this chapter—is dependent on the discretion of people, at multiple levels of government, interpreting, deciding, and carrying out their idea of the law.

References

Ahmed, A. (Sep 19, 2022). Torn Apart In Houston, a generations-deep community is being dismantled by mandatory buyouts. Grist. https://grist.org/housing/torn-apart-mandatory-buyout-flood-houston-allen-field/

Alaska Institute for Justice. (2020). Rights of Indigenous People in addressing climate-forced displacement. Submitted to the United Nations. https://assets.documentcloud.org/documents/6656724/Louisiana-Tribes-Complaint-to-UN.pdf

Becher, D. (2014). *Private property and public power: Eminent domain in Philadelphia*. Oxford University Press.

Bell, A., & Parchomovsky, G. (2017). Partial takings. *Columbia Law Review, 117*(8), 2043–2093.

Berke, P. R., Lyles, W., & Smith, G. (2014). Impacts of federal and state hazard mitigation policies on local land use policy. *Journal of Planning Education and Research, 34*(1), 60–76.

Connolly, K. (2003). A retrospective on Lucas v. South Carolina Coastal Council: Public policy implications for the 21st century. *Southeastern Environmental Law Journal, 12*, 1.

Craig, R. K. (2011). Public trust and public necessity defenses to takings liability for sea level rise response on the Gulf Coast. *Journal of Land Use & Environmental Law, 26*, 395–432.

Davis, J. E. (2010). Origins and evolution of the community land trust in the United States. In J. E. Davis (Ed.), *The community land trust reader* (pp. 3–47). Lincoln Institute of Land Policy.

DeFilippis, J., Williams, O. R., Pierce, J., Martin, D. G., Kruger, R., & Esfahani, A. H. (2019). On the transformative potential of community land trusts in the United States. *Antipode, 51*(3), 795–817.

Dyca, B., Muldoon-Smith, K., & Greenhalgh, P. (2020). Common value: Transferring development rights to make room for water. *Environmental Science & Policy, 114*, 312–320.

Ely, J. W., Jr. (2008). *The guardian of every other right: A constitutional history of property rights*. Oxford University Press.
FEMA. (2021) 2021 International Codes: Summary of Changes to Flood Provisions. https://www.fema.gov/sites/default/files/documents/fema_flood-i-code-changes_2021.pdf
Fitzpatrick, D. (2006). Evolution and chaos in property rights systems: The third world tragedy of contested access. *Yale Law Journal, 115*, 996–1048.
Foster, S. (2022, May 25). *From vacancy to decommodification: Co-cities and the enabling state*. LPE Blog. https://lpeproject.org/blog/from-vacancy-to-decommodification-co-cities-and-the-enabling-state/
Foundation for Community Association Research. (2021). *2021–2022 U.S. national and state statistical review*. U.S. Community Associations, Housing Units, and Residents.
Frank, T. (2022a, May 27). *How FEMA helps white and rich Americans escape floods*. Politico. https://www.politico.com/news/2022/05/27/unfair-fema-climate-program-floods-00032080
Frank, T. (2022b). *Hundreds of thousands drop flood insurance as rates rise*. E&E News: Climate Wire. https://www.eenews.net/articles/hundreds-of-thousands-drop-flood-insurance-as-rates-rise/
Freund, D. M. P. (2007). *Colored property: State policy and white racial politics in suburban America*. University of Chicago Press.
Georgetown Climate Center (GCC). (2020). Developing a Managed Retreat Toolkit, June 17, 2020, available July 5, 2020 at https://www.georgetownclimate.org/articles/building-resources-for-managed-retreat.html
Godsil, R. D. (2005). Environmental justice and the integration ideal. *NYLS Law Review, 49*(4), 6.
Jane Place Neighborhood Sustainability Initiative. (n.d.). *Our approach: Community land trust*. https://www.jpnsi.org/
Kamin, D. (2022). Home appraised with a black owner: $472,000. With a white owner: $750,000. *New York Times*.
Kendall, Douglas T. & Lord, Charles P. (2017). The takings project: A critical analysis and assessment of the progress so far. *Boston College Environmental Affairs Law Review, 25*(3).
Lamb, Z., Shi, L., Silva, S., & Spicer, J. (2022). Resident-Owned Resilience: Can Cooperative Land Ownership Enable Transformative Climate Adaptation for Manufactured Housing Communities? *Housing Policy Debate*, 1–23.
Lovett, J. A. (2020a). Community land trusts: Institutionalizing the human flourishing theory of property. *Cornell Journal of Law and Public Policy, 29*(3), 621.
Lovett, J. A. (2020b). Towards sustainable community ownership: A comparative assessment of Scotland's new compulsory community right to buy. In M. M.

Combe, J. Glass, & A. Tindley (Eds.), *Land reform in Scotland: History, law, and policy* (pp. 177–212). Edinburgh University Press.

Meltz, R. (2007). Takings law today: A primer for the perplexed. *Ecology Law Quarterly, 34*(2), 307–380.

Moore, J., & Acker, L. (2018). Recurrent flooding, sea level rise, and the relocation of at-risk communities: Case studies from the commonwealth of Virginia. *Virginia Coastal Policy Center, 26*. https://scholarship.law.wm.edu/vcpclinic/26

Moran, D., & Mihaly, E. (2018). Climate adaptation and liability: A legal primer and workshop summary report. Conservation Law Foundation (CLF) and Boston Green Ribbon Commission. https://www.clf.org/wpcontent/uploads/2018/01/GRC_CLF_Report_R8.pdf

Murr v. Wisconsin. (2017). COMMENT ON: 137 S. Ct. 1933. https://harvardlawreview.org/print/vol-131/murr-v-wisconsin/

Peloso, M. R., & Caldwell, M. R. (2011). Dynamic property rights: The public trust doctrine and takings in a changing climate. *Dynamic Property Rights, 30*(51), 51–119.

Phillips, B., Stukes, P. A., & Jenkins, P. (2012). Freedom Hill is not for sale—and neither is the lower ninth ward. *Journal of Black Studies, 43*(4), 405–426.

Project Recovery. (2023). *Post disaster relocation and buyout program*. https://harrisrecovery.org/post-disaster-relocation-and-buyout-program/

Platt, R. H. (1999a). From flood control to flood insurance: Changing approaches to floods in the United States. *Environments, 27*(1), 67.

Platt, R. H. (1999b). *Disasters and democracy: The politics of extreme natural events*. Island Press.

Robb, A., Stocker, L., Payne, M., & Middle, G. J. (2020). Enabling managed retreat from coastal hazard areas through property acquisition and transferable development rights: Insights from Western Australia. *Urban Policy and Research, 38*(3), 230–248.

Rodriguez-Dod, E. C., & Duhart, O. (2007). Evaluating Katrina: A snapshot of renters' rights following disasters. *Nova Law Review, 31*(3), 467.

Rothstein, R. (2017). *The color of law: A forgotten history of how our government segregated America*. Liveright.

Sanders, K. J. (2013). Re-assembling Osiris: Rule 23, the black farmers case, and reparations. *Penn State Law Review, 118*, 339.

Scottish Government. (2016). *Community right to buy guidance*. www.gov.scot

Serkin, C. (2014). Passive takings: The state's affirmative duty to protect property. *Michigan Law Review, 113*(3), 345–404.

Setyawan, K. (2021). Pointe-aux-Chenes parents file federal lawsuit over elementary school closure. *The Courier*. https://www.houmatoday.com/story/news/2021/06/18/pointe-aux-chenes-parents-federal-lawsuit-elementary-school-closure/7671482002/

Shoemaker, J. A. (2020). An introduction to American Indian land tenure: Mapping the legal landscape. *Journal of Law, Property, and Society, 5*(1).

Siders, A. (2013). *Managed coastal retreat: A legal handbook on shifting development away from vulnerable areas* (Columbia Public Law Research Paper, 14–365).

Siders, A. R., & Keenan, J. M. (2020). Variables shaping coastal adaptation decisions to armor, nourish, and retreat in North Carolina. *Ocean & Coastal Management, 183*, 105023.

Sogorea Te' Land Trust. (2023). https://sogoreate-landtrust.org/purpose-and-vision/

Somin, I. (2011). The judicial reaction to kelo. *Alb. Gov't L. Rev.*, 4, 1.

Sprankling, J. G. (1996). The antiwilderness bias in American property law. *The University of Chicago Law Review, 63*(2), 519–590. https://doi.org/10.2307/1600236

Stein, S. I. (2010). Wake up Fannie: I think I got something to say to you: Financing community land trust homebuyers without stripping affordability provisions. *Emory Law Journal, 60*(1), 209, 217–219.

Teirstein, Z. (2022). Biden's new vision for the National flood Insurance Program. *Grist*. https://grist.org/housing/bidens-new-vision-for-the-national-flood-insurance-program/

Underkuffler, Laura S. (2006). *Kelo's moral failure*. Cornell Law Faculty Publications. 891.

USACE. (2018). Planning Bulletin No. PB 2019-03: Further clarification of existing policy for USACE participation in nonstructural flood risk management and coastal storm risk management measures. https://planning.erdc.dren.mil/toolbox/library/PB/PB2019_03.pdf

Wuerthner, G. (2020). *The problem of conservation easements*. The Wildlife News. https://www.thewildlifenews.com/2020/04/15/the-problem-of-conservation-easements/

Legal References

Kelo v. City of New London, 545 U.S. 469 (2005). https://supreme.justia.com/cases/federal/us/545/469/

CHAPTER 9

Discretion and the Roles People Play in Interpreting and Applying the Law

Based on the relationships and work that have informed this book, it has become apparent to us that we ought to dedicate the last chapter to what we believe relocation scholars should know about how bureaucratic discretion works in conjunction with the law. Initially, we intended the latter part of this book to be a kind of a primer on laws, legal concepts, and legal tools that framed relocation. This was done in part so that relocation scholars and practitioners who have not had legal training could have a technical short course on some concepts; and to put legal constructs in conversation with the critical social sciences and critical social theory. As we were writing, though, we found ourselves over and over again reaching the end of a legal tool or concept's usefulness, saying, "… and then it's up to the discretion of the agency and the persons involved." Repeatedly, we ended up back where we started, with people; people in the context of their organizations, professional training, senses of legal possibility or constraint, and in power-laden relationships. As described in the previous two chapters and in the conclusion of Chapter 3, we believe that legal and regulatory possibilities already exist to enable more just community-led resettlement and to move away from processes that are entirely driven by the market. However, discretion and access to legal protections, tools, and strategies currently limit the realization of such possibilities. Moreover, there are very real costs to attempting to engage with the legal pathways we explore here, including time, financial costs, the risks of failure, and even the impacts to cultural and social

A. Jerolleman et al., *People or Property*,
https://doi.org/10.1007/978-3-031-36872-1_9

identities through the process of conforming to legal and bureaucratic framings of life, value, and community. We also realize that just listing legal possibilities is a piecemeal approach that does not address the range of needs and desires that the many people within a given social geographic context may have, and is not guaranteed to render equal assistance to all members of that community. Additionally, there are very few communities, community allies, and consultants who have a grasp of the many areas of the law that are required to render community-resettlement and justice together. Part of understanding the shifting risk landscape is thinking through the hows and whys of action and inaction, and what pursuing these paths mean for different people and existing struggles for justice and equity.

The concept of discretion is a highly theorized and important concept in the field of public administration. It refers to the ways in which public officials, or at times their contractors, make decisions, about seemingly very minor and inconsequential things, that greatly impact the implementation of public policies (Scott, 1997). Street-level bureaucracy, the exercise of discretion by front-line bureaucrats, such as those who interface with the public at regulatory agencies or facilities such as an Office of Motor Vehicles, can have a tremendous impact on the lived experiences of policies by the individuals who interact with government as citizens and consumers (Lipsky, 1980). In effect, these street-level bureaucrats become policymakers in a very literal sense. In the context of floodplain management, climate adaptation, and hazard mitigation, these interactions can lead to markedly different outcomes depending upon agency cultures and individual decisions. Real time, normative assumptions made by individuals taking calls for FEMA (as an example) about individuals seeking information or assistance (as an example) can have dramatic consequences on whose house is repaired and whose remains in disrepair (Jerolleman, 2019).[1] As these decisions accumulate, they can generate other assumptions, such as what is the highest and best use, whose neighborhood

[1] This discussion focuses primarily on bureaucratic discretion, but individuals and communities exercise discretion and agency as well, which also shapes processes and policy outcomes. Individual and group decisions, regarding what paths to pursue, for example, interact with agency processes in complex ways. The actions of government officials may encourage or discourage certain actions on the part of the community, similarly seeing the negative experiences of others who are navigating regulatory processes may also serve to discourage willing participation in such processes.

"shouldn't have been there in the first place," and where relocation seems like a foregone conclusion.

Discretion is often protected from legal challenges, unless it directly violates constitutional protections. For example, discretion is explicitly protected by the Stafford Act's non-liability provision:

> The Federal Government shall not be liable for any claim based upon the exercise or performance of or the failure to exercise or perform a discretionary function or duty on the part of a Federal agency or an employee of the Federal Government in carrying out the provisions of this chapter.[2]

Seen through the lens of "judicial ecology"—a heuristic to think not just about the courts, but how law is shaped by activism and social actions (Mahmood & Cousins, 2022)—administrative discretion alone does not determine access to resources, instead the courts and the administration of the law, including administrative law, influences and is influenced by the access and control that different individuals have to resources.

Therefore, any discussion of law and policy is incomplete without some consideration of the role of implementing agencies and governance (interactions between social systems and government via laws, regulations, etc.) more broadly. This book concerns itself primarily with law, how law, particularly property law, has operated in the distant past, in contemporary relocation scenarios, and whether the law can or cannot be put in service of community needs and aspirations relative to resettlement. However, laws are not created in a vacuum—and the creation of laws alone is not sufficient. Public administration scholarship has long recognized that the devil is in the details. Many well-intentioned legal and policy interventions fail due to a wide range of issues that emerge during implementation, including a failure to imagine unintended consequences and/or erroneous assumptions regarding local needs and desires (Hudson et al., 2018). Similarly, degrees of willing compliance across scales of government are also implicated in the success or failure of various policy interventions, particularly in the face of wicked and challenging social problems (May & Burby, 1996). Complex policy questions and legal issues require the exercise of discretion, but discretion can also bring in ethnocentric assumptions and perpetuate injustice.

[2] U.S. Code Title 42. Chapter 68. Subchapter III §5148.

If we, as authors, are exploring underutilized areas of the law (Chapter 8), and pointing to places in the law where reinterpretation may better foster justice (Chapter 7, for example), then we are also required to articulate an understanding of how laws are implemented, and the complex relationships between laws, regulations, and discretion. Implementation of law frequently transpires within federal agencies or the bureaucratic state. For example, the Stafford Act contains many instances in which a FEMA Regional Administrator can waive certain provisions. One example of incredible importance for our purposes here is that FEMA is broadly unable to build new, permanent housing after a disaster. If one of our arguments is that climate relocation implicates a broader housing crisis in the United States, then this legal restriction on building new houses is a unique obstacle to utilizing FEMA resources for just resettlement. However, a regional administrator can waive the restriction on building new housing, if certain conditions are met. Although this discretionary ability has only been used in certain circumstances, it is possible to imagine the role that such a discretionary ability could play for disaster affected communities that need new housing stock.

The bureaucratic state, also referred to as the administrative state or the fourth branch of government, does a great deal of policymaking via implementation of statutes, regulations, and other mechanisms.[3] Laws are created by Congress, signed into Law by the Executive branch, and then implemented via regulations—with the courts playing a role when challenges arise. Agencies promulgate both legally binding guidance, but also interpretive policy documents and memoranda that simply explain the more prevalent interpretations of regulations. Guidance documents are an important tool for agencies, as they can recommend and suggest, while still allowing implementation to occur in ways that make the most sense

[3] Federal agencies are a part of the Executive Branch, and are therefore also directed via Executive Orders which do not carry the same force of law. Executive Orders can, however, compel agency action and have a great deal of power over federal decision-making and federal assets. For example, recent efforts to ensure that the federal government complies with best practices for floodplain management with regard to its own facilities have been promulgated via Executive Order. The President often turns to Executive Orders when Congress is unwilling to act, but it is not a long-term strategy as an incoming administration can simply rescind it, a much easier process than modifying existing legislation. A more recent example is the Justice40 initiative, under the President Biden Administration, which is being promulgated entirely via executive orders. As such, any requirements that it places can simply be removed by the repeal of the executive orders.

locally. This creates several avenues for bureaucratic discretion, particularly when rules are purposefully left with a great deal of flexibility, in order to account for the substantially variability in state and local conditions. For example, regulations for hazard mitigation planning, contained in the Code of Federal Regulations, solely state that the public must be engaged but do not dictate much more than notice and meetings, leaving a great deal of discretion in how engagement is defined by states, counties, and their contractors (Jerolleman, 2013). Again, in our example of Isle de Jean Charles (Chapter 3) and Kinston (Chapter 4), we see that engagement is a critical part of relocations—that it is organized at the discretion of local agencies is important to remember.

All levels of government must be considered in an analysis of discretion and policy implementation. Planning processes are impacted by federal laws and regulations, creating a complex set of interactions between agencies and levels of government, with discretion present at all scales. Hazard mitigation planning, for example, occurs at the county and state level, but is reviewed by FEMA's regional offices. Hazard mitigation grant applications are submitted by counties to the state, which then typically makes decisions regarding which ones might move forward for FEMA's consideration. Additionally, as was previously described, any land use regulations are crafted and implemented at the local level while a great deal of environmental and climate regulation is done at the state and federal level. Although this chapter concerns itself primarily with federal processes, state governments typically mirror the national government, also creating statutes via legislative processes that are then implemented by state agencies. Similarly, local government entities exercise some discretion in how they implement state and federal programs, as well as with regard to whether to pursue resources for climate adaptation and hazard mitigation. This can include decisions regarding what areas to protect, where to focus resources, kinds of future development in geographies that overlap with state or federal planning initiatives, and even where and with whom to create access to funding mechanisms that require the state to serve as the grant recipient. Furthermore, regulatory mechanisms, protective measures, and development decisions across different scales are often in direct conflict. Along the east coast, for example, housing is being developed in vulnerable zones at a rate that is two to three times faster than in safer locations (Marandi & Man, 2021). This is occurring at the same time as buyout and acquisition efforts are underway in similarly situated neighborhoods and communities. In some cases, the acquisitions themselves are facilitating new development in neighboring locations.

Regulatory Mechanisms

Regulatory mechanisms are a frequently used tool for climate adaptation, along with incentive programs, and other bureaucratic mechanisms. In the United States, Congress often grants federal agencies the authority for the implementation of legislation, via the creation of regulations that carry the force of law. These regulations are created and promulgated via processes such as rulemaking, following procedures that are either established by the enabling legislation or by the Administrative Procedure Act (APA) (CRS, 2021). Under the rulemaking process, agencies provide notice and comment and receive feedback from interested parties. In practice, this feedback is often given by professional associations, think tanks, lobbying groups, and other entities who wish to promote their interests. Some public administration scholars have raised concerns about regulatory capture, where stakeholders that are intended to be regulated by rules, instead play a key role in writing those same rules. In some cases, such as hazard mitigation planning, there have been arguments made that the linkages are so tight between the rulemakers and the contractors who stand to benefit as to essentially constitute privatization of the service (Jerolleman, 2013). For example, the same firms that assisted with the creation of the regulations for hazard mitigation planning later bid on contracts to conduct the work locally and on contracts to be reviewers of those same plans on behalf of FEMA (Jerolleman, 2013).

There are also beneficial possibilities associated with the existing rulemaking process, including the opportunity for community leaders and their advocates to influence rules that directly impact their efforts at climate adaptation. Public comments can lead to minor victories with long-term implications. For example, several tribal entities responded to a rulemaking process relating to Environmental Justice within the EPA and requested language that read the agency would engage with Tribes and Indigenous persons. That change was made, increasing access for non-federally recognized tribes and also creating a model that other agencies might consider following. A major hurdle lies in the reality that this opportunity requires a substantial time and resource investment with little guarantee of a payout. For example, a recent promulgation of revised rules for hazard mitigation numbered over three hundred pages and only gave community members a few weeks in which to respond. Many such calls for comment may be in effect at the same time and across a range of agencies. In early 2023, for example, FEMA had multiple such calls as did HUD and the EPA. It is also often the case that comments are acknowledged but do not directly lead to changes in language.

Another advantage of the rulemaking process is the reduction of the burden on Congress and the opportunity for technical expertise to be brought to bear. The administrative state is tasked with the implementation of statutes and creation of rules in order to both prevent Congress from being bogged down in the minutia of how each and every law will be implemented and to allow agency expertise, as well as outside expertise, to be brought to bear on more technical problems (CRS, 2021). It also allows for dissenting voices in civil society to make themselves heard, and to have their comments on the record even if the agencies do not meet their requests. This dynamic may also provide a buffer from a changing political climate, leading to a greater level of stability as most mid-level personnel within agencies do not change over as presidential administrations change. Congress does though retain the power to pass statutes that compel agencies to repeal certain rules, limit their power, or expand it.

Courts can also play a role under judicial review processes, per the APA. While administrative law accords a great deal of deference to agencies, a court can compel agency action where it has either been withheld unlawfully or unreasonably delayed if the agency's actions were: arbitrary or capricious; exceeded statutory authority; contradicted statutory authority; or, violated procedures under the statute[4] (CRS, 2021). Agencies also promulgate interpretive rules, reports, and other products that serve as guidance regarding interpretations of the law, but lack the force of law (CRS, 2021). This type of guidance is subject to far fewer procedural requirements and not subject to the APA. The promulgation of guidance allows agencies to act more quickly, and to provide additional information to the public and other interested parties regarding how the

[4] One key issue in administrative law is the question of whether an agency has the requisite authority to perform a particular action, especially when state rights are implicated. As with many areas of the law, recent Supreme Court decisions and judicial trends are changing the landscape and, in this case, eliminating some of the deference that previously existed toward federal agencies.

agency intends to utilize its discretion in interpreting rules. However, the lack of legal authority behind guidance limits its application.

Communities interacting with federal and state agencies are often provided with federal guidance and rules, with no distinction being made between the two. One tool of bureaucratic power is to rely upon the lack of understanding and knowledge of bureaucratic processes among the general public. Community leaders and advocates are handed lengthy agency memos, reference to the Code of Regulations, and other similarly unapproachable documents and told that the law prevents the type of action that the community leaders are seeking. However, in some cases, there is ample discretion that bureaucrats choose not to exercise in support of flexible solutions for communities. The distinction between rules and guidance is a particularly important one in these situations. It is also worth noting that agencies become accustomed to treating certain types of guidance as law and lose, or "forget," their own flexibility over time as a series of interpretations of flexible rules become reified and delimit the bounds of future interpretations (Jerolleman, 2013).

Bureaucratic Discretion

Bureaucratic discretion, as well as political motivations that can influence bureaucratic decision-making, can play a substantial role in the determination of which communities should be encouraged to retreat in the face of climate risks and which communities should be assisted with their efforts at adapting in place (Marandi & Man, 2021). These decisions also play a role in the ways in which buyout programs are administered, including whether residents are given alternatives to relocation or permitted to act communally. Scholars have noted in the context of disaster recovery that "... discretion is likely to be used to the disadvantage of those least informed of their legal rights, particularly families with limited resources who lost personal records and had difficulty meeting documentary requirements, such as proof of occupancy, damage, personal poverty loss, and insurance coverage" (Hooks & Miller, 2006, 51). Even public planning processes often exacerbate existing inequities as they are led by administrators who better understand the regulatory limitations and often have predetermined solutions. The decision to go forward with a particular project, or utilizing a particular mechanism, represents an exercise of informed discretion and decision-making. There are several issues that agency representatives must consider to determine what regulatory mechanisms can be utilized by an agency or how their work is constrained by regulation. These include: identifying if the agency has the requisite authority, ensuring statutory and regulatory compliance, and taking into account constitutional compliance, in particular takings and due process (Georgetown Climate Center, 2020). Community members who engage with these processes are not fully conversant in the laws and regulations, and therefore cannot always adequately advocate for themselves, nor can they identify the discretionary points. Similarly advocates, social scientists, allies, and others may also not be fully conversant in the laws and regulations.

There are many other areas in which bureaucratic discretion plays a role in climate adaptation. One of these is with regard to disaster declarations. According to the federal General Accounting Office, "declaration decisions are not supported by standard factual data or related to published criteria" (Downton & Pielke, 2001). One scholar, Richard Sylves, has suggested that the bureaucratic politics model is the most appropriate for understanding disaster declarations where the decisions at the presidential level are the outcome of negotiations that involve elected officials and appointees (2020). However, he also noted that an organizational process model applied to routine events, where decisions are more often left to delegates and lower ranking officials (Sylves, 2020).

> ... the policies and policy recommendations generated in the executive branch of government and passed on to the chief executive [and often the legislature] are often the by-product of bureaucratic turf wars, interoffice competition, and expedient compromise between administrative chieftains rather than products of reasoned analysis about how to most effectively and efficiently carry out the law and policy commitments of the elected chief executive so as to serve the public interest. (Sylves, 2020, 53)

Disaster declarations have a direct impact on the availability of funds that are needed for climate adaptation and community resettlement efforts. FEMA has interpreted the Stafford Act to exclude slow-moving disasters from disaster declarations, limiting funding and assistance for slow-moving disasters such as drought and thawing permafrost. Both of these events have a direct impact on communities seeking to relocate (GAO, 2020). As mentioned before, a recent analysis of the use of FEMA elevation grants showed an alarming pattern in which, for the majority of the states analyzed, over half of the funding went to wealthy communities and to mostly white communities. In four states, over 75% of funds went to wealthy communities, and in six states almost half of all funds received had been spent in just one affluent or white community (Frank, 2022). The federal government exercises discretion in deciding how to allocate funds, while states exercise discretion in terms of where to promote programs, how much to assist counties, and even whether they will assist with matching requirements. In the case of these elevations, many recipients were able to leverage increased property values and decreased insurance costs to sell their newly elevated homes at a substantial profit. This outcome, the government subsidizing profit creation for wealthy homeowners as a hazard mitigation strategy, is avoidable. In the same analysis, North Carolina and Virginia made different decisions. These states covered the local match requirement for families, allowing lower-income families to access the program without a financial barrier, and the patterns of privilege did not hold (Frank, 2022). Discretionary decisions can be a powerful tool to change these patterns of racialized and income inequity without changing the law, as well as a tool for better utilizing the law in service of justice.

Higher-income communities have more political influence, more grant writing capacity, and the ability to generate proof of eligibility due to benefit–cost logistics, but as we see in the example above, this is not impossible to overcome. FEMA is attempting to direct a greater percentage of its hazard mitigation funds to communities that are considered socially vulnerable, as part of Justice40. This is an effort that, if successful, may also show the importance of bureaucratic intent in furthering more equitable outcomes. This effort, via BRIC, has so far been criticized as grants were still given to higher-income counties. For example, in fiscal year 2020, 94% of BRIC grants were awarded to wealthier coastal states and counties, and not to communities that lacked capacity for hazard mitigation (Headwater Economics, 2022). In fiscal year 2021, after a concerted effort to produce more equitable outcomes, only 80% of funds went to coastal states, but only two states in the interior received the bulk of the remaining mitigation funding (Headwater Economics, 2022).

A final example, described in Chapters 3 and 5, was evident in the Isle de Jean Charles resettlement. State planners conceptualized the resettlement as a complicated real estate transaction, focusing on the transfer of individual property ownership while dismissing the Tribal planning that had been instrumental in securing federal funding. The state asserted their discretion in a substantial amendment request to HUD in 2019, three years after the funding was awarded and deep into the fraught planning process. According to one state planner, maintaining good standing between the state agency (the grantee) and HUD (the granter) in order to ensure future funding was among their priorities. Community experiences and expectations were largely marginalized from the equation. Not only did state actors reframe the resettlement away from the Tribal community vision, but they were also permitted to do so by HUDs regulatory checks and balances such as amendment processes for action plans, relying on a HUD principle of "maximum feasible deference" to grantees. This principle essentially suggests that HUD permits the grantee, in this case the state, to apply its own discretion in interpreting regulations to the maximum extent possible.

Many federal agencies have sought to devolve control to the states in an effort to better account for local needs, but this does not necessarily guarantee more equitable outcomes. In fact, some of the authors of this book are increasingly interested in the origins of the "maximum feasible deference" principle and the shift from "maximum feasible participation" to "maximum feasible deference." The Housing and Community Development Act of 1974 established the Community Development Block Grant (CDBG) program, from which the CDBG-DR National Disaster Resilience funding has its roots. Before CDBG, during 1960s War on Poverty programs, HUD had advanced a principle of "Maximum Feasible Participation," which was embraced initially (Melish, 2010; Rubin, 1969), but then became a threat to local political regimes when Black communities asserted their rights to meaningful participation in ways that challenged local elites and racial structures. For example, Sherry Arnstein (1972) published the experiences of North City Area Wide Council of Philadelphia as they navigated the Model Cities program in the piece *Maximum Feasible Manipulation.* The piece chronicles the exploitation that troubled sanctioned participation and the tensions that emerged as actual participation in implementing federal program's challenged local power brokers and the status quo.[5]

[5] Authors would like to acknowledge and thank anthropologist Naomi Schiller, who introduced co-author Nathan Jessee to this particular Arnstein piece during collaboration and conversation about the pitfalls of participation.

Although several opportunities existed for state and federal partners to support the Tribe in retaining its core objectives, the state agency chose instead to apply a strict interpretation of existing regulations for the use of HUD funds, forgoing the spirit of innovation that was intended to be a hallmark of the National Disaster Resilience Competition. This is also a lesson in the limitations of innovation within existing mechanisms. The National Disaster Resilience Competition was envisioned as a partnership between the federal government and the Rockefeller Foundation intended to bring innovation to disaster risk reduction. "However, program implementation still relied on HUD's existing regulatory authorities and on the agency bureaucrats who had not been part of that visioning. For example, relinquishing title to previous land is typical when resettlement is funded via voluntary buyouts. Tribal community members, however, have advocated for retaining ownership of land from which the community is resettling and maintaining ongoing relationships to that ecology through seasonal or temporary habitation, subsistence fishing, ceremony, recreational and economic development, among other uses. After Tribal advocacy, the state eventually agreed with this innovation albeit with the use of restrictive homeowner agreements that prevent substantial repairs to Island houses, habitation, economic uses, and other activities (Jessee 2022; Simms et al. 2021)".

Administrative Evil

Just as Serkin raised the question of whether affirmative duties exist in the Constitution, one can also ask what duties the government, and its front-line representatives, have to the communities they serve. This includes the duty to exercise discretion in support of justice. The failure to exercise available discretion in the face of life threatening and lifeway destroying consequences, due to blind adherence to habitual interpretations of regulations, can also be understood as a form of administrative evil (Jerolleman, 2019). For example, blind application of rules and regulations with disregard for the tremendously destructive consequences of such rules and regulations, particularly when alternatives are available, is one frequent way in which administrative evil is perpetuated. Another clear way in which administrative evil is consistently perpetuated is through the unwillingness to consider the role of colonial logics and histories of disenfranchisement and genocide on the ability of Indigenous communities to successfully utilize and access resources.

In the case of the Isle de Jean Charles resettlement effort, for example, tribal citizens and leaders were penalized for a lack of federal recognition and for the limitations of the formal property ownership rights of the tribe. Even if the detrimental impacts to the Tribe were not intentional, though they clearly were (Baurick, 2022), the failure to consider harms caused by reducing the Jean Charles Choctaw Nation to but one of many stakeholders led the state to continue the pattern of historic violence that marks Indigenous/colonial encounters. One might imagine a scenario in which the potential concerns with the Fair Housing Act were immediately brought to the Tribe and HUD's attention by the state, and all three came together as partners in order to identify the best way to meet tribal primary needs and aims in the project. Historic examples of land dispossession were clearly intentional, and often justified by convoluted legal and normative gymnastics. More contemporary examples are often hidden in opaque technocratic processes and couched in the language of equality, community engagement, or public benefit. As Jessee notes (2022, 277): "... state efforts to transform the resettlement from what Tribal leaders viewed as 'an act of cultural survival' to a scalable model for managed retreat policy threatens to reproduce a frontier dynamic whereby colonial and capitalist futures are once again rested upon the erasure of indigenous peoples." Direct negative impacts are dismissed as coincidental or as a result of inherent capacity deficits within communities, such as a lack of knowledge or staff to manage processes, as described in Chapter 5, when Louisiana state planners and contractors repeatedly told the Tribe they could not mow the lawn of the new site and therefore should not be afforded the opportunity to own land or otherwise have a sustained institutionalized presence in the new development. Even when capacity deficits exist, which may be the result of a long history of colonization and displacement, one might envision government support for filling these gaps and investing in capacity building as a key role of government. Giving the Tribe office and museum space and collectively held land in the resettlement site, for example, could have been just this kind of support to enhance capacity.

Can Bureaucratic Discretion Be Used in Service of Community Desires?

There are examples of federal agencies working with community leaders to identify novel ways in which to apply rules and regulations. One such example took place on the Pine Ridge Indian Reservation, following a disaster declaration in 2019, where a Permanent Housing Mission was authorized.[6] Typically, following a disaster declaration under the Stafford Act that includes Individual Assistance, eligible families are assisted with temporary housing. This can include temporary trailers under the Direct Housing Authority, but these are typically only available for up to eighteen months. On Pine Ridge, the majority of the housing stock was manufactured homes and repairs were simply not feasible. Working with tribal leadership, FEMA field leadership made the decision to push for a permanent housing mission.

Permanent housing is only permitted under a certain set of circumstances: (1) bringing in temporary housing would be cost prohibitive; (2) infeasible; and (3) the supply is lacking. In the past, permanent housing had only been infrequently permitted and then only in places such as Alaska or island territories. FEMA leadership worked with the Office of Inspector General to make the argument that it was not possible to bring in travel trailers at the scale needed, or within a reasonable time window. Around 100 permanent units were brought in and Pine Ridge is considered a success story. Yet, front-line personnel at FEMA were at times uncomfortable stepping outside of traditional limits and other efforts to bring a permanent housing mission to states such as Florida and Louisiana have subsequently failed.

However, these examples depend on a complex array of actors, all of whom are willing to work in service of that community vision. While this is not an impossible scenario, it is quite unlikely and not one that is easily scaled or replicated. There are far more examples of discretion being utilized to deny assistance, such as the community of Pinhook that was flooded in 2011 and has struggled to receive any federal assistance. The homes were part of a USACE spillway, but had been the only ones that African Americans were permitted to purchase. Although the land could legally be flooded, residents were not even notified and were later denied assistance because the flooding was permissible. "They feel that they lived

[6] Based on an interview with a former FEMA official.

in peace, obeyed laws, paid their taxes, observed regulations and conventions; they established a respectable community that was self-sufficient and even prosperous. But when decisions were being made about whether or not to destroy their community, they were not consulted. They were never even notified" (Lawrence & Lawless, 2018, 142).

Conclusion

Discretion can make the best use of existing laws and policies while new ones are conceptualized and codified. The successful exercise of discretion within agencies can also point to new possibilities, as exceptions and pilot efforts become codified into the realm of the possible. One of the conclusions we have reached is that laws matter; but that people enacting, interpreting, and trying to foster new social space within the laws also matter. If people within an agency or state are trying to maximize the law's potential to protect people, especially overburdened people, from harm, then—while existing laws may make some actions more difficult—they may also be enough to produce just outcomes. If the laws change substantively in ways that are intended to protect overburdened and historically marginalized communities, but a city, state, or agency is trying to maximize the law's potential to protect property values—then any change to law may not be enough. On the other hand, changes to law, or interpretation of law by the courts, in some cases, can make material changes happen almost immediately. These spaces of interaction between law and people are critical; and justice and injustice is bound to both.

References

Arnstein, S. R. (1972). Maximum feasible manipulation. *Public Administration Review, 32*, 377–390.

Baurick, T. (2022, August 28). The last days of Isle de Jean Charles: A Louisiana tribe's struggle to escape the rising sea. *Times Picayune*. https://www.nola.com/news/environment/article_70ac1746-1f22-11ed-bc68-3bde459eba68.html

Bob Hudson, David Hunter & Stephen Peckham. (2018). Policy failure and the policy-implementation gap: can policy support programs help? *Policy Design and Practice*, *2*(1), 1-14.

Congressional Research Service. (2021). Agency Use of Guidance Documents. Report LSB10591

Downton, M. W., & Pielke, R. A., Jr. (2001). Discretion without accountability: Politics, flood damage, and climate. *Natural Hazards Review, 2*(4), 157–166.

Frank, T. (2022, May 27). *How FEMA helps white and rich Americans escape floods*. Politico. https://www.politico.com/news/2022/05/27/unfair-fema-climate-program-floods-00032080

Georgetown Climate Center. (2020). *Managed retreat toolkit*. https://www.georgetownclimate.org/adaptation/toolkits/managed-retreat-toolkit/introduction.html

Government Accountability Office. (2020). A climate migration pilot program could enhance the nation's resilience and reduce federal fiscal exposure. Washington, DC: GAO-20-488.

Headwater Economics. (2022). *Capacity-limited states still struggle to access FEMA BRIC grants*. https://headwaterseconomics.org/equity/capacity-limited-fema-bric-grants/

Hooks, J. P., & Miller, T. B. (2006). The continuing storm: How disaster recovery excludes those most in need. *California Western Law Review, 43*, 21.

Jerolleman, A. (2013). *The privatization of hazard mitigation: A case study of the creation and implementation of a Federal Program* (Doctoral dissertation). University of New Orleans.

Jerolleman, A. (2019). *Disaster recovery through the lens of justice*. Springer.

Jessee, N. (2022). Reshaping Louisiana's coastal frontier: Managed retreat as colonial decontextualization. *Journal of Political Ecology, 29*(1). https://doi.org/10.2458/jpe.2835

Lawrence, D. T., & Lawless, E. J. (2018). *When they blew the Levee: Race, politics, and community in Pinhook, Missouri*. University Press of Mississippi.

Lipsky, M. (1980). *Street-level bureaucracy: Dilemmas of the individual in public services*. Russell Sage Foundation.

Mahmood, A., & Cousins, J. J. (2022). Judicialising urban political ecologies: Post-politics and environmental governance in South Asia. *Antipode, 54*, 1944–1964. https://doi.org/10.1111/anti.12850

Marandi, A., & Man, K. L. (2021). Vulnerable city, recipient city, or climate destination? Towards a typology of domestic climate migration impacts in US cities. *Journal of Environmental Studies and Sciences, 11*, 465–480.

May, P. J., & Burby, R. J. (1996). Coercive versus cooperative policies: Comparing intergovernmental mandate performance. *Journal of Policy Analysis and Management, 15*, 171–201. https://doi.org/10.1002/(SICI)1520-6688(199621)15:2%3c171::AID-PAM2%3e3.0.CO;2-G

Melish, T. J. (2010). Maximum feasible participation of the poor: New governance, new accountability, and a 21st century war on the sources of poverty. *Yale Human Rights and Development Law Journal, 13*, 1.

Rubin, L. B. (1969). Maximum feasible participation: The origins, implications, and present status. *The Annals of the American Academy of Political and Social Science, 385*(1), 14–29.

Scott, P. G. (1997). Assessing determinants of bureaucratic discretion: An experiment in street-level decision making. *Journal of Public Administration Research and Theory: J-PART, 7*(1), 35–57.

Simms, J. R., Waller, H. L., Brunet, C., & Jenkins, P. (2021). The long goodbye on a disappearing, ancestral island: a just retreat from Isle de Jean Charles. *Journal of Environmental Studies and Sciences, 11*(3), 316-328.

Sylves, R. (2020). *Disaster policy and politics* (3rd ed.). Sage.

CHAPTER 10

Concluding Thoughts

We have come to the end of this broad-reaching book. It is 200 pages that attempt to weave together legal theories and contradictions within property law; case studies of relocated and relocating communities; the laws that shape those processes; and the bureaucratic discretion that interprets those laws, in order to see the tangled web of culture, law, assumption, property, power, race, and weather that create modern relocations in "response" to climate change. This book has many goals, but one is to offer a counter-balance to the ever-growing cacophony of voices that keep repeating the oversimplified notion that "Sea Level Rise is driving migration".

We understand that we must live within the bounds of the natural environment, indeed, many of the communities we live in or work in are fundamentally oriented toward the idea of living ecologically and sustainably. We also understand that the environment is changing: that hurricanes are stronger and intensify more rapidly, that wildfires are more severe, that the permafrost boundary is moving North, that the temperature is rising. We also know, by witness, research, and common sense, that simultaneous to these environmental changes, sand is trucked in to protect tourist areas (Marino, 2018); small islands are being built in the South China Sea; Manhattan is "too big" to drown. The goal of this book is to show that the future (and present) of climate relocations will be a social calculus, not an ecological one.

A. Jerolleman et al., *People or Property*,
https://doi.org/10.1007/978-3-031-36872-1_10

Who, how, and what relocations look like will be the product of whose lives are seen as deserving; which livelihoods are seen as worthy of recreating on higher ground; who will be made whole when faced with extreme risk, and what will be legible in that accounting. The position we have taken in this book is a critical position, but not a hopeless one. The creation of the property regime in the United States, and the Constitution itself, was ideologically tied to the desire to stem the power of the monarch. The discourse around property did draw deeply on Locke's view, but it also considered a social and civic function of property ownership. It is possible to reinterpret highest and best use again, to put people ahead of property value in our social calculus of what to protect; to let those people self-identify creative pathways forward into unknown futures; to not singularly interpret land as real estate, or a citizen as a property owner.

A second goal of this book is to bring diverse readers into conversation with one another around applied research directed at climate justice. It is likely, for example, that legal scholars are not all well versed in Indigenous histories; that ethnographers often misunderstand property law and processes of law making; that community leaders or allies do not have a working knowledge of how regulatory mechanisms and bureaucratic discretion function. We know that some ideas in this book will be elementary for some readers, while other ideas will be new and challenging. We hope that this book is a launching place, especially for young academics and policymakers, who want to marry (as we do) the best parts of social theory and criticism, with applied research, directed toward real climate justice outcomes. We wrote this book as a set of authors who at times disagreed with one another in different ways. We disagreed on the role of property, the emphasis on history, the use of relocation case studies, and the positionality of voice. Despite that, we came, more or less, to a happy and positive consensus on most of what you read here. This gives us hope. Property and property law is one of the most divisive topics in the United States—but we hope there is still space for agreement and consensus about the value of land as sacred; and the valuing of people as infinitely greater than property. We also hope that we have modeled how a consortium of ethnographers, community leaders, and legal and public administration scholars might come together and create something new, possibly fragmented, perhaps not exhaustive, but somehow both historically sweeping and immediately applicable.

A final goal of the book is about challenging the limits of the law. Scattered throughout the book are concrete suggestions, and references to the suggestions made by others, about possible ways forward under conditions of ecological and climatic change. They include:

1. Eliminate matching requirements for hazard mitigation grants in small and impoverished communities.
2. Test Community Land Trusts as a mechanism for collective property holding and advocacy.
3. Monitor and test the use of inclusionary zoning as a hazard mitigation strategy to ensure equitable outcomes.
4. Expand legal pathways for collective ownerships and communal processes.
5. Reconsider the benefit/cost calculations in hazard mitigation and other grant making processes, including mechanisms to recognize non-market value.
6. Monitor and test in court the inequitable distribution of hazard mitigation subsidies.
7. Continue to subsidize insurance for low-income families on the coast, despite changes to NFIP.
8. Create more low income and social housing stock.
9. Recognize and improve the rights of renters and other precarious possessors.
10. Use replacement value instead of fair market value in voluntary buyouts, especially in low-and-moderate income neighborhoods, or in historically overburdened neighborhoods.
11. Consider mechanisms of repair in neighborhoods where climate change exacerbates histories of neglect and oppression.
12. Generate long-term assessments and invest in self-stewarded assessments of relocated communities, including renters, to gauge the impacts of relocation.
13. Create community-based organizations that can hold representational power in relocation scenarios driven by state actors, particularly for people in more precarious relationships with property.
14. Fund Indigenous nations and tribal communities' self-determined efforts to regenerate ecological relations, steward adaptation planning processes, and ensure social and cultural futures on traditional and new lands.

Throughout the book there are others. We do not think any of these suggestions, if carried out, will be a panacea to long histories of oppression, or solutions to economic inequity. We also do not know if these suggestions would work—or what the unintended consequences of them would be. We do know that when the burden of testing these possibilities falls on communities, or community leaders, they are beset with procedural risk and exhaustion. However, we did not want to write a book that was just a critique. There are an ever-growing set of reports on the strategies governments should take when faced with habitual flooding and relocation. Many of these reports offer technocratic solutions, presented as best practices that only lack funding or scaling. The list offered above compromises some of our solutions and suggestions. They are informed by our collective wisdom, which is limited and imperfect, but is perhaps stronger by acknowledging that no one solution exists and that messy processes of mutual learning are necessary.

Reference

Marino, E. (2018). Adaptation privilege and voluntary buyouts: Perspectives on ethnocentrism in sea level rise relocation and retreat policies in the US. *Global Environmental Change, 49*, 10–13.

Correction to: People or Property

Correction to:
A. Jerolleman et al., *People or Property*,
https://doi.org/10.1007/978-3-031-36872-1

The original version of this book was inadvertently published without a few authors in each chapter, which have now been updated. The book has been updated with the changes.

The updated version of the book can be found at
https://doi.org/10.1007/978-3-031-36872-1

A. Jerolleman et al., *People or Property*,
https://doi.org/10.1007/978-3-031-36872-1_11

References

Agrawal, A. (2008). *The role of local institutions in adaptation to climate change*. The World Bank.

Agyeman, J., & Boone, K. (2020, June 18). *Land loss has plagued black America since emancipation—Is it time to look again at 'black commons' and collective ownership?* The Conversation. https://theconversation.com/land-loss-has-plagued-black-america-since-emancipation-is-it-time-to-look-again-at-black-commons-and-collective-ownership-140514

Agyeman, J., Devine-Wright, P., & Prange, J. (2009). Close to the edge, down by the river? Joining up managed retreat and place attachment in a climate changed world. *Environment and Planning, 41*, 509–513.

Ahenakew, C., Andreotti, V. D. O., Cooper, G., & Hireme, H. (2014). Beyond epistemic provincialism: De-provincializing Indigenous resistance. *AlterNative: An International Journal of Indigenous Peoples, 10*(3), 216–231.

Aidoo, F. S. (2021). Architectures of mis/managed retreat: Black land loss to green housing gains. *Journal of Environmental Studies and Sciences, 11*(3), 451–464.

Alexander, G. S. (1997). *Commodity & propriety: Competing visions of property in American legal thought 1776–1970*. University of Chicago Press.

Alexander, G. S. (2009). The social-obligation norm in American property law. *Cornell Law Faculty Publications, 94*(4), 745–819. https://scholarship.law.cornell.edu/lsrp_papers/92

American Civil Liberties Union. (2018). *ACLU Annual Report 2018*. Retrieved July 7, 2022, from https://www.aclu.org/other/aclu-annual-report-2018

Anderson, D. (June 11, 2020). Redlining's Legacy of Inequality: $212,000 Less Home Equity, Low Homeownership Rates For Black Families. Redfin News. https://www.redfin.com/news/redlining-real-estate-racial-wealth-gap/

A. Jerolleman et al., *People or Property*,
https://doi.org/10.1007/978-3-031-36872-1

Angelo, H., & Wachsmuth, D. (2015). Urbanizing urban political ecology: A critique of methodological cityism. *International Journal of Urban and Regional Research, 39*(1), 16–27.

Anguelovski, I., Connolly, J. J., Pearsall, H., Shokry, G., Checker, M., Maantay, J., Gould, K., Lewis, T., Maroko, A., & Roberts, J. T. (2019). Why green "climate gentrification" threatens poor and vulnerable populations. *Proceedings of the National Academy of Sciences, 116*(52), 26139–26143.

Ansfield, B. (2015). Still submerged: The uninhabitability of urban redevelopment. In K. McKittrick (Ed.), *Sylvia Wynter: On being human as praxis* (pp. 124–141). Duke University Press.

Arnstein, S. R. (1972). Maximum feasible manipulation. *Public Administration Review, 32*, 377–390.

Arruñada, B., & Lehavi, A. (2011). Prime property institutions for subprime era: Towards innovative models of homeownership. *Berkeley Business Law Journal, 8*, 1. https://doi.org/10.2139/ssrn.1601172

Atoba, K. O., Brody, S. D., Highfield, W. E., Shepard, C. C., & Verdone, L. N. (2020). Strategic property buyouts to enhance flood resilience: A multi-criteria spatial approach for incorporating ecological values into the selection process. *Environmental Hazards*, 1–19. https://doi.org/10.1080/17477891.2020.1771251

Baja, K. (2022). Rethinking process and reframing language for climate-inducted relocation. In I. J. Ajibade & A. R. Siders (Eds.), *Global views on climate relocation and social justice* (pp. 19–33). Routledge.

Baker, C. K., Binder, S. B., Greer, A., Weir, P., & Gates, K. (2018). Integrating community concerns and recommendations into home buyout and relocation policy. *Risk, Hazards & Crisis in Public Policy, 9*(4), 455–479. https://doi.org/10.1002/rhc3.12144

Banner, S. (2005). *How the Indians lost their land: Law and power on the frontier*. Harvard University Press.

Barile, J. P., Binder, S. B., & Baker, C. K. (2020). Recovering after a natural disaster: Differences in quality of life across three communities after Hurricane Sandy. *Applied Research in Quality of Life*. https://doi.org/10.1007/s11482-019-09722-3

Barker, J. (Ed.). (2005). *Sovereignty matters: Locations of contestation and possibility in indigenous struggles for self-determination*. University of Nebraska Press.

Barker, J. (2008). Gender, sovereignty, rights: Native women's activism against social inequality and violence in Canada. *American Quarterly, 60*(2), 259–266.

Barrios, R. E. (2017). *Governing affect: Neoliberalism and disaster reconstruction*. University of Nebraska Press.

Baurick, T. (2022, August 28). The last days of Isle de Jean Charles: A Louisiana tribe's struggle to escape the rising sea. *Times Picayune*. https://www.nola.com/news/environment/article_70ac1746-1f22-11ed-bc68-3bde459eba68.html

Becher, D. (2014). *Private property and public power: Eminent domain in Philadelphia*. Oxford University Press.

Bell, A., & Parchomovsky, G. (2017). Partial takings. *Columbia Law Review, 117*(8), 2043–2093.

Berke, P. R., Lyles, W., & Smith, G. (2014). Impacts of federal and state hazard mitigation policies on local land use policy. *Journal of Planning Education and Research, 34*(1), 60–76.

Berkhofer, R. F., Jr. (1978). *The White Man's Indian*. Knopf.

Bezgrebelna, M., McKenzie, K., Wells, S., Ravindran, A., Kral, M., Christensen, J., Stergiopoulos, V., Gaetz, S., & Kidd, S. A. (2021). Climate change, weather, housing precarity, and homelessness: A systematic review of reviews. *International Journal of Environmental Research and Public Health, 18*(11), 5812. https://doi.org/10.3390/ijerph18115812

Bhandar, B. (2018). *Colonial lives of property: Law, land, and racial regimes of ownership*. Duke University Press.

Bier, V. M. (2017). Understanding and mitigating the impacts of massive relocations due to disasters. *Economics of Disasters and Climate Change, 1*(2), 179–202. https://doi.org/10.1007/s41885-017-0003-4

Binder, S. B., Baker, C. K., & Barile, J. P. (2015). Rebuild or relocate? Resilience and postdisaster decision-making after Hurricane Sandy. *American Journal of Community Psychology, 56*(1–2), 180–196.

Binder, S. B., Barile, J. P., Baker, C. K., & Kulp, B. (2019). Home buyouts and household recovery: Neighborhood differences three years after Hurricane Sandy. *Environmental Hazards, 18*(2), 127–145.

Binder, S. B., & Greer, A. (2016). The devil is in the details: Linking home buyout policy, practice, and experience after Hurricane Sandy. *Politics and Governance, 4*(4), 97–106.

Binder, S. B., Greer, A., & Zavar, E. (2020). Home buyouts: A tool for mitigation or recovery? *Disaster Prevention and Management, 29*(4), 497–510. https://doi.org/10.1108/DPM-09-2019-0298

Black, J. E. (2009). Native resistive rhetoric and the decolonization of American Indian removal discourse. *Quarterly Journal of Speech, 95*(1), 66–88.

Blomley, N. (2004). *Unsettling the city: Urban land and the politics of property*. Routledge.

Blomley, N. (2020). Precarious territory: Property law, housing, and the socio-spatial order. *Antipode, 52*(1), 36–57.

Blunt, A., & Dowling, R. (2006). *Home*. Routledge.

Boas, F. C., Adams, H., Sterly, H., Bush, S., van der Geest, K., Wiegel, H., Ashraf, H., Baldwin, A., Bettini, G., Blondin, S., de Bruijn, M., Durand-Delacre, D., Fröhlich, C., Gioli, G., Guaita, L., Hut, E., Jarawura, F., Lamers, M., Lietaer, S., … Hulme, M. (2019). Climate migration myths. *Nature Climate Change, 9*(12), 901–903. https://doi.org/10.1038/s41558-019-0633-3

Bolin, R. C., & Stanford, L. (1991). Shelter, housing and recovery: A comparison of U.S. disasters. *Disasters, 15*(1), 24–34.

Bowes, J. P. (2014). American Indian removal beyond the removal act. *Native American and Indigenous Studies, 1*(1), 65–87.

Braamskamp, A., & Penning-Rowsell, E. C. (2018). Managed retreat: A rare and paradoxical success, but yielding a dismal prognosis. *Environmental Management and Sustainable Development, 7*(2), 108–136. https://doi.org/10.5296/emsd.v7i2.12851

Breunlin, R., & Regis, H. A. (2006). Putting the ninth ward on the map: Race, place, and transformation in Desire, New Orleans. *American Anthropologist, 108*(4), 744–764. https://doi.org/10.1525/aa.2006.108.4.744

Bronen, R., & Chapin, F. S., III. (2013). Adaptive governance and institutional strategies for climate-induced community relocations in Alaska. *Proceedings of the National Academy of Sciences, 110*(23), 9320–9325.

Bronen, R., Maldonado, J. K., Marino, E., & Hardison, P. (2018). Climate change and displacement: Challenges and needs to address an imminent reality. In M. M. Cernea & J. K. Maldonado (Eds.), *Challenging the prevailing paradigm of displacement and resettlement* (pp. 252–272). Routledge.

Brown, D. L. (2002). Migration and community: Social networks in a multilevel world. *Rural Sociology, 67*(1), 1.

Browne, K. E. (2015). *Standing in the need: Culture, comfort, and coming home after Katrina*. University of Texas Press.

Bryson, L., & Mowbray, M. (1981). 'Community': The spray-on solution. *Australian Journal of Social Issues, 16*(4), 255–267.

Bullard, R. D., Mohai, P., Saha, R., & Wright, B. (2008). Toxic wastes and race at twenty: Why race still matters after all of these years. *Environmental Law, 38*, 371.

Burkett, M. (2011). The nation ex-situ: On climate change, deterritorialized nationhood and the post-climate era. *Climate Law, 2*(3), 345–374.

Burkett, M. (2018). Behind the veil: Climate migration, regime shift, and a new theory of justice. *Harvard Civil Rights—Civil Liberties Law Review, 53*, 446–492.

Burkett, M. (2007). Reconciliation and nonrepetition: A new paradigm for African-American reparations. *Oregon Law Review, 86*, 99.

Burkett, M., & Flores, D. (2018, September 13). *From surviving to thriving: Relocation and migration*. CPR Blog. http://progressivereform.org/cpr-blog/surviving-thriving-relocation-and-migration/
Byrne, J. P., & Grannis, J. (2012). Coastal retreat measures. In M. B. Gerrard & K. Fischer Kuh (Eds.), *The law of adaptation to climate change: US and international aspects* (pp. 267–306). American Bar Association.
Callison, C. (2017). Climate change communication and indigenous publics. In M. Nisbet (Ed.), *The Oxford encyclopedia of climate change communication*. Oxford University Press.
Cardwell, J. (2021). Community perceptions of a floodplain buyout program in Charlotte, North Carolina. *Natural Hazards, 115*, 2141–2160.
Carlson, L. A. (1981). *Indians, bureaucrats, and land: The Dawes Act and the decline of Indian farming*. Greenwood Press.
Carson, B. S. (2015, July 23). Experimenting with failed socialism again. *The Washington Times*. https://www.washingtontimes.com/news/2015/jul/23/ben-carson-obamas-housing-rules-try-to-accomplish-/
Case, D. S., & Voluck, D. A. (2012). *Alaska natives and American laws*. University of Alaska Press.
Cave, A. A. (2003). Abuse of power: Andrew Jackson and the Indian removal act of 1830. *The Historian, 65*(6), 1330–1353.
CEQ. (2021). Executive Order 14008: Tackling the Climate Crisis at Home and Abroad (January 27, 2021).
Cernea, M. (1997). The risks and reconstruction model for resettling displaced populations. *World Development, 25*(10), 1569–1587.
Chakrabarty, D. (2009). The climate of history: Four theses. *Critical Inquiry, 35*(2), 197–222.
Checker, M. (2011). Wiped out by the "greenwave": Environmental gentrification and the paradoxical politics of urban sustainability. *City & Society, 23*(2), 210–229.
Checker, M. (2020). *The sustainability myth: Environmental gentrification and the politics of justice*. New York University Press.
Chemnick, J. (2022, June 1). *Experts to "White House: EJ screening tool should consider race"*. E&E News, ClimateWire. https://www.eenews.net/articles/experts-to-white-house-ej-screening-tool-should-consider-race/
Clipp, A., Gentile, B., Green, M., Galinski, A., Harlan, R., Rosen, Z., & Saucier, M. (2017). *2017 coastal master plan. Appendix B. People and the landscape*. Coastal Protection and Restoration Authority. http://coastal.la.gov/wp-content/uploads/2017/04/Appendix-B_People-and-the-Landscape_FINAL.pdf
Comardelle, C. (2020, October 19). Preserving our place: Isle de Jean Charles. *Nonprofit Quarterly*. https://nonprofitquarterly.org/preserving-our-place-isle-de-jean-charles

Connolly, K. (2003). A retrospective on Lucas v. South Carolina Coastal Council: Public policy implications for the 21st century. *Southeastern Environmental Law Journal, 12*, 1.

Cottar, S., Doberstein, B., Henstra, D., & Henstra, D. (2021). Evaluating property buyouts and disaster recovery assistance (rebuild) options in Canada: A comparative analysis of Constance Bay, Ontario and Pointe Gatineau, Quebec. *Natural Hazards, 109*, 201–220. https://doi.org/10.1007/s11069-021-04832-4

Craig, R. K. (2011). Public trust and public necessity defenses to takings liability for sea level rise response on the Gulf Coast. *Journal of Land Use & Environmental Law, 26*, 395–432.

Dalbom, C., Hemmerling, S. A., & Lewis, J. (2014). Community resettlement prospects in Southeast Louisiana: A multidisciplinary exploration of legal, cultural, and demographic aspects of moving individuals and communities. *Tulane Institute on Water Resources Law & Policy, New Orleans, 49.*

Davis, J. E. (2010). Origins and evolution of the community land trust in the United States. In J. E. Davis (Ed.), *The community land trust reader* (pp. 3–47). Lincoln Institute of Land Policy.

DeFilippis, J., Williams, O. R., Pierce, J., Martin, D. G., Kruger, R., & Esfahani, A. H. (2019). On the transformative potential of community land trusts in the United States. *Antipode, 51*(3), 795–817.

Deininger, K., Byerlee, D., Lindsay, J., Norton, A., Selod, H., & Stickler, M. (2011). *Rising global interest in farmland: Can it yield sustainable and equitable benefits?* World Bank. https://openknowledge.worldbank.org/handle/10986/2263

Deloria, V., Jr. (1969). *Custer died for your sins: An Indian manifesto.* Macmillan.

Denevan, W. (1992). The pristine myth: The landscape of the Americas in 1492. *Annals of the Association of American Geographers, 82*(3), 369–385.

Dermanksy, J. (2022, September 8). *Isle de Jean Charles community members moved into the first federally funded resettlement project in Louisiana despite visible engineering issues*. Desmog. https://www.desmog.com/2022/09/08/isle-de-jean-charles-relocation-new-isle-climate-change/

De Vries, D. H. (2008). *Temporal vulnerability: Historical ecologies of monitoring, memory, and meaning in changing United States floodplain landscapes* (Publication No. 3304420) (Doctoral dissertation). University of North Carolina at Chapel Hill. ProQuest.

De Vries, D. H. (2011). Temporal vulnerability to flood hazards: Recurrence, risk and referentiality along the eastern North Carolina Neuse River. *Global Environmental Change, 21*(1), 154–164. https://doi.org/10.1016/j.gloenvcha.2010.09.006

De Vries, D. H. (2017). Historical waterscape trajectories that need care: The unwanted refurbished flood homes of Kinston's devolved disaster mitigation program. *Journal of Political Ecology, 24*, 931–950.

De Vries, D. H. (2019). Surprise ecologies: Case studies on temporal vulnerability in four North American floodplains. *Ecology and Society, 24*(4), 37. https://doi.org/10.5751/ES-11274-240437

De Vries, D. H., & Fraser, J. C. (2012). Citizenship rights and voluntary decision making in post disaster U.S. floodplain buyout mitigation programs. *International Journal of Mass Emergencies and Disasters, 30*(1), 1–33.

De Weger, E., Van Vooren, N., Luijkx, K. G., Baan, C. A., & Drewes, H. W. (2018). Achieving successful community engagement: A rapid realist review. *BMC Health Services Research, 18*(285).

Dineen, J. K. (2016, August 17). Feds reject housing plan meant to help minorities stay in SF. *San Francisco Chronicle*.

Dobbs, D. B. (2000). *The law of torts*. West Group.

D'Oro, R. (2014, January 17). Residents of eroding Alaska village seek federal help. *Fairbanks Daily News Miner*. https://www.newsminer.com/news/alaska_news/residents-of-eroding-alaska-village-seek-federal-help/article_9ce9b1b6-7fc0-11e3-80e6-0019bb30f31a.html

Downton, M. W., & Pielke, R. A., Jr. (2001). Discretion without accountability: Politics, flood damage, and climate. *Natural Hazards Review, 2*(4), 157–166.

Dunbar-Ortiz, R. (2014). *An indigenous peoples' history of the United States*. Beacon Press.

Dundon, L. A., & Camp, J. S. (2021). Climate justice and home-buyout programs: Renters as a forgotten population in managed retreat actions. *Journal of Environmental Studies and Sciences, 11*(3), 420–433. https://doi.org/10.1007/s13412-021-00691-4

DuPuis, E. M., & Greenberg, M. (2019). The right to the resilient city: Progressive politics and the green growth machine in New York City. *Journal of Environmental Studies and Sciences, 9*(3), 352–363.

Durst, N. J., & Wegmann, J. (2017). Informal housing in the United States. *International Journal of Urban and Regional Research, 41*(2), 282–297.

Dyca, B., Muldoon-Smith, K., & Greenhalgh, P. (2020). Common value: Transferring development rights to make room for water. *Environmental Science & Policy, 114*, 312–320.

Echo-Hawk, R. C. (2010). *The magic children racial identity at the end of the age of race*. Routledge.

Elam, S. (2019, July 17). *A flood forced this town to move. It could be a model for others hit by the climate crisis*. CNN. https://www.cnn.com/2019/07/17/us/valmeyer-flooding-climate-crisis-midwest/index.html

Ellickson, R. C. (2011). Two cheers for the bundle-of-sticks metaphor, three cheers for Merrill and Smith. *Econ Journal Watch, 8*(3), 215–222.

Elliott, J. R., Brown, P. L., & Loughran, K. (2020). Racial inequities in the federal buyout of flood-prone homes: A nationwide assessment of environmental adaptation. *Socius, 6*.

Elliott, J. R., & Howell, J. (2017). Beyond disasters: A longitudinal analysis of natural hazards' unequal impacts on residential instability. *Social Forces, 95*(3), 1181–1207.

Ely, J. W., Jr. (2008). *The guardian of every other right: A constitutional history of property rights*. Oxford University Press.

Epstein, R. A. (1985). *Takings: Private property and the power of eminent domain*. Harvard University Press.

Erikson, K. (1978). *Everything in its path*. Simon and Schuster.

Estes, N. (2019). *Our history is the future: Standing rock versus the Dakota access pipeline, and the long tradition of indigenous resistance*. Verso Books.

Esteves, L. (2018, September 13). *Climate change: We need to start moving people away from some coastal areas, warns scientist*. The conversation. https://theconversation.com/climate-change-we-need-to-start-moving-people-away-from-some-coastal-areas-warns-scientist-101351

Fadel, L., & Lopez, A. (2022). *Texas GOP platform embraces far-right and anti-gay rhetoric*. Morning Edition. NPR Oregon Public Broadcasting. https://wwngw.npr.org/ng2022/06/24/1107244492/texas-gop-platform-embraces-far-right-and-anti-gay-rhetoric

Fagen, P. W. (2006). *Remittances in conflict and crises: How remittances sustain livelihoods in war, crises and transitions to peace*. International Peace Institute.

Farbotko, C. (2022). Anti-displacement mobilities and re-emplacements: Alternative climate mobilities in Funafala. *Journal of Ethnic and Migration Studies, 48*, 3380–3396.

Farrell, J., Burow, P. B., McConnell, K., Bayham, J., Whyte, K., & Koss, G. (2021). Effects of land dispossession and forced migration on Indigenous peoples in North America. *Science, 374*(6567).

FEMA. (2003). *Innovative floodplain management case studies: Kinston, North Carolina. Mitigation case studies*. https://www.fema.gov/pdf/casestudys/kinston_cs.pdf

FEMA. (2011, December). *A whole community approach to emergency management: Principles, themes, and pathways for action* (FDOC 104-008-1). https://www.fema.gov/sites/default/files/2020-07/whole_community_dec2011__2.pdf

FEMA. (2017, October 6). *Fact Sheet: NFIP "substantial damage"—What does it mean?* (R4 DR-4338-GA FS 008). https://www.fema.gov/press-release/20210318/fact-sheet-nfip-substantial-damage-what-does-it-mean-0

FEMA BRIC. (2021). https://www.fema.gov/sites/default/files/documents/fema_fy21-bric-technical-criteria-psm_111521.pdf

FEMA CRS. (2017). Community rating system coordinators manual. https://www.fema.gov/sites/default/files/documents/fema_community-rating-system_coordinators-manual_2017.pdf

FEMA CRS. (2023). Eligible communities database. https://www.fema.gov/sites/default/files/documents/fema_crs_eligible-communities_oct-2023.pdf

Fitzpatrick, D. (2006). Evolution and chaos in property rights systems: The third world tragedy of contested access. *Yale Law Journal, 115*, 996–1048.

Fixico, D. L. (1986). *Termination and relocation. Federal Indian policy, 1945–1960*. University of New Mexico Press.

Flavelle, C. (2020a, March 11). Trump administration presses cities to evict homeowners from flood zones. *The New York Times*.

Flavelle, C. (2020b, August 26). U.S. flood strategy shifts to 'unavoidable' relocation of entire neighborhoods. *The New York Times* https://www.nytimes.com/2020/08/26/climate/flooding-relocation-managed-retreat.html

Foster, S. (2022, May 25). *From vacancy to decommodification: Co-cities and the enabling state*. LPE Blog. https://lpeproject.org/blog/from-vacancy-to-decommodification-co-cities-and-the-enabling-state/

Fothergill, A., & Peek, L. A. (2004). Poverty and disasters in the United States: A review of recent sociological findings. *Natural Hazards, 32*, 89–110.

Foundation for Community Association Research. (2021). *2021–2022 U.S. national and state statistical review*. U.S. Community Associations, Housing Units, and Residents.

Frank, T. (2022a, May 27). *How FEMA helps white and rich Americans escape floods*. Politico. https://www.politico.com/news/2022/05/27/unfair-fema-climate-program-floods-00032080

Frank, T. (2022b). *Hundreds of thousands drop flood insurance as rates rise*. E&E News: Climate Wire. https://www.eenews.net/articles/hundreds-of-thousands-drop-flood-insurance-as-rates-rise/

Fraser, J., Elmore, R., Godshalk, D., & Rohe, W. (2003). *Implementing floodplain land acquisition programs in urban localities*. University of North Carolina at Chapel Hill.

Freudenberg, R., Calvin, E., Tolkoff, L., & Brawley, D. (2016). *Buy-in for buyouts: The case for managed retreat from flood zones*. Lincoln Institute of Land Policy report. https://www.lincolninst.edu/publications/policy-focus-reports/buy-in-for-buyouts

Freund, D. M. P. (2007). *Colored property: State policy and white racial politics in suburban America*. University of Chicago Press.

Fullilove, M. T. (2005). *Root shock: How tearing up city neighborhoods hurts Americans and what we can do about it*. One World Press.

Fussell, E. (2012). Help from family, friends, and strangers during Hurricane Katrina: Finding the limits of social networks. In L. Weber & L. Peek (Eds.),

Displaced: Life in the Katrina diaspora (pp. 150–166). University of Texas Press.

Gass, H. (2017, August 2). Tactical retreat? As seas rise, Louisiana faces hard choices. *Christian Science Monitor*. https://www.csmonitor.com/Environment/Inhabit/2017/0802/Tactical-retreat-As-seas-rise-Louisiana-faces-hard-choices

Georgetown Climate Center. (2020). *Managed retreat toolkit*. https://www.georgetownclimate.org/adaptation/toolkits/managed-retreat-toolkit/introduction.html

Gerber, J. D., & Gerber, J. F. (2017). Decommodification as a foundation for ecological economics. *Ecological Economics, 131*, 551–556. https://doi.org/10.1016/j.ecolecon.2016.08.030

Gilbert, J., Wood, S. D., & Sharp, G. (2002). Who owns the land? Agricultural land ownership by race/ethnicity. *Rural America/Rural Development Perspectives, 17*(4), 55–62. https://doi.org/10.22004/ag.econ.289693

Gilman, D., & Steglich, E. (2018). The unending floods. Disaster recovery and immigration policy. *Texas Law Review Online, 96*, 91–101. https://texaslawreview.org/the-unending-floods/

Godsil, R. D. (2005). Environmental justice and the integration ideal. *NYLS Law Review, 49*(4), 6.

Goffman, E. (1974). *Frame analysis: An essay on the organization of experience*. Harvard University Press.

Gold, A. G. (2005, May). *Conceptualizing community: Anthropological reflections*. Brown University. Retrieved July 14, 2022, from https://www.brown.edu/research/research-ethics/conceptualizing-community-anthropological-reflections

Goldstein, A. (2014).*Formations of United States Colonialism*. Duke University Press

Gramling, R., Laska, S., Wooddell, G., Forsyth, C., Darlington, J., Green, B., Kappel, B., & Boudreaux, B. (2006). *Anticipating social effects of coastal restoration projects*. Louisiana Department of Natural Resources.

Grandinetti, T. (2019). Urban aloha ʻaina: Kakaʻako and a decolonized right to the city. *Settler Colonial Studies, 9*(2), 227–246.

Greenberg, M. (2013). The disaster inside the disaster: Hurricane Sandy and post-crisis redevelopment. *New Labor Forum, 23*(1), 44–52. https://doi.org/10.1177/1095796013513239

Greenfield, N. (2021). *Alaska natives lead a unified resistance to the pebble mine*. NRDC. https://www.nrdc.org/stories/alaska-natives-lead-unified-resistance-pebble-mine

Green, T. F., & Olshansky, R. B. (2012). Rebuilding housing in New Orleans: The Road Home Program after the Hurricane Katrina disaster. *Housing Policy Debate, 22*(1), 75–99.

Greer, A., & Binder, S. B. (2017). A historical assessment of home buyout policy: Are we learning or just failing? *Housing Policy Debate, 27*(3), 372–392. https://doi.org/10.1080/10511482.2016.1245209

Greer, A., Sherri, B. B., & Zavar, E. (2021). From hazard mitigation to climate adaptation: A review of home buyout program literature. *Housing Policy Debate*. https://doi.org/10.1080/10511482.2021.1931930

Guijt, I., & Shah, M. K. (1998). *The myth of community: Gender issues in participatory development*. Intermediate Technology Publications.

Hall, A. J. (2003). *American empire and the fourth world: The bowl with one spoon*. McGill-Queen's University Press. https://doi.org/10.2307/j.ctt80p73

Hall, L. K. (2008). Strategies of erasure: US colonialism and native Hawaiian feminism. *American Quarterly, 60*(2), 273–280.

Halperin, R. H. (1998). *Practicing community: Class culture and power in an urban neighborhood*. University of Texas Press.

Haney, T. (2019). Move out or dig in? Risk awareness and mobility plans in disaster-affected communities. *Journal of Contingencies and Crisis Management, 27*(3), 224–236. https://doi.org/10.1111/1468-5973.12253

Hardy, D., Bailey, M., & Heynen, N. (2022). "We're still here": An abolition ecology blockade of double dispossession of Gullah/Geechee land. *Annals of the American Association of Geographers, 112*(3), 867–876.

Harris, C. I. (1993). Whiteness as property. *Harvard Law Review, 106*(8), 1707–1791.

Harrison, A. (1991). *Black exodus: The great migration from the American South*. University Press of Mississippi.

Hartman, C. W. (1971). Relocation: Illusory promises and no relief. *Virginia Law Review, 57*(5), 745–817.

Harvey, D. (2008). The right to the city. *The City Reader, 6*(1), 23–40.

Hatcher, L. D. S. (2006). *A case for reparations: The plight of the African-American World War II veteran concerning federal discriminatory housing practices* (Vol. 2). The Modern American.

Headwater Economics. (2022). *Capacity-limited states still struggle to access FEMA BRIC grants*. https://headwaterseconomics.org/equity/capacity-limited-fema-bric-grants/

Heinsohn, G., & Steiger, O. (1996). *Eigentum, Zins und Geld: Ungelöste Rätsel der Wirtschaftswissenschaft*. Rowohlt.

Heinsohn, G., & Steiger, O. (2013). *Ownership economics: On the foundations of interest, money, markets, business cycles and economic development*. Routledge.

Heller, M., & Hills, R. (2008). Land assembly districts. *Harvard Law Review, 121*(6), 1465–1527.

Henry, J. (2013). Return or relocate? An inductive analysis of decision-making in a disaster. *Disasters, 37*(2), 293–316. https://doi.org/10.1111/j.1467-7717.2012.01303.x

Hersher, R. (2019, October 9). *Sweeping study raises questions about who benefits from buyouts of flood-prone home*. NPR Oregon Public Broadcasting. https://www.npr.org/2019/10/09/767920427/sweeping-study-raises-questions-about-who-benefits-from-buyouts-of-flood-prone-h

Hooks, J. P., & Miller, T. B. (2006). The continuing storm: How disaster recovery excludes those most in need. *California Western Law Review, 43*, 21.

Horton, L. (2012). Nowhere to turn: Obstacles for immigrants seeking disaster assistance. *National Lawyers Guild Review, 69*, 140–159.

Howell, J., & Korver-Glenn, E. (2021, November). The increasing effect of neighborhood racial composition on housing values, 1980–2015. *Social Problems, 68*(4), 1051–1071. https://doi.org/10.1093/socpro/spaa033

Hudson, B., Hunter, D., & Peckham, S. (2019). Policy failure and the policy-implementation gap: Can policy support programs help? *Policy Design and Practice, 2*(1), 1–14. https://doi.org/10.1080/25741292.2018.1540378

Isacoff, R. (2021). Identity and power: How cultural values inform decision-making in climate-based relocation. In I. J. Ajibade & A. R. Siders (Eds.), *Global views on climate relocation and social justice* (pp. 194–208). Routledge.

Jackson, K. T. (1985). *Crabgrass frontier: The suburbanization of the United States*. Oxford University Press.

Jane Place Neighborhood Sustainability Initiative. (n.d.). *Our approach: Community land trust*. https://www.jpnsi.org/

Jerolleman, A. (2013). *The privatization of hazard mitigation: A case study of the creation and implementation of a Federal Program* (Doctoral dissertation). University of New Orleans.

Jerolleman, A. (2019). *Disaster recovery through the lens of justice*. Springer.

Jerolleman, A., & Graves, J. (2020). Personal and institutional timelines for hurricane preparedness, recovery and mitigation. *International Journal of Mass Emergencies and Disasters, 38*(1), 77–88.

Jessee, N. (2020). Community resettlement in Louisiana: Learning from histories of horror and hope. In S. Laska (Ed.), *Louisiana's response to extreme weather—A test case for coastal resilience*. Springer.

Jessee, N. (2021). *Tribal leaders raise 'serious concerns' about plans to turn their shrinking Louisiana Island home into a 'sportsman's paradise'*. Desmog. https://www.desmog.com/2021/07/23/isle-de-jean-charles-tribe-louisiana-sportsmans-paradise/

Jessee, N. (2022). Reshaping Louisiana's coastal frontier: Managed retreat as colonial decontextualization. *Journal of Political Ecology, 29*(1). https://doi.org/10.2458/jpe.2835

Jin, D., Hoagland, P., Au, D. K., & Qiu, J. (2015). Shoreline change, seawalls, and coastal property values. *Ocean & Coastal Management, 114*, 185–193.

Kades, E. (2000). The dark side of efficiency: Johnson v. M'Intosh and the expropriation of American Indian lands. *University of Pennsylvania Law Review, 148*(4), 1065–1190. https://doi.org/10.2307/3312840

Kaiman, C. M. (2016). Environmental justice and community-based reparations. *Seattle University Law Review, 39*, 1327–1338.

Kamel, N. M. O., & Loukaitou-Sideris, A. (2004). Residential assistance and recovery following the Northridge Earthquake. *Urban Studies, 41*(3), 533–562.

Kamin, D. (2022). Home appraised with a black owner: $472,000. With a white owner: $750,000. *New York Times*.

Kapp, K. W. (1950). Political economy and psychology. *Kyklos, 4*(4), 291–315. https://doi.org/10.1111/j.1467-6435.1950.tb01418.x

Kasakove, S. (2019, May 17). The tenants' rights movement is expanding beyond big cities. *The New Republic*. https://newrepublic.com/article/153929/tenants-rights-movement-expanding-beyond-big-cities

Kawash, S. (1998). Bodies at risk: The architecture of reversible destiny. *PAJ: A Journal of Performance and Art, 20*(2), 17–27.

Keenan, J. M., & Bradt, J. T. (2020). Underwaterwriting: From theory to empiricism in regional mortgage markets in the US. *Climatic Change, 162*(4), 2043–2067.

Keenan, J. M., Hill, T., & Gumber, A. (2018). Climate gentrification: From theory to empiricism in Miami-Dade County, Florida. *Environmental Research Letters, 13*(5), 054001–054001. https://doi.org/10.1088/1748-9326/aabb32

Keene, E. (2017). Lessons from relocations past: Climate change, tribes, and the need for pragmatism in community relocation planning. *American Indian Law Review, 42*(1), 259–289.

Keene, E. (2018). Resources for relocation: In search of a coherent federal policy on resettling climate-vulnerable communities. *Texas Environmental Law Journal, 48*, 119.

Kick, E. L., Fraser, J. C., Fulkerson, G. M., McKinney, L. A., & De Vries, D. H. (2011). Repetitive flood victims and acceptance of FEMA mitigation offers: An analysis with community–system policy implications. *Disasters, 35*(3), 510–539.

King, M. (2017). A tribe faces rising tides: The resettlement of Isle de Jean Charles. *LSU Journal of Energy Law and Resources, 6*, 295.

Kinston Daily Free Press. (1976, July 4, Sunday). Historical highlight. *Kinston Daily Free Press* by M. Maynard.

Kniffen, F. B., Gregory, H. F., & Stokes, G. A. (1987). *Tribes of Louisiana from 1542 to the present*. Louisiana State University Press.

Knuth, S. (2016). Seeing green in San Francisco: City as resource frontier. *Antipode, 48*(3), 626–644.

Koslov, L. (2016). The case for retreat. *Public Culture, 28*(2), 359–387.

Kraan, C. M., Hino, M., Niemann, J., Siders, A. R., & Mach, K. J. (2021). Promoting equity in retreat through voluntary property buyout programs. *Journal of Environmental Studies and Sciences, 11*(3), 481–492. https://doi.org/10.1007/s13412-021-00688-z

Krakoff, S. (2013). Settler colonialism and reclamation: Where American Indian law and natural resources law meet. *Colorado Natural Resources, Energy & Environmental Law Review, 24*(2), 261.

Krueckeberg, D. A. (1995). The difficult character of property: To whom do things belong? *Journal of the American Planning Association, 61*(3), 301–309. https://doi.org/10.1080/01944369508975644

Kuo, S. S., & Means, B. (2016). Collective Coercion. *Boston College Law Review, 57*, 1599.

Laplante, L. J. (2015). Just repair. *Cornell International Law Journal, 48*, 513.

Lasley, C. E. (2012). *Catastrophes and the role of social networks in recovery: A case study of St. Bernard Parish, LA, residents after Hurricane Katrina* (Doctoral dissertation). University of New Orleans. https://scholarworks.uno.edu/td/1504

Lawrence, D. T., & Lawless, E. J. (2018). *When they blew the Levee: Race, politics, and community in Pinhook, Missouri*. University Press of Mississippi.

Lee, J. Y., & Van Zandt, S. (2019). Housing tenure and social vulnerability to disasters: A review of the evidence. *Journal of Planning Literature, 34*(2), 156–170.

Lefebvre, H. (1974). *The production of space*. Wiley-Blackwell.

Lein, L., Angel, R., Beausoleil, J., & Bell, H. (2012). The basement of extreme poverty: Katrina Survivors and poverty programs. In W. Lynn & L. Peek (Eds.), *Displaced: Life in the Katrina diaspora* (pp. 47–62). University of Texas Press.

Li, J., & Spidalieri, K. (2021). Home is where the safer ground is: The need to promote affordable housing laws and policies in receiving communities. *Journal of Environmental Studies and Sciences, 11*(4), 682–695.

Lipsky, M. (1980). *Street-level bureaucracy: Dilemmas of the individual in public services*. Russell Sage Foundation.

Locke, J. (1948). *The second treatise of civil government and a letter concerning toleration*. B. Blackwell.

Locke, J. (1961). *Two treatises of government: With a supplement, patriarcha, by Robert Filmer* (Vol. 2). Simon and Schuster.

Loughran, K., Elliott, J. R., & Kennedy, S. W. (2019). Urban ecology in the time of climate change: Houston, flooding, and the case of federal buyouts. *Social Currents, 6*(2), 121–140.

Louis-Charles, H. M., Howard, R., Remy, L., Nibbs, F., & Turner, G. (2020). Ethical considerations for postdisaster fieldwork and data collection in the Caribbean. *American Behavioral Scientist, 64*(8), 1129–1144.

Louisiana Department of Administration (LDOA). (2017). *The resettlement of Isle de Jean Charles: Report on data gathering and engagement phase*. Louisiana Department of Administration. http://isledejeancharles.la.gov/sites/default/files/public/IDJC-Final-Report-Update.pdf

Louisiana Department of Administration (LDOA). (2019). *Substantial Amendment 5: Introduction of new activities and project narrative clarifications for the utilization of community development block grant funds under the National Disaster Resilience Competition (NDRC) Resettlement of Isle de Jean Charles*. LDOA. https://www.doa.la.gov/media/3wwj2iyx/ndr_idjc_substantial_amendment_5-hud-approved.pdf

Lovett, J. A. (2007). Property and radically changed circumstances. *Tennessee Law Review, 74*(4), 463–566.

Lovett, J. A. (2017). Moving to higher ground: Protecting and relocating communities in response to climate change. *Vermont Law Review, 42*(1), 25.

Lovett, J. A. (2020a). Community land trusts: Institutionalizing the human flourishing theory of property. *Cornell Journal of Law and Public Policy, 29*(3), 621.

Lovett, J. A. (2020b). Towards sustainable community ownership: A comparative assessment of Scotland's new compulsory community right to buy. In M. M. Combe, J. Glass, & A. Tindley (Eds.), *Land reform in Scotland: History, law, and policy* (pp. 177–212). Edinburgh University Press.

Lovett, J. A., & Combe, M. M. (2019). The parable of Portobello: Lessons and questions from the first urban acquisition under the Scottish community right-to-buy regime. *Montana Law Review, 80*(2), 211.

Lustgarten, A. (2020, September 15). *Climate change will force a new American migration*. ProPublica. https://www.propublica.org/article/climate-change-will-force-a-new-american-migration

Lynn, K. A. (2017). Who defines "whole": An urban political ecology of flood control and community relocation in Houston, Texas. *Journal of Political Ecology, 24*(1), 951.

Mach K. J., Kraan C. M., Hino M., Siders A. R., Johnston E. M., & Field C. B. (2019, October 9). Managed retreat through voluntary buyouts of flood-prone properties. *Science Advances, 5*(10). https://doi.org/10.1126/sciadv.aax8995

Mahmood, A., & Cousins, J. J. (2022). Judicialising urban political ecologies: Post-politics and environmental governance in South Asia. *Antipode, 54*, 1944–1964. https://doi.org/10.1111/anti.12850

Mahmud, L. (2016, October 27). *We have never been liberal: Occidentalist myths and the impending fascist apocalypse*. Society for Cultural Anthropology.

Retrieved July 15, 2022, from https://culanth.org/fieldsights/we-have-never-been-liberal-occidentalist-myths-and-the-impending-fascist-apocalypse
Make the Road New York. (2014, December 17). *Treading water: Renters in post-Sandy New York City*. Retrieved July 13, 2022, from https://maketheroadny.org/treading-water-renters-in-post-sandy-new-york-city/
Maldonado, J. K. (2019). *Seeking justice in an energy sacrifice zone: Standing on vanishing land in coastal Louisiana*. Routledge.
Maldonado, J. K., & Peterson, K. (2018). A community-based model for resettlement: Lessons from coastal Louisiana. In R. McLeman & F. Gemenne (Eds.), *Routledge handbook of environmental displacement and migration* (pp. 289–299). Routledge.
Maldonado, J. K., Shearer, C., Bronen, R., Peterson, K., & Lazarus, H. (2013). The impact of climate change on tribal communities in the US: Displacement, relocation, and human rights. *Climate Change, 120*(3), 601–614.
Maldonado, J. K., Wang, I. F. C., Eningowuk, F., Lesley, I., Lascurain, A., Lazrus, H., Naquin, C. A., Naquin, J. R., Nogueras-Vidal, K. M., Peterson, K., Rivera-Collazo, I., Souza, M. K., Stege, M., & Thomas, B. (2021). Addressing the challenges of climate-driven community-led resettlement and site expansion: Knowledge sharing, storytelling, healing, and collaborative coalition building. *Journal of Environmental Studies and Sciences, 11*(3), 294–304. https://doi.org/10.1007/s13412-021-00695-0
Manda, S., Dougill, A., & Tallontire, A. (2019). Large-scale land acquisitions and institutions: Patterns, influence and barriers in Zambia. *Geographical Journal, 185*(2), 194–208.
Manda, S., Jerolleman, A., & Marino, E. (2023). Assumptions and understanding of success in home buyout programs.*International Journal of Disaster Risk Reduction,*103863.
Marandi, A., & Man, K. L. (2021). Vulnerable city, recipient city, or climate destination? Towards a typology of domestic climate migration impacts in US cities. *Journal of Environmental Studies and Sciences, 11*, 465–480.
Marino, E. (2015). *Fierce climate, sacred ground: An ethnography of climate change in Shishmaref*. University of Alaska Press.
Marino, E. (2018). Adaptation privilege and voluntary buyouts: Perspectives on ethnocentrism in sea level rise relocation and retreat policies in the US. *Global Environmental Change, 49*, 10–13.
Marino, E., & Lazrus, H. (2015). Migration or forced displacement?: The complex choices of climate change and disaster migrants in Shishmaref, Alaska and Nanumea, Tuvalu. *Human Organization, 74*(4), 341–350.
Marino, E. K., & Faas, A. J. (2020). Is vulnerability an outdated concept? After subjects and spaces. *Annals of Anthropological Practice, 44*(1), 33–46.
Martinich, J., Neumann, J., Ludwig, L., & Jantarasami, L. (2012). Risks of sea level rise to disadvantaged communities in the United States. *Mitigation and*

Adaptation Strategies for Global Change, 18(2), 169–185. https://doi.org/10.1007/s11027-011-9356-0

Marx, K. (1859). *A contribution to the critique of political economy* (S. W. Ryazanskaya, Trans.). Lawrence & Wishart.

Maskovsky, J. (2006). Governing the "new hometowns": Race, power, and neighborhood participation in the new inner city. *Identities: Global Studies in Culture and Power, 13*(1), 73–99.

Matz, D., Vogel, E. B., Mattar, S., & Montenegro, H. (2015). Interrupting intergenerational trauma: Children of Holocaust survivors and the Third Reich. *Journal of Phenomenological Psychology, 46*(2), 185–205. https://doi.org/10.1163/15691624-12341295

May, P. J., & Burby, R. J. (1996). Coercive versus cooperative policies: Comparing intergovernmental mandate performance. *Journal of Policy Analysis and Management, 15*, 171–201. https://doi.org/10.1002/(SICI)1520-6688(199621)15:2%3c171::AID-PAM2%3e3.0.CO;2-G

McAdam, J. (2012). *Climate change, forced migration, and international law*. Oxford University Press.

McAdam, J., & Ferris, E. (2015). Planned relocation in the context of climate change: Unpacking the legal and conceptual issues. *Cambridge Journal of International and Comparative Law, 4*(1), 137–166.

McCloskey, D. J., McDonald, M. A., Cook, J., Heurtin Roberts, S., Updegrove, S., Sampson, D., Gutter, S., & Milton, (M.) E. (2011). Community engagement: Definitions and organizing concepts from the literature. In D. J. McCloskey, S. Aguilar-Gaxiola, & J. L. Michener (Eds.), *Principles of community engagement. Clinical and translational science awards consortium community engagement key function committee task force on the principles of community engagement* (2nd ed.). NIH Publication No. 11-7782. Retrieved July 15, 2022, from https://www.atsdr.cdc.gov/communityengagement/pce_intro.html

McConnell, E. D. (2017). Rented, crowded, and unaffordable? Social vulnerabilities and the accumulation of precarious housing conditions in Los Angeles. *Housing Policy Debate, 27*(1), 60–79.

McDonald, J. (2010). Mapping the legal landscape of climate change adaptation. In T. Bonyhady, A. Macintosh, & J. McDonald (Eds.), *Adaptation to climate change: Law and policy* (pp. 1–37). The Federation Press.

McGhee, D. (2017). *Were the post-Sandy Staten Island buyouts successful in reducing national vulnerability?* (Master's Project). Duke University. Retrieved July 13, 2022, from https://hdl.handle.net/10161/14168

Melish, T. J. (2010). Maximum feasible participation of the poor: New governance, new accountability, and a 21st century war on the sources of poverty. *Yale Human Rights and Development Law Journal, 13*, 1.

Meltz, R. (2007). Takings law today: A primer for the perplexed. *Ecology Law Quarterly, 34*(2), 307–380.

Messias, D. K. H., Barrington, C., & Lacy, E. (2012). Latino social network dynamics and the Hurricane Katrina disaster. *Disasters, 36*(1), 101–121.

Miller, R. J. (2005). The doctrine of discovery in American Indian law. *Idaho Law Review, 42*(1), 1.

Mironova, O. (2014, April 29). *The value of land: How community land trusts maintain housing affordability*. Urban Omnibus. Retrieved July 12, 2022, from https://urbanomnibus.net/2014/04/the-value-of-land-how-community-land-trusts-maintain-housing-affordability/

Mol, A. (2008). *The logic of care: Health and the problem of patient choice*. Routledge.

Mol, A., Ingunn M., & Pols, J. (2010). Care: Putting practice into theory. In A. Mol, I. Moser, & J. Pols (Eds.), *Care in practice: On tinkering in clinics, homes and farms*. Transcript.

Moore, J., & Acker, L. (2018). Recurrent flooding, sea level rise, and the relocation of at-risk communities: Case studies from the commonwealth of Virginia. *Virginia Coastal Policy Center, 26*. https://scholarship.law.wm.edu/vcpclinic/26

Moran, D., & Mihaly, E. (2018, January). *Climate and liability: A legal primer and workshop summary report*. Conservation Law Foundation (CLF) and Boston Green Ribbon Commission.

Moreton-Robinson, A. (2015). *The white possessive: White possession and Indigenous sovereignty matters*. University of Minnesota Press.

Morris, D. H. (2021). The climate crisis is a housing crisis: Without growth we cannot retreat. In I. J. Ajibade & A. R. Siders (Eds.), *Global views on climate relocation and social justice* (pp. 142–151). Routledge.

Mufson, S. (2015, September 1). Obama visits receding glacier in Alaska to highlight climate change. *The Washington Post*. https://www.washingtonpost.com/politics/obama-visits-receding-glacier-in-alaska-to-highlight-climate-change/2015/09/01/dfacfe1e-50f6-11e5-9812-92d5948a40f8_story.html

Muñiz, B. (2006). *In the eye of the storm: How the government and private response to Hurricane Katrina failed Latinos*. National Council of La Raza.

Nagata, D. K., Kim, J. H. H., & Nguyen, T. U. (2015). Processing cultural trauma: Intergenerational effects of the Japanese American Incarceration. *Journal of Social Issues, 71*(2), 56–370. https://doi.org/10.1111/josi.12115

National Congress of American Indians (NCAI). (2021). The National Congress of American Indians Resolution #SAC-21-037 Additional Tribal Disaster Resilience and Climate Change Common Principles. https://ncai.assetbank-server.com/assetbank-ncai/assetfile/177.pdf

Naylor, L., Fall, V., & Fox, A. (2020). The power of place in disaster recovery: Heritage-based practice in the post-Matthew landscape of Princeville, North

Carolina. *Parks Stewardship Forum, 36*(1), 128–136. https://doi.org/10.5070/P536146398

NCDEM. (1999). *Hazard mitigation in North Carolina: Measuring success: Sustainable housing, sustainable business, sustainable infrastructure, sustainable environment*. Division of Emergency Management & Federal Emergency Management Agency. https://digital.ncdcr.gov/digital/collection/p249901coll22/id/638829

Nelson, M. (2014). Using land swaps to concentrate redevelopment and expand resettlement options in post-Hurricane Katrina New Orleans. *Journal of the American Planning Association, 80*(4), 426–437.

Newcomb, S. T. (2008). *Pagans in the promised land: Decoding the doctrine of Christian discovery*. Fulcrum Publishing.

Newkirk, V., II. (2019). The great land robbery: The shameful story of how 1 million black families have been ripped from their farms. *The Atlantic*.

NYU Furman Center. (2017). *Housing in the US floodplain: A data brief*. NYU Furman Center. Retrieved December 19, 2021, from https://furmancenter.org/files/NYUFurmanCenter_HousingInTheFloodplain_May2017.pdf

Olivera McCan, M. (2006). *case study of floodplain acquisition/relocation in Kinston, NC after Hurricane Fran (1996) and Floyd (1999)* (Master's thesis). University of North Carolina at Chapel Hill. https://doi.org/10.17615/rhp8-te06

Oulahen, G., & Doberstein, B. (2012). Citizen participation in post-disaster flood hazard mitigation planning in Peterborough, Ontario, Canada. *Risks, Hazards, and Crisis in Public Policy, 3*(1), 1–26. https://doi.org/10.1515/1944-4079.1098

Panfil, Y. (2020, July 14). *The case for 'managed retreat'*. Politico. Retrieved July 15, 2022, from https://www.politico.com/news/agenda/2020/07/14/climate-change-managed-retreat-341753

Parchomovsky, G., & Siegelman, P. (2004). Selling Mayberry: Communities and individuals in law and economics. *California Law Review, 92*(1), 75–146.

Pardee, J. W. (2012). Living through displacement: Housing insecurity among low-income evacuees. In L. Weber & L. Peek (Eds.), *Displaced life in the Katrina diaspora* (pp. 63–78). University of Texas Press.

Park, K. S. (2021). The history wars and property law: Conquest and slavery as foundational to the field. *Yale Law Journal, 131*, 1062.

Peacock, W. G., Van Zandt, S., Zhang, Y., & Highfield, W. E. (2015). Inequities in long-term housing after disaster. *Journal of the American Planning Association, 80*(4), 356–371.

Peloso, M. R., & Caldwell, M. R. (2011). Dynamic property rights: The public trust doctrine and takings in a changing climate. *Dynamic Property Rights, 30*(51), 51–119.

Pettus, K. (2019). The first American climate refugees and the need for proactive relocation. *The George Washington Law Review, 87*(1), 172.

Phillips, B., Stukes, P. A., & Jenkins, P. (2012). Freedom hill is not for sale—and neither is the lower ninth ward. *Journal of Black Studies, 43*(4), 405–426. https://doi.org/10.1177/0021934711425489

Piguet, E. (2013). From "primitive migration" to "climate refugees": The curious fate of the natural environment in migration studies. *Annals of the Association of American Geographers, 103*(1), 148–162.

Plastrik, P., & Cleveland, J. (2019, March). *Can it happen here? Improving the prospect for managed retreat by US Cities*. Innovation Network for Communities.

Platt, R. H. (1999a). From flood control to flood insurance: Changing approaches to floods in the United States. *Environments, 27*(1), 67.

Platt, R. H. (1999b). *Disasters and democracy: The politics of extreme natural events*. Island Press.

Poirier, M. R. (2002). The virtue of vagueness in takings doctrine. *Cardozo Law Review, 24*(1), 93–192.

Polanyi, K. (1944). The self-regulating market and the fictitious commodities: Labor, land and money. In *The great transformation* (pp. 71–80). Beacon Press.

Project Recovery. (2023). *Post disaster relocation and buyout program*. https://harrisrecovery.org/post-disaster-relocation-and-buyout-program/

Purdy, J. (2007). Property and empire: The law of imperialism in Johnson v. M'intosh. *The George Washington Law Review, 75*(2), 329.

Qaqeemasq, C. C. (2020, March 27). *Message from the chairman: We will take action to prevent the loss of our land*. Mashpee Wampanoag Tribe. Retrieved July 16, 2022, from https://mashpeewampanoagtribe-nsn.gov/news/2020/3/27/message-from-the-chairman-we-will-take-action-to-prevent-the-loss-of-our-land

Rebotier, J. (2012). Vulnerability conditions and risk representations in Latin-America: Framing the territorializing urban risk. *Global Environmental Change, 22*(2), 391–398.

Reuveny, R. (2007). Climate change-induced migration and violent conflict. *Political Geography, 26*(6), 656–673.

Right To The City Alliance. (n.d.). Retrieved July 7, 2022, from https://righttothecity.org/

Rising Voices. (2018). *Rising voices 6. Rising together: Mobilizing and learning from local actions workshop report*. Rising Voices. Retrieved July 16, 2022, from https://risingvoices.ucar.edu/sites/default/files/RV6%20Report_final_1.pdf

Rising Voices. (2019). *7th annual rising voices workshop. Converging voices: Building relationships & practices for intercultural science*. Rising Voices.

Retrieved July 16, 2022, from https://risingvoices.ucar.edu/sites/default/files/RV7%20Workshop%20Report.pdf

Rizzi, N. (2014, April 11). State won't add any more neighborhoods to Sandy buyout program. *DNAinfo*. Retrieved July 16, 2022, from https://www.dnainfo.com/new-york/20140411/new-dorp-beach/state-will-add-no-more-neighborhoods-sandy-buyout-program/

Robb, A., Stocker, L., Payne, M., & Middle, G. J. (2020). Enabling managed retreat from coastal hazard areas through property acquisition and transferable development rights: Insights from Western Australia. *Urban Policy and Research, 38*(3), 230–248.

Robbie, J., & van de Sidje, E. (2020). Assembling a sustainable system: Exploring the systemic constitutional approach to property in the context of sustainability. *Loyola Law Review, 66*, 553–616.

Robinson, C. S., Davidson, R. A., Trainor, J. E., Kruse, J. L., & Nozick, L. K. (2018). Homeowner acceptance of voluntary property acquisition offers. *International Journal of Disaster Risk Reduction, 31*, 234–242. https://doi.org/10.1016/j.ijdrr.2018.05.002

Rodriguez-Dod, E. C., & Duhart, O. (2007). Evaluating Katrina: A snapshot of renters' rights following disasters. *Nova Law Review, 31*(3), 467.

Ronald, W. P., & Lindell, M. K. (1997). Principles for managing community relocation as a hazard mitigation measure. *Journal of Contingencies and Crisis Management, 5*(1), 49–59. https://doi.org/10.1111/1468-5973.00036

Rose, C. M. (1994). *Property and persuasion: Essays on the history, theory and rhetoric of ownership*. Routledge.

Rothstein, R. (2017). *The color of law: A forgotten history of how our government segregated America*. Liveright.

Roy, A. (2003). Paradigms of propertied citizenship: Transnational techniques of analysis. *Urban Affairs Review, 38*(4), 463–491. https://doi.org/10.1177/1078087402250356

Roy, A. (2005). Urban informality: Toward an epistemology of planning. *Journal of the American Planning Association, 71*(2), 147–156.

Rubin, L. B. (1969). Maximum feasible participation: The origins, implications, and present status. *The Annals of the American Academy of Political and Social Science, 385*(1), 14–29.

Rumbach, A. J., & Kudva, N. (2011). Putting people at the center of climate change adaptation plans: A vulnerability approach. *Risks, Hazards, and Crisis in Public Policy, 2*(4), 1–23. https://doi.org/10.2202/1944-4079.1096

Rumbach, A., Sullivan, E., & Makarewicz, C. (2020). Mobile home parks and disasters: Understanding risk to the third housing type in the United States. *Natural Hazards Review, 21*(2).

Salvesen, D., BenDor, T. K., Kamrath, C., & Ganser, B. (2018). *Are floodplain buyouts a smart investment for local governments*. Final Report for the UNC Policy Collaboratory.

Sanders, K. J. (2013). Re-assembling Osiris: Rule 23, the black farmers case, and reparations. *Penn State Law Review, 118*, 339.

Sand-Fleischmann, M. G. (2019). *Circumventing the next trail of tears: Re-approaching planning and policy for the climatologically displaced indigenous communities of coastal Louisiana* (Doctoral dissertation). Cornell University.

Sand, M. (2017). Costs and benefits: Why economic quantification in hazard mitigation policy threatens culture in coastal Louisiana. In F. van Straalen, T. Hartmann, & J. Sheehan (Eds.), *Property rights and climate change: Land use under changing environmental conditions* (pp. 86–97). Routledge.

Savloy, S. (2008, June 17). A town that looked at leaving the floodplain but stayed on. *The New York Times*. Retrieved July 12, 2022, from https://www.nytimes.com/2008/06/17/us/17iowa.html

Schragger, R. C. (2001). The limits of localism. *Michigan Law Review, 100*(2), 371–472. https://doi.org/10.2307/1290541

Schutt, A. M. (2016). ANCSA Section 7 (I): $40 million per word and counting. *Alaska Law Review, 33*, 229.

Schutz, A., & Sandy, M. (2011). *Collective action for social change: An introduction to community organizing*. Springer.

Scottish Government. (2016). *Community right to buy guidance*. www.gov.scot

Scott, J. C. (1986). *Seeing like a state: How certain schemes to improve the human condition have failed*. Yale University Press.

Scott, P. G. (1997). Assessing determinants of bureaucratic discretion: An experiment in street-level decision making. *Journal of Public Administration Research and Theory: J-PART, 7*(1), 35–57.

Serkin, C. (2014). Passive takings: The state's affirmative duty to protect property. *Michigan Law Review, 113*(3), 345–404.

Setyawan, K. (2021). Pointe-aux-Chenes parents file federal lawsuit over elementary school closure. *The Courier*. https://www.houmatoday.com/story/news/2021/06/18/pointe-aux-chenes-parents-federal-lawsuit-elementary-school-closure/7671482002/

Shi, L., & Moser, S. (2021). Transformative climate adaptation in the United States: Trends and prospects. *Science, 372*(6549), eabc8054.

Shi, L., & Varuzzo, A. M. (2020). Surging seas, rising fiscal stress: Exploring municipal fiscal vulnerability to climate change. *Cities, 100*, 102658.

Shoemaker, J. A. (2020). An introduction to American Indian land tenure: Mapping the legal landscape. *Journal of Law, Property, and Society, 5*(1).

Shriver, T. E., & Kennedy, D. K. (2005). Contested environmental hazards and community conflict over relocation. *Rural Sociology, 70*(4), 491–513.

Siders, A. (2013). *Managed coastal retreat: A legal handbook on shifting development away from vulnerable areas* (Columbia Public Law Research Paper, 14-365).

Siders, A. R. (2018a). Social justice implications of US managed retreat buyout programs. *Climatic Change, 152*(2), 239–257.

Siders, A. R. (2018b, October 19). *Government-funded buyouts after disasters are slow and inequitable—Here's how that could change*. The Conversation. Retrieved July 16, 2022, from https://theconversation.com/government-funded-buyouts-after-disasters-are-slow-and-inequitable-heres-how-that-could-change-103817

Siders, A. R. (2019). Social justice implications of US managed retreat buyout programs. *Climatic Change, 152*(2), 239–257. https://doi.org/10.1007/s10584-018-2272-5

Siders, A. R., Hino, M., & Mach, K. J. (2019). The case for strategic and managed climate retreat. *Science, 365*(6455), 761–763.

Siders, A. R., & Keenan, J. M. (2020). Variables shaping coastal adaptation decisions to armor, nourish, and retreat in North Carolina. *Ocean & Coastal Management, 183*, 105023.

Singer, J. W. (2006). After the flood: Equality & humanity in property regimes. *Loyola Law Review, 52*(2), 243.

Singer, J. W. (2014). Property as the law of democracy. *Duke Law Journal, 63*(6), 1287–1335. https://doi.org/10.2139/ssrn.2407966

Smith, H. E. (2012). Property as the law of things. *Harvard Law Review, 125*(7), 1691–1726.

Sogorea Te' Land Trust. (2023). https://sogoreate-landtrust.org/purpose-and-vision/

Spidalieri, K., & Bennett, A. (2020). *Managed retreat toolkit*. Georgetown Climate Center. Retrieved July 14, 2022, from https://www.georgetownclimate.org/adaptation/toolkits/managed-retreat-toolkit/introduction.html

Sprankling, J. G. (1996). The antiwilderness bias in American property law. *The University of Chicago Law Review, 63*(2), 519–590. https://doi.org/10.2307/1600236

Stanton, T. (2018). John Locke and the fable of liberalism. *The Historical Journal, 61*(3), 597–622.

Starna, W. A. (1992). "Public ethnohistory" and native-American communities: History or administrative genocide? *Radical History Review, 1992*(53), 126–139.

Stein, S. I. (2010). Wake up Fannie: I think I got something to say to you: Financing community land trust homebuyers without stripping affordability provisions. *Emory Law Journal, 60*(1), 209, 217–219.

Stein, S. (2019). *Capital city: Gentrification and the real estate state*. Verso Books.

Stoler, A. L., & McGranahan, C. (2007). Introduction: Refiguring imperial terrains. In A. L. Stoler, C. McGranahan, & P. C. Perdue (Eds.), *Imperial formations* (pp. 3–42). SAR Press.

Sullivan, E. (2018). *Manufactured insecurity: Mobile home parks and Americans' tenuous right to place*. University of California Press.

Sutley, E. J., & Hamideh, S. (2020). Postdisaster housing stages: A Markov chain approach to model sequences and duration based on social vulnerability. *Risk Analysis, 40*(12), 2675–2695. https://doi.org/10.1111/risa.13576

Sylves, R. (2020). *Disaster policy and politics* (3rd ed.). Sage.

Tate, E., Strong, A., Kraus, T., & Xiong, H. (2016). Flood recovery and property acquisition in Cedar Rapids, Iowa. *Natural Hazards, 80*(3), 2055–2079.

Taylor, K.-Y. (2019). *Race for profit: How banks and the real estate industry undermined black homeownership*. UNC Press Books.

Taylor, Z. J., & Aalbers, M. B. (2022). Climate gentrification: Risk, rent, and restructuring in Greater Miami. *Annals of the American Association of Geographers, 112*(6), 1685–1701.

Teicher, J. G. (2021). This land is their land. *The Baffler*. https://thebaffler.com/latest/this-land-is-their-land-teicher

Teirstein, Z. (2022). Biden's new vision for the National flood Insurance Program. *Grist*. https://grist.org/housing/bidens-new-vision-for-the-national-flood-insurance-program/

Thornton, R. (1984). Cherokee population losses during the Trail of Tears: A new perspective and a new estimate. *Ethnohistory, 31*, 289–300.

Titz, A., Cannon, T., & Krüger, F. (2018). Uncovering 'community': Challenging an elusive concept in development and disaster related work. *Societies, 8*(3), 71.

Tolnay, S. E. (2003). The African American "great migration" and beyond. *Annual Review of Sociology, 29*, 209–232

Trujillo-Pagán, N. (2007). Katrina's Latinos: Vulnerability and disasters in relief and recovery. In K. A. Bates & R. S. Swan (Eds.), *Through the eye of Katrina: Social justice in the United States* (pp. 147–168). Carolina Academic Press.

Tulane Institute of Water Resources Law & Policy. (2014, September). *Community resettlement: Prospects in Southeast Louisiana. A multidisciplinary exploration of legal, cultural, and demographic aspects of moving individuals and communities*. Tulane University Law School.

Tully, J. (1980). *A discourse on property: John Locke and his adversaries*. Cambridge University Press.

Turner, E. (2012). Introduction. In E. Turner, *Communitas: Contemporary anthropology of religion*. Palgrave Macmillan. https://doi.org/10.1057/9781137016423_1

United States Department of Housing and Urban Development (HUD). (2016). *National disaster resilience competition grantee profiles*. https://www.hud.gov/sites/documents/NDRCGRANTPROFILES.PDF

USGENWEB. (2007). *Vertical File Bell 02433-5. Original copy found at Heritage Place*. Lenoir County Community College, Kinston, NC. Retrieved December 2007, from http://ftp.rootsweb.com/pub/usgenweb/nc/lenoir/bios/jamcdaniel.txt

U.S. Senate Hearing 111-470. (2009, November 4). *Fixing the federal acknowledgment process*. U.S. Government Publishing Office. https://www.govinfo.gov/content/pkg/CHRG-111shrg56575/html/CHRG-111shrg56575.htm

Vreeland, A. (2019). *Hazard mitigation strategy application: An evaluation of the town of Princeville's future mitigation strategies* (Masters dissertation). University of North Carolina at Chapel Hill. https://doi.org/10.17615/663f-v695

Wachtendorf, T., Nelan, M. M., & Blinn-Pike, L. (2013). Households and families. In D. S. K. Thomas, B. D. Phillips, W. E. Lovekamp, & A. Fothergill (Eds.), *Social vulnerability to disasters* (pp. 281–310). CRC Press.

Walls, M. L., & Whitbeck, L. B. (2012). The intergenerational effects of relocation policies on indigenous families. *Journal of Family Issues, 33*(9), 1272–1293. https://doi.org/10.1177/0192513X12447178

Watkinson-Schutten, M. (2022). Decolonizing climate adaptation by reacquiring fractionated tribal lands. In M. Walter, T. Kukutai, A. A. Gonzales, & R. Henry (Eds.), *The Oxford handbook of indigenous sociology*. Oxford University Press. https://doi.org/10.1093/oxfordhb/9780197528778.013.42

Watts, M. (2003). Alternative modern—Development as cultural geography. In K. Anderson, M. Domosh, & S. Pile (Eds.), *Handbook of cultural geography* (pp. 433–454). Sage. https://doi.org/10.4135/9781848608252.n31

Weber, L., & Peek, L. (2012). *Displaced: Life in the Katrina diaspora*. University of Texas Press.

Wegmann, J., Schafran, A., & Pfeiffer, D. (2017). Breaking the double impasse: Securing and supporting diverse housing tenures in the United States. *Housing Policy Debate, 27*(2), 193–216.

Weinstein, L., & Ren, X. (2009). The changing right to the city: Urban renewal and housing rights in globalizing Shanghai and Mumbai. *City & Community, 8*(4), 407–432.

Werner, E., & McMullen, T. (2021). Advocates push nationwide movement for land return to Blacks after victory in California. *The Washington Post*.

Weyiouanna, T., Sr. (2007). *Shishmaref erosion and relocation coalition concerns*. Immediate Action Workgroup Hearing.

White, G. F. (1945). *Human adjustment to floods* (Research Paper no. 29, Doctoral dissertation). The University of Chicago. https://biotech.law.lsu.edu/climate/docs/Human_Adj_Floods_White.pdf

White, M. M. (2020). Race, land, and the law: Black farmers and the limits of a politics of recognition. In *Black food matters: Racial Justice in the wake of food justice*. University of Minnesota Press.
Whyte, K. P. (2016). Is it colonial déjà vu? Indigenous peoples and climate injustice. In *Humanities for the environment* (pp. 102–119). Routledge.
Wikerson, I. (2010). *The warmth of other suns: The epic story of America's great migration*. Vintage Book.
Williams, B. (2002). The concept of community. *Reviews in Anthropology, 31*, 339–350.
Williams, R. (1995). *The sociology of culture*. University of Chicago Press.
Wilmsen, B., & Webber, M. (2015). What can we learn from the practice of development-forced displacement and resettlement for organized resettlements in response to climate change? *Geoforum, 58*, 76–85.
Wolfe, P. (2006). Settler colonialism and the elimination of the native. *Journal of Genocide Research, 8*(4), 387–409.
Wuerthner, G. (2020). *The problem of conservation easements*. The Wildlife News. https://www.thewildlifenews.com/2020/04/15/the-problem-of-conservation-easements/
Wyman, K. M. (2018). The new essentialism in property. *Journal of Legal Analysis, 9*(2), 183–246. https://doi.org/10.1093/jla/lay002
Yamato, S. (2020, August 24). *Civil liberties act of 1988*. Densho Encyclopedia. Retrieved July 16, 2022, from https://encyclopedia.densho.org/Civil%20Liberties%20Act%20of%201988
Yoder, J. (2020). Does property ownership lead to participation in local politics? Evidence from property records and meeting minutes. *American Political Science Review, 114*(4), 1213–1229.
Young, I. M. (2011). *Responsibility for justice* (p. 40). Oxford University Press.
Zhang, Y., & Peacock, W. G. (2010). Planning for housing recovery? Lessons learned from Hurricane Andrew. *Journal of the American Planning Association, 76*(1), 5–24.

Legal References

Allain-Lebreton Co. v. Department of the Army, 670 F.2d 43 (5th Cir. 1982). https://law.resource.org/pub/us/case/reporter/F2/670/670.F2d.43.80-3451.html
Cherokee Nation v. Georgia, 30 U.S. 5 Pet. 1 1 (1831). https://supreme.justia.com/cases/federal/us/30/1/
City of Sherrill v. Oneida Indian Nation of N.Y., 125 S. Ct. 1478 (2005). https://www.supremecourt.gov/oral_arguments/argument_transcripts/2004/03-855.pd

Eagle Bear, Inc. v. The Blackfeet Indian Nation, CV-21-88-GF-BMM (D. Mont. Nov. 17, 2021). https://casetext.com/case/eagle-bear-inc-v-the-blackfeet-indian-nation

Federally Recognized Indian Tribe List Act of 1994, Pub. L. 103-454, title I (Nov. 2, 1994). https://www.govinfo.gov/content/pkg/STATUTE-108/pdf/STATUTE-108-Pg4791.pdf

Johnson & Graham's Lessee v. McIntosh, 21 U.S. 543 (1823). https://supreme.justia.com/cases/federal/us/21/543/

Jones v. Alfred H. Mayer Co., 392 U.S. 409 (Warren Court 1968). https://supreme.justia.com/cases/federal/us/392/409/

Kelo v. City of New London, 545 U.S. 469 (2005). https://supreme.justia.com/cases/federal/us/545/469/

Murr v. Wisconsin, 137 S. Ct. 1933 (2017). https://www.supremecourt.gov/opinions/16pdf/15-214_f1gj.pdf

Pennsylvania Coal Co. v. Mahon, 260 U.S. 393 (1922). https://supreme.justia.com/cases/federal/us/260/393/

Replacement housing of last resort, 49 CFR §24.404 (2005). https://www.ecfr.gov/current/title-49/subtitle-A/part-24/subpart-E/section-24.404

Shelley v. Kraemer, 334 U.S. 1 (Vinson Court 1948). https://tile.loc.gov/storage-services/service/ll/usrep/usrep334/usrep334001/usrep334001.pdf

Tee-Hit-Ton Indians v. United States, 348 U.S. 272 (1955). https://supreme.justia.com/cases/federal/us/348/272/

Uniform Relocation Assistance and Real Property Acquisition Policies Act, 42 U.S.C. § 4601 (1970).

Uniform Relocation Assistance and Real Property Acquisition Policies Act, 42 U.S.C. § 4601, seq. and 49 C.F.R. pt. 24 (1970).

Index

A. Jerolleman et al., *People or Property*,
https://doi.org/10.1007/978-3-031-36872-1

R

S

FSC
www.fsc.org
MIX
Papier | Fördert
gute Waldnutzung
FSC® C083411

Kolibri 360 GmbH
Ferdinand-Jühlke-Straße 7
99095 Erfurt, Deutschland
produktsicherheit@kolibri360.de